God Hates You:
The Worst Religious Leaders of the Western World

By Roger Bauman

Illustrations by Roger Bauman
Illustrations edited by Nicky Torkzadeh

Copyright © 2013 by Roger Bauman

This book is dedicated to the memory of Jill D. Mullaney, whose enthusiasm for this project was a great source of encouragement to me.

Table of contents

Preface

Part 1: One True Faith................................7

Constantine The Great
Pope Stephen VI
Pope Sergius III
What the Hell??? Pope Joan
Pope John XI
Pope Benedict IX
Pope Urban II
What the Hell??? The Rest of the Crusades
Pope Innocent III
What the Hell??? The End of the Cathars
Pope Boniface VIII
What the Hell??? Lost and Found
Pope Urban VI
Torquemada
What the Hell??? Human Sacrifice in the Aztec Faith
Pope Alexander VI
Savonarola
Pope Leo X

Part II: The Battle for Souls..........................101

Martin Luther
What the Hell??? The Fall of Rome
John Calvin
King Henry VIII
What the Hell??? The Battle for Souls
Pope Urban VIII
What the Hell??? This is Turning into a Witch-Hunt!
Oliver Cromwell
Maximilien Robespierre
Joseph Smith
What the Hell??? The Mountain Meadows Massacre
Pope Pius IX
What the Hell??? The Protocols of the Elders of Zion
Fr. Charles Coughlin
Bob Jones

What the Hell??? Snake Handlers
Pope Pius XII
What the Hell??? The Magdalene Laundries

Part III: The Marketplace of Salvation.................206

L. Ron Hubbard
Jim Jones
What the Hell??? Faith Healers
David Koresh
Jerry Falwell
Bhagwan Shree Rajneesh (a.k.a. Osho)
Sun Myung Moon
What the Hell??? Make a Joyful Noise Unto the Lord!
Jimmy Swaggart
Jim and Tammy Faye Bakker
Pat Robertson
Louis Farrakhan
What the Hell??? Space, The Final Frontier
Sheikh Omar Abdel-Rahman
Warren Jeffs
What the Hell??? Sexual Child Abuse in the Catholic Church
Fred Phelps
What the Hell??? The Ten Commandments in Uganda
My Cup Runneth Over

Preface

In as much as possible, this is not a theology book. If you want to delve into parsing meanings of scripture or to search for the historical Jesus, this isn't the book for you. If you have big theological questions such as "could God make a slice of pizza so hot that even he couldn't eat it?" then again, this is the wrong book. Nor is this book intended to promote one faith over the other. Admittedly, the Roman Catholic Church takes it on the chin pretty hard in this book, especially in the first section. Since the Catholic Church was pretty much the only game in town in Western Europe for centuries, however, it is only reasonable that it would monopolize the crappy leaders of that era. The Catholic Church's hierarchical structure, which invests so much power in the hands of the pope, also lends itself to creating especially visible bad leaders. Protestant's can take pride that none of their own make this book... until Martin Luther.

You will also note that this book steers clear of using the word "cult." All creeds are more or less equal in these pages regardless of how many worshippers they have attained or how long they have been around. As far as this book is concerned, maybe the pope can speak with infallibility, maybe Joseph Smith was chosen as a prophet of the Lord, maybe a space alien named Xenu is imprisoned in an underground cell and maybe the Antichrist is a Jew who walks amongst us today as Jerry Falwell once claimed. Then again, maybe not.

I also want to stress that I won't dismiss these people as a bunch of lunatics. Most—if not all—of the villains in these pages knew full well what they were doing. To call them insane would excuse them from their crimes and misdeeds.

So why a book concentrating on awful religious leaders? Not to diminish the failings of secular authorities, but people rely on the leaders of their churches and temples for more than the practical matters of state. Society looks to them as moral guides. The faithful arrange their worldviews and voting habits around their teachings and place their souls in their care. In many cases, people have felt that the only way they could find salvation was to kill or die based on the utterances of their religious superiors.

The vile deeds described in these pages are not only moral failings—and in many cases crimes against humanity—but also a betrayal of the faith good intentioned people place in religion.

Part I

One True Faith

Constantine The Great

Normally, rulers earn the title "Great" by virtue of their success on the battlefield—and by that measure, Constantine certainly qualified. But it was his ardent support of Christianity rather than his military conquests that won him his moniker. Though he was not baptized until his dying days, Constantine's impact on Christianity rivals even that of St. Paul. He was also a hot-tempered, cruel, war-mongering murderer. As the first Christian Emperor of the Roman Empire, he is also an ideal person with which to start this book.

Christians had suffered mightily in Rome since the time of the Great Fire in the year 64. Rightly or wrongly, Emperor Nero blamed Christian agitators for the devastating conflagration, and all Christians were made to pay for it. Christians were rounded up and executed *en masse*, often in the most horrific manners imaginable. As the years and centuries went by, the fervor of the persecution ebbed and flowed, but Christianity remained illegal, and public professions of Christian faith were always dangerous. In the year 303, the Emperor Diocletian launched a massive crackdown against Christians that even claimed the lives of some of his most trusted government officials. Conservative Romans believed that the survival of their empire depended upon pleasing the traditional Roman gods. They feared the Empire was in danger of being undermined by Christians who rejected those deities. A young Constantine (who was then still a pagan) was on hand to witness all of this.

Constantine had some fairly interesting parents. His mother Helena (now known as St. Helena) was most likely a former prostitute. After she converted to Christianity, she picked up the hobby of discovering holy relics. Amongst her claimed discoveries were remnants the "True Cross" upon which Jesus was crucified and the nails used to attach him to it (there will be much more on this later).

Constantine's father was an emperor ruling over the western portion of the Roman Empire. Upon his father's death, Constantine inherited most of his dad's turf. While this was a lofty position to hold, Constantine was just one of a handful of emperors who each controlled pieces of the vast Roman Empire.

Amongst these mini-emperors, Constantine was the youngest and the least powerful.

But he was still a force to be reckoned with. Anyone who dared to challenge him in his section of the empire came to regret it. He rounded up a large number of his enemies and had them torn apart by beasts in an amphitheater; mostly, it seems, for his own amusement. The animals were said to have killed until they staggered from exhaustion. He also put his own father-in-law to death after he led a failed rebellion against Constantine.

For the most part, however, Constantine laid low and waited for his chance at greater glory to present itself. In 312 he saw his opportunity. The part of the empire controlled by his brother-in-law, Maxentius, was sliding into disarray. Constantine headed to Italy to take advantage of the situation. As he drew closer to Rome, he claimed that he saw a vision of Christ in a dream. The next day he ordered his troops to mark their shields with the Chi-Rho, a Christian symbol that looks like a "P" and an "X" overlapping one another. It's possible a good chunk of Constantine's men didn't even know this was a Christian symbol, but no matter. The battle went well for Constantine. Maxentius' troops became disorganized, and the battle turned into a route in which numerous men, including Maxentius himself, were thrown from the Milvian Bridge into the Tiber River where they drowned. Constantine had Maxentius' corpse fished out of the river and beheaded. The head was then taken to Rome to demonstrate his victory. After the Roman populace had their chance to admire this vile trophy, it was taken on a tour of North Africa.

The Battle of the Milvian Bridge turned out to be the turning point for Christianity. Constantine quickly legalized the religion in return for the solid favor the Christian God had done for him. Christians went from cowering in fear of persecution to triumphant overnight. Their churches were now even funded by Constantine himself. It is unknown if Constantine had really bought into Christianity at this point, or if the whole thing was just a ploy to win support from the growing number of Christians in the empire. His embrace of Christianity may also have been motivated by a need to justify his military cause, which was on shaky legal ground. In any event, Constantine milked the move for all it was worth. He even went as far as to declare himself "the equal of the apostles."

Constantine's vision didn't go unnoticed in the rest of empire. In the East, Caesar Licinius (who was another of Constantine's brothers-in-law) also claimed to see a divine Christian vision before he went into battle against his main rival. He too emerged victorious, and he grabbed the entire eastern half of the Empire for himself. Despite their both being chosen by God for holy visions, the two rulers soon butted heads and started plotting against each other. Constantine wanted war even more than Licinius did and when it inevitably came he got the better of him in battle. He was only able to take a bit of Licinius' territory, however, before he had to settle for peace. During the war, both sides blew off their devotion to the God they had praised beforehand.

Meanwhile, the Christians were spreading their wings in their newfound freedom, and they started ruffling each other's feathers in the process. During the time of persecution, any differences between Christian groups were easily ignored, as mere survival was the preeminent concern. In the new climate, however, bitter disputes broke out over theological matters that few people would care about today. In North Africa, a group called the Donatists arose. The Donatists were entirely unforgiving of Christians who had renounced their faith to save their skins during the time of the Roman persecution. They also refused to recognize the authority of bishops in cities such as Carthage who did not conform to their views. They pleaded with Constantine to support their cause, but ultimately he decided against them. He even sent an army to Africa to clamp down upon them. When his troops arrived in Carthage, the Donatists tried to defend their churches, but the soldiers burned them down with men, women, and children inside. The soldiers moved from city to city attacking the Donatists, but rather than stamping out the movement, they only strengthened the resolve of the Donatists' resistance to Rome. Constantine was ultimately forced to tolerate the Donatists. They would continue to practice their version of Christianity until they were wiped out by Arabs centuries later.

Notwithstanding his divine vision, Licinius had grown tired of the Christians in his chunk of the empire, and he started persecuting them again. This, amongst other things, gave Constantine an excuse to renew hostilities with his rival. At the battlefront, Constantine had a tent put up for the purpose of receiving word from heaven as to when and where to attack his foe. God apparently wanted Constantine to launch attacks at Hadrianopolis and Chrysopolis where he inflicted a total of 59,000 fatalities upon Licinius' armies. Constantine went on to capture Byzantium thanks in large part to the heroic military efforts of his son, Crispus. He then renamed the city "Constantinople" in honor of the greatest person he could think of. Though weakened by all these defeats, Licinius remained a dangerous opponent. The threat of more battles between the two emperors was averted, however, when Constantine's beloved sister Constantina (who was the wife of Licinius) helped to broker a deal of clemency that ended the fighting. A feast was held to celebrate the deal before Licinius was sent off to his retirement estate/prison where he would spend the rest of his days. Those days didn't add up to a whole lot, however, as Constantine quickly reneged on the deal and had Licinius decapitated.

For those of you keeping score at home, Constantine had now killed one father-in-law and two brothers-in-law, but as it turns out he was only warming up.

In 325 Constantine ordered the murders of Licinius' son as well as his own favorite son, Crispus. A few months later he had his wife Fausta killed by ordering his thugs to drown her in a scalding bath. He forbade any mention of his son or wife ever again. Why he did this will likely never be known. He may have feared a plot against him or he may have believed that Crispus had gotten intimate with his stepmother, Fausta.

This theory gains credence when one considers Constantine's concern with sexual purity, an interest that turned into an obsession that went beyond all bounds of rationality. Among the draconian sexual laws he created was a prohibition of elopement that ordered women who eloped to be burned alive and any guardians who assisted in elopements to be put to death by means of having molten metal poured down their throats.

In the same year that Constantine was wiping out his family, he was again confronted with disagreements between various factions of Christians in the Empire. In order to finally get all Christians on the same page, he convened a council of bishops to meet in Nicea with the goal of reaching agreement on various aspects of Christian theology. It was a lavish affair, especially when one considers that many of the guests had spent time in Roman prisons for the crime of being Christians earlier in their lives. All of Constantine's wining and dining wasn't enough to bring about a consensus, however, so he told the assembly he would tolerate no sedition in the Church. He threatened to exile the bishops whose objections were preventing agreements from being reached. Under these threats, the council approved the Nicene Creed, which is still recited by Christians to this day.

They also reached an agreement upon when Easter was to be observed which also remains in place.

Constantine continued to mold Christianity to his will in this way. In 326 he ordered the destruction of all books he considered to be heretical. He exiled troublesome clergy for the rest of his life.

Despite his constant attention to the Church, his divine visions, and his promotion of Christianity, Constantine had never actually been baptized as a Christian himself. Finally, at the age of sixty-two as his life was slipping away from him, he consented to baptism. Why did he wait so long? We can't say for sure, but it's a pretty good bet that he saw baptism as a washing away of all his sins, and he wanted to make sure he got done with all his sinning before his baptism.

After mulling over all the sordid details of Constantine's life you may conclude that he was something short of the ideal in the morality department. That, however, is not the way he would be remembered by religious communities. The Catholic Church revered the memory of Constantine. In the Middle Ages it even went so far as to hold him up as the model of Christian leadership that kings were expected to aspire to. In the Eastern Church he came to be held in even higher regard. Today both Eastern Orthodox Christians and Roman Catholics know him as St. Constantine.

One of the most lasting contributions Constantine (inadvertently) made to the Church was the *Donation of Constantine*. This is a document created long after his death that claimed that Constantine offered his crown to the Bishop of Rome (who is now known as Pope Sylvester although the term "pope" would not be used until many years after Constantine's time). Sylvester refused the honor, allowing Constantine to continue his reign. The moral of the story was that Constantine ruled only at the pleasure of Sylvester. Moreover, the document asserted that Constantine moved his capitol from Rome to Constantinople because he felt no earthly ruler could share Rome with the leader of the Church. The only problem with the document is that it was a forgery. Constantine never offered his power to Sylvester or to anyone else. The document was widely accepted as genuine. It became the foundation for the tradition of secular rulers seeking papal blessing before ascending to their thrones. Eventually, prospective rulers started lavishing favors upon the popes to gain their approval. It also set the stage for the creation of what would become the Papal States, a territory that provided the popes with income from tax collections and a base from which real power could be wielded. With these benefits, the papacy was transformed into a highly lucrative position that was worth fighting for. And fight people did. Things got particularly bad in 767 when several aspirants to the throne got involved in a battle-royal over the papacy. One candidate had his eyes gouged out and another was murdered. A third had the good sense to bring an army with him to Rome, so he won the job.

Pope Stephen VI

The Papacy has seen murderers, womanizers, and loathsome characters of every sort. When it comes to flat-out strangeness, however, no one can lay a finger on Pope Stephen VI, who is sometimes called Stephen VII. The numbering of Popes is more of an art than a science.

First, some background is necessary. In the mid-ninth century, the man who would eventually become Pope Formosus was a big shot in the Church doing missionary work in the fledgling Christian land of Bulgaria. He was also tied up in the political machinations of the French court, where he persuaded Charles the Bald to be crowned by the Pope. Somehow Formosus stepped on some high-powered toes in the process and was put on trial by Pope John VIII. John charged Formosus with a wide variety of crimes including aspiring to become Pope, deserting his priestly duties, and conspiracy. Formosus was supposed to have been excommunicated, but he was allowed to dodge that fate by promising to leave Rome and never to practice as a priest again.

Pope John eventually gave up the ghost and his successor, Pope Marinus, dismissed the charges against Formosus. By and by, Formosus himself was elected Pope, apparently proving that he did aspire to the papacy. His five-year reign was marked by various political intrigues, shifting alliances, violence, and mayhem—all of which were par-for-the-course in the Middle Ages. Of particular note was his conflict with the noble Spoleto family. To gain relief from the pressure this clan put on him, Formosus reached out for help from the Frankish King, Arnulf who invaded Italy to aid Formosus. For this and other reasons, Formosus became an extremely divisive figure in the Church for years to come. He died on April 4, 896.

End of story—or so you would think.

Boniface VI was elected to succeed Formosus. Boniface's election was hurriedly forced upon the Church by a mob rioting in Rome at the time of the election. His papacy is remarkable for two reasons. First, he is the only pope elected despite having been defrocked for immoral behavior—*twice*. Second, he died of gout after serving as pope for about two weeks.

Enter Stephen, who at least partially owed his election as pope to the aforementioned Spoleto family who still had a bone to pick with Pope Formosus. Stephen shared his sponsors' contempt for Formosus, and he wasn't going to let a detail like the fact that Formosus was dead stand in the way of his need for vengeance. But how do you get revenge against a dead man? Stephen put his creative skills to work and devised what would come to be known as the Cadaver Synod. Yes, it means what you think it means.

In 897 Stephen ordered Formosus' corpse exhumed after it had been in the ground for over eight months. He demanded that Formosus' rotting remains be dressed in papal vestments, had him propped up on a throne and put him on trial for the same type of charges Pope John had charged him with years earlier. Formosus was appointed a defender who, it seems, barely got a word in edgewise as Stephen raged against his predecessor. This all took place in front of an assembly of Church bigwigs who remained silent during the proceedings, but who undoubtedly had a great deal to say about the affair when they were out of earshot of the Pope—the live one, that is.

Stephen's debating skills were on full display for all to admire. Every point he raised in the trial left Formosus utterly speechless. There are sources that claim a person was appointed to crouch behind Formosus and "talk" for the dead Pontiff, but come on, *that* would have been crazy! After Stephen's clever arguments had reduced Formosus to a crumpled heap on the stand, the accused was found guilty on all counts.

There would be no mercy for poor Formosus. Stephen ordered the papal vestments torn from his body, had three fingers cut off of his right hand (the one used for blessing), voided everything Formosus had done as Pope and had him reburied. Then he reconsidered that move and had Formosus exhumed again. This time his body was thrown into the Tiber River where it languished for some time until a fisherman pulled it out and gave it an impromptu burial. The Roman populace, unaware that the corpse had been retrieved, reported seeing a resurrected Pope

Formosus walking through the city and performing miracles amongst the citizenry.

Stephen wasn't allowed to bask in the glow of his victory over Formosus for long, however. An earthquake that struck shortly after the trial devastated the Basilica of St. John Lateran. The temblor was widely seen as proof of God's displeasure with Steven's actions. More importantly, a pro-Formosus faction existed within the Church's leadership, and it wasn't as impressed by the macabre spectacle of the trial as Stephen apparently had been. When the political winds shifted in their favor, they deposed Stephen and had him imprisoned. He was strangled to death shortly thereafter.

End of story—or so you would think.

After Stephen's murder, the pro-Formosus faction of the Church elected Romanus Pope. After he proved to be an ineffective leader, he was deposed, and Theodore II was made Pope. Pope Theodore revoked the judgment against Formosus. He had Formosus exhumed yet again, dressed in Papal vestments yet again, and held yet another funeral for the Pope who wouldn't stay in the ground—or the water for the matter. This was pretty much all Theodore did as he died after only twenty days in office. He may have been murdered, but facts are hard to come by in his case

After a great amount of intrigue, Pope John IX then succeeded to the Holy See. For some reason, he felt the need to reopen the Formosus case and affirmed Theodore's findings, not once, but twice. He also forbade anyone else from ever putting a dead person on trial.

During the reign of Pope Sergius III, the pontiff saw fit to revisit the case that—unlike the Popes involved— refused to die. He overturned the previous rulings, re-condemned Formosus, and heaped praise upon Stephen VI.

And that was the last time the Church addressed this case. So technically, the verdict against Formosus still stands today although no one takes it seriously. I think we can understand why the Church is hesitant to, ahem, unearth this case again.

> There has never been a Pope Formosus II. About 500 years after the Cadaver Synod (also poetically known as the *Synod Horrenda*), Pope Paul II seriously considered taking the name before he was talked out of it.

The Pornocracy

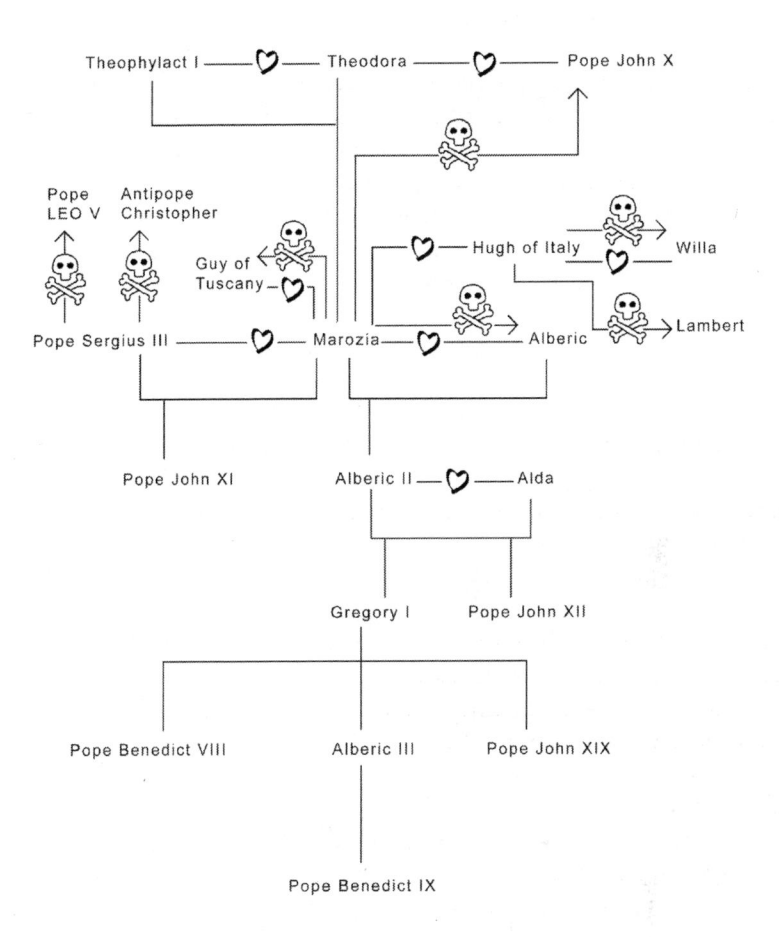

```
Theophylact I —♥— Theodora —♥— Pope John X
                                  ☠
Pope      Antipope
LEO V     Christopher
  ↑         ↑       Guy of ☠          ♥— Hugh of Italy —♥— Willa
  ☠         ☠       Tuscany—♥                ☠
                                                              ♥— Lambert
Pope Sergius III —♥— Marozia —♥— Alberic  ☠

         |                |
    Pope John XI     Alberic II —♥— Alda
                            |
                     Gregory I    Pope John XII
                            |
              Pope Benedict VIII   Alberic III   Pope John XIX
                                       |
                                 Pope Benedict IX
```

Pope Sergius III

Pope Sergius III participated in the trial of Pope Formosus before he became pope. He then perpetuated that debacle by re-condemning the dead Pope after he took office. What's more, some sources claim that Sergius had Formosus exhumed again and then had his corpse beheaded, but this is doubtful. In any case, his involvement in the whole dreadful Formosus episode is little more than a footnote in his papacy, which ranks among worst of all time.

Sergius was elected pope in 897 when the anti-Formosus party of the church had once again gained the upper hand in that ongoing political fray. That didn't last long, however, as the pro-Formosus candidate, John IX found some military backing which he used to depose Sergius. After being ousted from the papacy, Sergius was forced into exile. Leo V succeeded John upon his death. He only reigned for one month before he was deposed by Pope (now Antipope) Christopher.

All the while, Sergius was gathering an army of his own. When the turmoil surrounding Christopher's power grab broke out in Rome, he saw his chance to act. He marched into Rome and deposed Christopher. He had both Leo and Christopher arrested and thrown into dungeons where they languished for some time before Sergius had both of them killed. Other popes murdered their predecessors, but Sergius is the only one to murder two of them.

Sergius then denounced Leo, Christopher, John, and of course, Formosus. He also invalidated all the acts performed by any of them. This meant that all the bishops any of these popes had appointed were invalidated, and in turn, anyone ordained as priests by such bishops were also invalid. This had the effect of creating complete chaos within the Church. Under the threat of violence, Sergius ordered everyone to be re-ordained by people of whom he approved.

Sergius' skullduggery and viciousness were not enough to navigate the dangerous political waters of Rome solo, however. He needed allies, and he found them in the form of the noble Theophylact family. He became so close to this family that he inadvertently initiated a period of Church history that would come to be known as the "Pornocracy."

Before you get all hot and bothered over the term "Pornocracy," you should know that it wasn't nearly as titillating as its name would suggest. It was not a time when medieval sexpots ruled the Church; rather, it was a period in which the women of the Theophylact family exerted so much influence over the Church that people wondered where the real power lay. I would say they wondered who was wearing the pants in the relationship, but of course, popes don't wear pants.

None of these women were more influential than Theodora, who was the formidable matriarch of the family. She somehow overshadowed her husband and became the most powerful person in Rome. She even set up an illicit love affair for Sergius with her teenaged daughter Marozia in order to secure an alliance with the Pope. After he died, it was Theodora who personally chose his papal successors. One of these men was Pope John X, who also was Theodora's lover. This was all perfectly sleazy of course, but at least it spared Rome and the Church from more violence related to papal succession battles.

At this point, Theodora and her husband both disappear from history without a trace. What happened to them is unknown. When the dust cleared, it was their daughter, Marozia, who was left in charge of the Theophylact family and the city of Rome. She would prove to be even more ruthless than her mother had been.

One of her first tasks was to get rid of her mom's lover, Pope John, whom she hated. It didn't take long for her to outmaneuver and imprison him. John rotted in a dungeon for about a year until Marozia's second husband, Guy of Tuscany, smothered him to death with pillows.

Marozia was in such a powerful position that she was able to appoint popes herself, just like her mother had done. She appointed a couple of elderly, pliant popes to fill the office until her own son was old enough to put on the throne. When he did he took the name of Pope John XI. The new pope's father, by the way, was none other than Pope Sergius, who had impregnated Marozia when she was only fifteen years old. So

Pope Sergius managed the spectacular feat of not only killing two of his predecessors, but also fathering one of his successors.

But Marozia wasn't finished with her plotting. She got it into her head that she wished to be crowned as an empress. She found a suitable man to rule by her side in the form of a stooge named Hugh, who came with a nice pedigree; in fact, he was the King of Italy. There was a bit of a problem with the match, however, in that both she and Hugh were already married. To complicate matters further, Marozia's husband Guy was Hugh's half-brother. But the convenient, suspicious deaths of both their spouses left Marozia and Hugh swinging singles again. When Lambert, who was another of Hugh's half-brothers, protested this unseemly relationship, Hugh had his eyes gouged out. Then he had him imprisoned until he died shortly thereafter. Hearing no more objections, the lovebirds were married. The wedding took place in a castle and was performed by none other than Pope John XI, himself. This remains the only time in history that a pope presided over his mother's marriage.

But alas, the couple would not live happily ever after. In fact, their relationship didn't even survive their wedding reception. At the post-wedding celebration, Hugh arrogantly asserted his authority by smacking Marozia's other son, Alberic, across the face. Alberic exploded in anger, marched out of the party and into the streets. There, he assembled a mob to storm the castle where the wedding party was being held. Hugh bravely looked down from the castle upon the rabble assembling in the streets below, and he panicked. In his terror, he abandoned his new wife and any hope of being made emperor. He fled Rome never to return. Alberic seized power for himself and became known as Alberic II. He had his mother thrown into prison where she languished until her death not long thereafter. He also imprisoned his half-brother, the pope. John would spend the rest of his papacy taking his orders from Alberic. After John died, it was Alberic who would choose the popes.

The story of Pope Sergius III raises a question: who is an antipope? Serving as pope in good standing until death is no guarantee that the Church will continue to honor your papacy after you're gone. Sometimes, the Church doesn't drop the antipope hammer until many years later. The aforementioned Antipope Christopher was not demoted to antipope until the twentieth century, a thousand years after he had served as pope.

The surest way to become an antipope is to be elected in a canonically dubious method. This is what eventually got Christopher kicked off the papal list. As you shall see throughout this book, however, some pretty questionable elections are still held as valid.

Then there is the case of Antipope Boniface VII. In 973 Boniface murdered pope Benedict VI and got himself elected pope. Rioting forced him to flee Rome, but he returned when his replacement, Pope John XIV, died. John had also probably been murdered on the order of Boniface. If so, this would mean that Sergius was not the only pope to kill two of his predecessors, but as Boniface is considered an antipope today, it could be argued that he doesn't count. In any case, Boniface's return to the papacy was a short one. He himself died under mysterious circumstances shortly after resuming his holy duties.

Pope Sergius III was not the only pope who fathered one of his successors, either. Pope Hormisdas had fathered Pope Silverus many years earlier.

What the Hell???

Pope Joan

Sometime in the middle of the ninth century a young woman disguised herself as a male and undertook a course of religious education. She was a quick study and worked her way up through the Church until she was elected Pope. This cross-dressing imposter took the papal name of John, and her ploy worked brilliantly until she became pregnant. The female pope, who was apparently ignorant of the nine-month gestational period, went into labor and gave birth while in a public procession from St. Peter's to St. John Lateran. The good people of Rome—aghast at this moral outrage—righteously stoned the female interloper to death.

Seriously?

Hell no. The misogynistic story of "Pope Joan" is pure hogwash. How do we know this? First off, there are significantly different versions of the tale. Some claim Joan died in childbirth rather than from stoning. Still others say she died of shame. Secondly, the earliest reliably dated, written account of this story dates from 1255—four hundred years after the "fact." Thirdly, there are no gaps in papal history during the 850s when this supposedly happened.

Oh, another red flag is that the whole thing is utterly ludicrous. It is implausible that a woman advancing through the stages of pregnancy could cavort around the Vatican every day without anyone noticing that she was a female.

The myth of Pope Joan appears to have been born out of the Pornocracy. The outrage over this period festered until it took the form of this kooky yarn.

Notwithstanding the stupidity of the tale, it was almost universally believed in the Middle Ages, and the Church did nothing to discourage belief in it. The legend served as a cautionary example of what would happen if women were allowed too much fancy book learning. It worked to the male-dominated Church's advantage to have people buying into it.

The myth came back to haunt the Church, however, when the Protestant Reformation occurred. The Protestants (and the Hussites before them) were quick to throw the story of the female pope in the face of the Catholic Church as an example of the gross immorality that went on in Rome.

If that weren't enough, the Pope Joan story has left us with another fanciful belief that perseveres to this day; namely the chairs known to scholars as the *sedes stercoraria* and to pretty much everyone else as the "ball-checking chairs." These strange-looking chairs have large holes in the centers of their seats. It is said that after the debacle of Pope Joan, all future popes were required to sit on the chair so a Church official could reach under and cop a feel of the holy tackle to assure that no ladies were trying to sneak out of the kitchen and into the Holy See.

Like the story of Joan herself, the ball-checking chair is total bunk. While the Church did have chairs with holes in them, they were in use long before the time the Joan incident allegedly took place. What the odd design with the hole is for is unknown, but there is no reason to believe it was for checking gender.

There are reports of genital check taking place at papal ordinations to this day, but claims from "witnesses" can be broken into two categories; one, hearsay and two, people claiming their view was obstructed during the ceremony, which, they conclude, is when the crotch grab must have occurred. In other words, *not* seeing the act take place is presented as proof that it happened.

In 1978, French author Maurice Clavel, writing in the pages of *Nouvel Observateur*, rapturously hailed the newly elected Pope John Paul II with the words "He has them. *Duas et bebe pendentes* (two, well hung) for sure." He went on to praise other aspects of John Paul's physique and his "eye for the girls."

Pope John XII

What did your folks give you when you got out of high school? A stereo? Money for college? Maybe even a car? If you were Octavian of the Theophylact clan you got the papacy.

Young Octavian was the son of the Alberic II, the brutal Patrician of Rome who we met in the chapter on Sergius III. Alberic made his son a Prince, but that wasn't enough to satisfy him. Alberic forced the Roman nobility to swear an oath that his son would be made pope as soon as an opening occurred. That opening presented itself in quick order when Pope John XI kicked the bucket, and as promised, Octavian was elected pope at the ripe old age of eighteen or so. He got to keep his royal title, so he was both pope and prince. He was the nephew of his predecessor, John XI, and the grandson of Sergius III and Marozia.

There were four main problems with John, however, that undermined his chances of being a good pope.

1) He was immature, inexperienced, and poorly educated.
2) He cared very little about the Church, religious matters or morality in general.
3) He was a horny teenager.
4) He was an idiot.

Handed the keys to the kingdom, John wasted no time in embarking on a campaign of decadence, debauchery, and mayhem that might have made Caligula blush.

John filled the Vatican with so many loose women—with whom he fornicated openly—that he was said to have turned the papal apartments into a brothel. He was reputed to have had sex with pilgrims while they were in the Basilica of St. Peter's. He gave one of his mistresses golden crosses and chalices that he had stolen from the Church. Since he was still a prince, he made her a feudal lord for good measure. It was said that he even got it on with his own niece and his father's widow.

He ordained a ten-year-old boy as a bishop, and he ordained a deacon in a horse stable. He ordained bishops for pay. He raised a glass of wine to toast Satan. He invoked the aid of pagan gods while gambling. He also celebrated mass without communion, and he never made the sign of the cross. But in light of his other transgressions, it's a little hard to get worked up over that.

Yet there was more to John's papacy than gross immorality and total disregard for Catholic tradition. He also found the time to get the stuffing beaten out of him in the political arena.

As usual, there were lots of intrigues and plots floating around Rome at the time, but after Alberic's death, John didn't have his father around to protect him anymore. When he got into trouble, he looked to Germany for an ally. He pledged an oath to the German King Otto I and crowned him Holy Roman Emperor in return for Otto's saving of the holy bacon from rivals within Italy. No sooner had the deal been done, however, than John realized he had made himself a virtual vassal to the more powerful Otto. So John foolishly started making awkward attempts to form an alliance against him. Otto tried to ignore John's insane plotting, but John made a point of shoving his betrayal into Otto's face, eventually leaving him with no choice but to march on Rome. In a panic, John stole everything he could carry from the Church and headed for the hills, literally, with the papal treasury in tow. When Otto got to Rome he convened a synod, which put John on trial in absentia. The synod was really little more than a show trial with a predetermined outcome. Nevertheless, there was no shortage of witnesses willing to testify to John's appalling behavior. So it came as no surprise when John was deposed by the synod and Otto's handpicked man, Leo VIII, was placed on the papal throne.

The potential difficulty with Leo was that he wasn't a cardinal, or a bishop, or even a priest for that matter. *No problemo!* Under pressure from Otto, Leo was first elected pope by acclaim and *then* ordained a priest. He was then promoted through the lower orders of the church. He got a new promotion roughly every two hours, until he was ordained the Bishop of Rome. This whole process consumed two days.

With his man on the throne, Otto confidently headed back north, but he failed to take into account the popular opinion of the Roman populace. Leo's papacy was such an obvious fraud—

and Leo himself was such a heel—that the people began to revolt against him even before Otto's departure. John helped stoke the flames of unrest by encouraging dissent in Rome from the safety of his mountain hideout. Widespread rioting erupted in Rome, forcing Leo to flee to Germany where Otto could protect him. John was thus able to stroll back into Rome and retake the papal throne for himself. John then deposed Leo and declared null and void all of his papal acts.

Once he was back in Rome, John went about the business of brutalizing those who had supported Otto and Leo. It is alleged that during this period one cardinal was fatally castrated, another had his hand cut off, another Church official was scourged, and one who had testified against John at the synod had his tongue cut out, his nose torn off, and his fingers removed. John also excommunicated Leo and everyone associated with him. What John didn't understand, however, was that there was nothing stopping Otto from returning to Rome, which is what he did. Once again, John had to hightail it out of town.

At this point, the story takes a curious turn, even when compared to everything that had occurred up to this point. John died suddenly on May 14, 964 before Otto even got to Rome. The reputed cause of his death referred to the devil striking him upon his temple. This explanation is sometimes interpreted as John suffering a stroke. The stroke story is dubious for two reasons, however. First, John was only in his mid-twenties at the time, and strokes are mighty uncommon at that age. Second, he is believed to have died in the bed of a married woman. It seems much more likely that the strike upon his temple was provided courtesy of the lady's husband.

When Otto arrived in Rome he found that a new pope, Benedict V, had been elected, despite Otto's clearly stated wish that Leo be restored to the papacy. The Roman people and the clergy had rush-elected Benedict precisely to prevent Leo's return. Otto expressed his anger with this development by laying siege to the city. Faced with starvation, the people relented and allowed Leo to become pope once again. Benedict was forced to hand his papal staff over to Leo and lie prostrate before him. Leo then broke the staff by smashing it over poor Benedict's head. Leo also stripped Benedict of his papal vestments and deposed him.

Otto then forced Benedict to move to Hamburg where he would spend the rest of his life under the emperor's thumb.

> Despite Leo VIII's dubious rise to the top, his papacy is still recognized as valid by the Catholic Church today.

Pope Benedict IX

In 1032 another Theophylact, this one named Tusculan, was elected pope and took the name Benedict IX. It would not be the last time he would assume the papacy in what would be one of the more bizarre and corrupt episodes in papal history.

Papacy I: Benedict IX and the Temple of Dumb

Benedict was a layperson; in fact, he was the third layman in a row to be elected pope. The two popes previous to Benedict were both the sons of Count Gregory of the infamous Theophylact dynasty. When his first-born son died, Gregory replaced him as pope with his next son. When he also died, he put his grandson on the throne. Benedict was somewhere between the age of eleven and twenty when the papacy was purchased for him. His predecessor had been his uncle.

Given the circumstances of his election, it is not surprising that Benedict was a crappy pope who lived as he pleased and used the Church as a vehicle to promote the interests of his family.

He also had to watch his back, as there were plenty of people who resented Gregory's ability to pick everyone in his family to be pope, thereby monopolizing access to the Church treasury. Soon after Benedict became pope, a plan was hatched to assassinate him while he attended mass in St. Peter's. The assassins intended to strangle the wet-behind-the-ears pontiff at the church because that was the only time he could be found outside the confines of his heavily defended home. The pope's life was saved, however, by a wildly improbable bit of luck. At the moment when he was to be killed, a solar eclipse occurred. The sudden, unexpected darkness cast the scene into confusion and gave the superstitious a bad omen to fear. The plotters' hesitation in carrying out their murderous plan won the pope's bodyguards enough time to figure out what was going on, and they whisked him away to safety.

Despite the dog-eat-dog nature of papal politics he was thrust into, it's hard to feel too terrible for Benedict. He was a massive womanizer who raided the Church's funds to support a lavish lifestyle. He was variously labeled as an adulterer, murder and rapist. St. Peter Damian later described him as "feasting on immorality" and "a demon from hell in the disguise of a priest." He was so bad, in fact, that after four years as pope, a dissatisfied populace briefly chased him out of Rome until the Holy Roman Emperor, Conrad II, threw his weight around to get Benedict back into the city. Eight years later, Benedict sparked a more serious popular revolt that forced him to flee the city for a longer period.

While he was out of town on this second occasion, a rival family of the Theophylacts installed their own pope, Sylvester III, to replace him. Benedict excommunicated Sylvester while in exile and started raising an army to overthrow him.

Papacy II: Benedict Strikes Back!

Benedict marched on Rome and kicked Sylvester to the curb. After going to all that trouble to get the papacy back, what did Benedict then do? He turned around and gave it all away two months later! Well, he didn't really *give* it away so much as he *sold* it to a man who took the name Pope Gregory VI. Benedict never really wanted to be pope in the first place, and he had his eye on a young lady he wished to marry. Besides, he had cleaned out all the money from the holy coffers by this time; so selling the office was a reasonable way to keep the cash flowing. He got the better part of a ton of gold for the papacy. That sounds like a pretty steep price, but since the new pope was Benedict's godfather, it might have actually reflected a family discount.

Papacy III: The Return of the Ding-A-Ling

In 1047 Henry III ascended to the top of the Holy Roman Empire and wished to be crowned emperor by the pope. But there he faced a problem. Gregory and Sylvester both claimed to be pope. More importantly, Benedict still seemed to be the real pope, as his sale of the papacy might not have been entirely valid under cannon law. He summoned all three claimants to a synod in Rome to sort out the mess. Henry deposed both Sylvester and Gregory at the synod. Benedict hadn't bothered to show up for the festivities, so his deposition had to wait for four more days. Henry then named his own man to be pope. This pope took the name Clement II. While in exile, Benedict's marriage plans had fallen through, so he changed his mind about not wanting to be pope anymore. He rejected Clement's claim to the papacy, apparently forgetting that he had kind of forfeited his own claim when he sold the office.

Clement only lasted as pope for eight months before he cast off this mortal coil. The people of Rome then clamored for Benedict's return. Since this is the same citizenry that had twice previously chased Benedict out of town, it's worth asking why the change of heart took place. First off, the Romans were always quick to reject any pope pushed on them by German rulers. Furthermore, it seems Benedict had bribed people to demand his return. The ploy worked, and Benedict was made pope yet again, but it wouldn't last long. Nine moths into Benedict's third term, Henry finally succeeded in ousting him for good. Sylvester was imprisoned, Gregory and Benedict were forced to abdicate, and Henry placed yet another pope, Damasus II, onto the throne. Damasus convened a trial of Benedict in which he was charged with buying and selling the papacy, but Benedict ignored the proceedings. He was excommunicated without offering a defense.

Benedict's final years are largely lost to history. Some say he tried once more to get the papacy back, but evidence for this is wanting. He died somewhere between 1055 and 1085.

> One more Theophylact would briefly serve as pope after Benedict, but that would be the end of the family's popes. The Theophylact's rein of terror in the Church had lasted on and off for over a hundred years.

Pope Urban II

In March of 1088 Otho of Lagery was unanimously elected pope and took the name of Urban II. Unfortunately for the new pope, an antipope by the name of Guibert was already on the throne, and he had the backing of several notables, most significantly the Holy Roman Emperor, Henry IV. With friends like these, Guibert had no reason to step aside for the less-powerful Urban. Urban went to Sicily where he secured the support of King Roger I and then undertook his quest to claim his place in Rome. After six years of warfare and bribery, he managed to oust Guibert, excommunicate Henry, and take the reins of the Church.

Urban wasted no time in making his mark upon the Church. He convened several councils; the most famous of these was in Clarmount, France. There were several items on the docket for this meeting, which involved hundreds of clergymen. Marriage amongst the clergy was condemned, the King of France was excommunicated, and the matter of a Crusade to the Holy Land was brought up.

Before the council had convened, the Byzantine Emperor Alexius I had petitioned Urban for help against the Turks who were threatening his realm. Normally an appeal from the leader of the Orthodox Christian Byzantines would have been dismissed out of hand by Rome, but Urban lent a sympathetic ear to this request. There were probably several factors influencing this. Muslims were in control of Spain and Portugal and had pushed into France before being turned back at Tours. They had also established bases in southern France and Italy at the time. The Muslim threat must have appeared very real to Catholics as well as to Orthodox Christians. Furthermore, the symbolic significance of the Holy Land could not have been lost on Urban. If he were able to liberate the holy city of Jerusalem, his legacy as one of the greatest popes of all time would be secured.

So Urban implored a large crowd gathered in Clarmount to take up arms against the infidels who were threatening the East. What exactly Urban said is a matter of great debate. It is commonly claimed that the crowd shouted, "God wills it" after his speech, but this too cannot be confirmed. What is beyond debate, however, is that the speech was an absolute hit. Men both rich and poor were practically falling over each other in a rush to sign up for the holy war to come. The hysteria quickly spread throughout Europe, helped at least in part by letters Urban sent to bishops near and far proclaiming the mission. Urban granted forgiveness of sins to those who took up arms for the Crusade, and he gave the banner of St. Peter to one of the leaders of the expedition. Only men judged to be of sufficient moral standing were allowed to go on the Crusade.

Zealots such as Peter the Hermit and Walter the Penniless stoked the flames of passion even beyond what Urban had. Countless thousands of men flocked to armies they were hastily throwing together. So great was the response to the call to arms that a problem arose. The raw recruits were entirely impatient to get started on their inevitable victory against the infidels. So rather than waiting for proper leadership and provisions to be arranged, they marched off to war in two huge mobs led by the completely unqualified Peter and Walter. This fiasco came to be known as the "Peasants' Crusade."

The mobs compensated for their lack of supplies by pillaging their way across Hungary and Bulgaria, destroying the livelihoods of whatever farmers whose lands happened to be in their way. It is said an argument over a pair of shoes erupted into a fight amongst the crusaders that left thousands of people dead. One can only imagine what Emperor Alexius must have thought when he got a load of this motley assemblage as it approached Constantinople. This was the army he had pleaded with Urban to send? The real army of the First Crusade was on its way, but he had no way of knowing that.

The peasants made their way south into Muslim lands, giving them the chance to kill people who weren't Christians for a change. They even managed to capture the lightly defended castle of Xerigordon from the Turks. The Turks naturally responded to this invasion by sending out an army to destroy it. When confronted by a real army, the peasants total lack of preparedness made itself clear. The Turks laid siege to the castle leaving the Crusaders with no water supply. Driven mad with thirst, the men drank their blood and urine in a futile attempt to stay alive. The Turks then offered stark terms of surrender to the desperate peasant crusaders. Those who converted to Islam were allowed to live, while those who refused were killed to a man. The men who accepted Islam were sold into slavery where they remained for the rest of their lives.

A second group of the peasant rabble was cut down at the town of Civetot with the loss of tens of thousands of men. Only a small percentage of the original force ever made it back to Europe. Peter the Hermit was one of the few survivors.

When the actual army of the Crusade made its way into enemy territory, the Turks expected it to be another assemblage of idiots playing soldier. They launched multiple failed attacks against them before they realized the threat they posed was serious. The Crusaders captured Nicea and catapulted the decapitated heads of several defenders over the city walls as an exclamation point on their victory. The Christians then quickly made their way to the city of Antioch where the Turks were waiting for them behind heavy fortifications. The Crusaders laid siege to the Muslims, and a long standoff ensued. Both sides suffered terribly as the months dragged on. The crusading army nearly broke down. Yet just when the Crusade seemed ready to fail, an operative who had been bribed by the Christian army found a way to let them into the city. The Crusaders poured into Antioch and promptly laid waste to it before regrouping for a push toward their ultimate goal—Jerusalem.

Though Jerusalem was well defended, the city fell to the Crusaders with relative ease. The Crusaders then proceeded to kill nearly everyone there, including men, women, and children. Jews were killed along with Muslims on the theory they were all infidels. Many of the victims were tortured before they were dispatched to the great beyond.

Meanwhile back in Rome, Urban had been making periodic pronouncements praising the divine mission to the Holy Land. He died shortly after the capture of Jerusalem and the ensuing massacre. Word of the victory did not reach Rome until after Urban's death, however, so he never learned how his holy war turned out.

Urban is venerated as a saint today.

> If Urban had hoped the Crusade would cement his name in history he certainly succeeded. Everything else he did as pope is completely overshadowed by the Crusade. But while he might have expected to be remembered as the hero who brought Jerusalem into the Christian realm, the eventual verdict on his Crusade turned out to be sharply negative. The Crusades poisoned relations between Christians and Muslims in a way that continues to this day. They are almost universally cited as one of the greatest atrocities ever committed in the name of God.

What the Hell???

The Rest of the Crusades

The Crusades went on for over a century after the fall of Jerusalem. Things started going south for the Christian cause not long after the triumph of the First Crusade, however. The alliance between the Catholic and Orthodox Christians started breaking down in no time. The lack of unity on both the Christian and Muslim sides would become an almost constant theme throughout the Crusades.

A second Crusade was called to shore up Christian gains and expand their territories. The now-legendary Knights Templar had been formed by this time. They not only paid for a good-sized chunk of the Crusade, but also played a big role in a Christian offensive designed to capture Damascus. The bid for Damascus failed, however, and the Crusade withered away.

Jerusalem fell back into Muslim hands after the crusaders lost 20,000 men at the disastrous Battle of Hattin, so the Third Crusade was launched to get it back. This campaign featured the marquee match up of the English King Richard "Lionheart" and the Arab Sultan Saladin. Richard won the showdown between the two at Acre although he was in no position to even try to retake Jerusalem. Saladin knew Richard's real interests lay in England, so he decided to simply wait him out. When the king went back to care of matters on the home front, Saladin easily retook the lands Richard had captured from him. For his trouble, Richard was kidnapped twice while on his way back to England by Europeans who apparently weren't all that impressed with his godly mission in the Middle East.

Then the story of the Crusades takes a turn for the bizarre. The Children's Crusade took place between the Third and Fourth Crusades. Details are sketchy as to what actually happened, but it seems there may have been two young men named Stephen and Nicholas who whipped up support for another Crusade in France and Germany respectively. According to legend, they attracted armies of kids to march off to the Holy Land, but met with disaster. The concept of armies of children is, however, pretty implausible. This concept may stem from a too-literal reading of descriptions of the forces. When contemporary people refer to soldiers as "the boys" they certainly don't mean to suggest the troops are children, yet it seems a similar term used in the Middle Ages has lead to the notion there were actually armies of whippersnappers on the march. It's probably better to think of the so-called "Children's Crusade" as more of a second Peasant's Crusade, only without the combat. The leaders of the expedition marched their armies—if they can be called that—to the Mediterranean Sea where they had promised that the waters would part before them in the same way they believed they had for Moses. When this miracle failed to occur, the mob disintegrated. A couple of no accounts with the charming names of William the Pig and Hugh the Iron promised some of the few remaining combatants they could get them to the Holy Land. Rather than sending them on their pilgrimage though, the hucksters sold the would-be crusaders into slavery.

The Fourth Crusade was arguably the most pathetic of the Crusades. A Christian army was assembled in Venice with the goal of once again capturing the Holy Land from the infidels. The army was completely reliant on the Venetians for transportation, however, and they soon found themselves taking orders from their hosts who had bigger concerns than religious wars. They forced the crusaders to invade Hungary rather than the Holy Land to win territory for their city-state. When Pope Innocent III heard that his army had been diverted to attack a Christian kingdom, he went ballistic and excommunicated the whole force. With the concept of a holy war effectively flushed down the toilet, the Crusaders turned their attention to Constantinople. They captured the city and raped and pillaged it to their hearts' content. The fall of the greatest city in Orthodox Christendom was good enough news to cheer up Innocent, but his improved mood didn't last long as reports got to him relating how the whole Byzantine assault had once again been orchestrated by Venice for its own massive financial gain. It's worth remembering at this point that the original impetus for the Crusades was to protect the Byzantine Empire. Now it's capitol was laid to waste by the very crusaders who were ostensibly protecting it. The Fourth Crusade ended without ever venturing into Muslim territory.

A fifth Crusade accomplished nothing, but that didn't stop a sixth from being organized. Strong leadership was an ingredient that had been missing in many of the preceding Crusades. That issue was addressed by recruiting the Holy Roman Emperor Frederick II to lead this campaign. The problem was that Frederick hated Pope Gregory IX even more than he hated the Muslims. When Frederick and a big chunk of his army came down with malaria he had to postpone the planned invasion of the Middle East. Gregory took this as dithering on Frederick's part, and he excommunicated him. The excommunication rendered Frederick unfit for the Crusade, but he didn't care. When he had recovered from his illness he led his troops on the Crusade anyway. This so angered Gregory that he nonsensically excommunicated Frederick a second time for the offense of crusading while excommunicated. Undeterred, Frederick was able to win back Jerusalem from the Muslims without the bother of having to fight for it. He negotiated his way into town with a Muslim ruler who was so concerned about being attacked elsewhere by other Muslims that he figured he could live with a Christian presence in Jerusalem more easily than he could try to fight a war on two fronts.

Nevertheless, Frederick proved to be an unpopular ruler with the locals. When he got word that things were going poorly for his interests back in Europe, he decided to sneak out of town and head home. The townsfolk caught wind of his flight, however, and bombarded him with feces as he made his way through the streets. When he got back to Europe, Frederick waged war against the pope.

The Christians lost Jerusalem once more, and a seventh Crusade was launched to take it yet again. This failed, and it marked the end of the major Crusades. By now a new force, the Mongols, had appeared from the East had beaten the daylights out of Christians and Muslims alike. In the face of such a threat, continued crusading didn't seem like the greatest idea. The Crusades did continue, however, but with diminishing vigor until they finally petered out for good. One can't help but think that European kings had gotten sick of sending their armies off on missions that were not enriching them. In the end, the Christians lost all the territory they had gained in the Crusades.

On March 12, 2000 Pope John Paul II made headlines when he sort of apologized for the Crusades. What he actually said was...

While we praise God who, in his merciful love, has produced in the Church a wonderful harvest of holiness, missionary zeal, total dedication to Christ and neighbor, we cannot fail to recognize the infidelities to the Gospel committed by some of our brethren, especially during the second millennium. Let us ask pardon for the divisions which have occurred among Christians, for the violence some have used in the service of the truth and for the distrustful and hostile attitudes sometimes taken towards the followers of other religions.

He never actually mentioned the Crusades anywhere in his sermon, and he maintained that the unspecified actions were undertaken in "service of the truth." He was trying to denounce the unsavory actions of the crusaders without undermining the moral authority of the Church that ordered the Crusades in the first place.

Pope Innocent III

A lot of the popes in his book are characters the Church would rather forget, but such is not the case with Pope Innocent III. Innocent was an iron-willed man who restored much of the political prestige to the Church that had been lost in the years leading up to his papacy. Under his rule, the Church rose to a level of power that had been almost unimaginable up until that point. Innocent was also deeply devoted to his faith, an attitude that was far from the norm for popes in those days. The *Catholic Encyclopedia* refers to him as "one of the greatest popes of the Middle Ages." Yet what is greatness in the eyes of some is villainy in the eyes of others, and such is the case with Innocent.

Lotario Dei Conti di Segni was crowned pope in 1198 amidst great celebration. He took the name Innocent for what might now seem like ironic reasons. He was lucky in the sense that the Holy Roman Emperor had just died, and his heir was far too young to rule. The resulting power vacuum left no one in Germany who was strong enough to push around the pope. It also created a situation in which the various aspirants to power in Germany and elsewhere were in great need of papal blessing to shore up their positions. Innocent took full advantage of this situation. He made it clear that he was not only the absolute ruler of the Church, but of the temporal world as well.

It was Innocent who launched the tragicomic Fourth Crusade that never set foot in the Middle East. In his rage, he excommunicated the Venetians who had diverted his army. His anger subsided, however, when he realized that this turn of events could allow him to bring the Orthodox dissidents of the East back into the one true faith. He began an effort to Latinize the Eastern Church and return it to Catholicism. This effort, of course, eventually ended in failure.

Of far greater interest to Innocent than the goings on in the East, was the situation in the Languedoc area of what is now southern France. A new faith had taken root there, and he viewed it as an intolerable heresy.

The new religion, called "Catharism," had probably originated in Eastern Europe and migrated across the continent until it reached fertile soil in the Languedoc. The Cathars were dualists; they saw all of creation as being divided into good (spiritual) and evil (material) realms. They viewed the entire material world as sinful and considered the renunciation of materialism as the only path to salvation. They saw the God of the Old Testament as an evil God and the God of the New Testament as a good one. They believed Jesus had existed only in spiritual form. Life on this earth was hell in their eyes. They believed that sinners were punished by being reincarnated again and again into our awful world. They believed all people had led many past lives in both genders. Since they felt there was little difference between men and women, they became pioneers of gender equity. The hardcore followers of the faith were known as "perfects." The perfects engaged in fasting and prayer on a near-constant basis, stayed celibate, and were what we might call vegans today, except that they did eat fish. They were also pacifists who would not defend themselves even if attacked. The faith spread fast and had come to be accepted in the Languedoc. Innocent, however, was determined to put an end to it.

His first tactic was an appeal to reason. Public debates were held between priests and perfects while at the same time, Cistercian monks were sent out to convert the heretics. All of this ended in spectacular failure. The fact of the matter was that the avaricious behavior that was readily apparent in so many Catholic officials only served to increase the appeal of the anti-materialistic Cathars. The heavy-handed Cistercians succeeded only in offending the people they encountered. Innocent then sent Domingo de Guzman (who would later be canonized as St. Dominic) to preach to the heretics. Like the perfects, Domingo lived a life without material comfort. He was more appealing to the people of the Languedoc than those Innocent had sent before him, but he too made little headway in bringing Cathars back into the Church. Another Monk named Peter of Castelnau was sent to the Languedoc as a sort of last chance to let the people see the holy light. When he was murdered, things took a turn for the worse.

The first course of business in Innocent's new get-tough scheme was to let Count Raymond VI know who was boss. Raymond was ruler of much of the Languedoc. Though he was a Catholic himself, he had no interest in persecuting the Cathars. He was a tolerant type of man who drew the ire of the Church for his soft treatment of both the Cathars and the Jews. In his lands, Jews were allowed to live on more equal terms with the rest of society than anywhere else in Christendom. He had Jews in his court and—in violation of Church law—allowed Jews to own property and hire Christian employees. A game called "Strike the Jew" (which was merely a public beating of Jews) was banned in his domain despite protests from the Catholic clergy who demanded that the tradition be allowed to continue.

Raymond was blamed for the death of Peter of Castelnau without evidence or a trial. He was then subjected to a humiliating act of contrition. He was partially stripped in public before his subjects and scourged by clergy members. He was then forced to announce that he would condemn heretics and dismiss Jews from his employment. In return, Raymond would be allowed to keep his lands, provided of course, that he didn't offend the Church any further.

But this was only the start of Innocent's crackdown. In 1209 he called for a new crusade, not to wrest the Holy Land from the Muslims, but to exterminate the heresy in the Languedoc. The appeal of this "Albigensian Crusade" was strong. It promised guaranteed salvation and great riches to prospective warriors, and they didn't have to traipse all the way to Jerusalem to get them. This Crusade would be fought right in the combatants' back yard. Tens of thousands of men answered Innocent's call to arms, and a massive army led by a man named Arnold Amaury marched toward the Languedoc. It would mark the second crusade of Innocent's papacy in which only Christian cities were attacked. Innocent made it a crime to tolerate the presence of Cathars, so the Catholics in the area who had lived peacefully with their Cathar neighbors were in the crosshairs of the crusade just as much as the Cathars themselves.

The first city in the way of the crusaders was Béziers. The townspeople retreated behind the city's formidable walls while the crusaders set up a siege. They offered to spare the town if its citizens would turn over 222 Cathars for punishment. Catholics made up the majority of the town's population, but they refused to turn anyone over to the pope's army, and they braced themselves for the inevitable onslaught. The crusading army was powerful, but the town's fortifications were solid. They stood a real chance of turning back an attack. Furthermore, most of the crusaders were only signed up for forty-day terms of service, so the prospect of holding off the crusaders until they went home was promising. The town fell, however, when some of its defenders stupidly left the city gates open just long enough to let the opportunistic crusaders charge inside.

Once they had breached the town's defenses, the massacre was on. It was said that Amaury gave the command "Kill them all, God will know his own!" Whether or not he actually said this will never be known, but his men did kill everyone in Béziers. They killed men, women, children, and even babies. They killed Cathars and Catholics alike. They killed the town's Catholic clergy who were dressed in their vestments. They even killed the people who had sought sanctuary by crowding into the town's Catholic Church. All told, about 20,000 people died in the slaughter. After all this murdering, the crusaders were still able to find the strength to bicker over whom should reap the spoils of their conquest. When it was decided that the rich men in their ranks were entitled to nearly all the swag, the less well-off decided to express their disappointment with the decision by burning the city to the ground before the loot could be pillaged. The crusaders walked away from the flaming carnage without the treasure they had coveted, but were comforted by the knowledge that they were now assured of entry into heaven.

Yet the destruction of Béziers was just a prelude to the carnage that was to come. Next up was the huge fortress of Carcassone. The crusaders advanced steadily toward the castle, inflicting heavy losses upon those who dared to get in their way. They laid siege to Carcassone, leaving the defenders without water. When their leader, Raymond Roger, was offered the chance to negotiate surrender, he took it. The crusaders reneged on their promise of safe passage to Raymond Roger, however, and imprisoned him. He was killed, and Carcassone surrendered quickly thereafter. The crusaders magnanimously decided to let the defenders live. They did, however, seize every single possession the people had and turned them out into the wilderness with nothing to their names.

The crusaders had cut the heart out of the Languedoc. But they didn't have enough men to police all the territory they had conquered, so rebellions broke out in various places. The crusaders responded to the uprisings with appalling cruelty. At the town of Bram, the crusaders put down one such conflagration, gathered the surviving defenders, stabbed their eyes out, chopped their noses off, and cut off their lips. One man was left with one eye to guide the pathetic group to another town where everyone could behold what happened to those who defied the army of the Church.

In his zeal to exterminate the heretics, Innocent renewed the crusade year after year. And he was getting results. At the town of Lavaur, 400 Cathar perfects were captured and set afire in what was the largest mass burning of humanity in the Middle Ages.

By now, a man named Simon de Montfort had taken control of the crusading army, and he used it with lethal force against his opponents. In the process, he managed to enrich himself to no end. He actually amassed more land than was owned by the king of France. Such a meteoric rise to the top of the social order made some of the old blue bloods in Europe a bit nervous. This concern caused Innocent to call a halt to the crusade in 1213. His hatred of the heretics soon got the better of him, however, and he quickly reinstated it.

In 1215 Innocent convened the Fourth Lateran Council to hash out some dogmatic issues that had been debated within the Church for some time. It was to be the most important theological meeting of the entire Middle Ages. Thousands of dignitaries descended upon Rome for the event. So great was the throng that one bishop died of suffocation at the opening ceremony. The first order of business was to condemn the heretics once more, but that was by no means the end of it. The council made decisions that still are at the core of the Church today. Under Innocent's fierce guidance, the issue of the nature of the Holy Trinity was permanently resolved, and the Eucharist was declared to be the actual body and blood of Christ. Additionally, it was decreed that Jews would have to wear yellow patches on their clothes to identify themselves so that people would not unknowingly fail to discriminate against them.

Also in 1215, Innocent injected himself into a political uprising against King John in England. John was a famously inept ruler who had been forced to sign the Magna Carta, a document that greatly curtailed the power of the king and made small steps in the direction of democracy. Innocent lashed out at the Magna Carta calling it a "shameful and demeaning agreement, forced upon the King by violence and fear." He made it clear that kings were to answer to the pope, not to their subjects.

Innocent was only thirty-seven years old when he was elected pope, so he was still a relatively young man in his mid-fifties at the time, but he surprisingly dropped dead on July 16, 1216. The "great" pope was gone, but his crusade against the Cathars would live on.

The term "Cathar" is actually an insult. It comes from a German play on words that alludes to cat worshiping. It was widely believed that the Cathars included cats in dark ceremonies they were supposed to have held. The Cathars were thought to have ritually kissed the cats on their anuses. Outlandish stories such as this helped to dehumanize the Cathars in the eyes of those who were out to slaughter them. The Cathars referred to themselves only as "good Christians."

Another contribution to our lexicon from this debacle is the term "buggar." This stems from a corruption of "Bulgar" which referred to an Eastern heresy that came to be associated with Catharism. As you might guess, it was rumored that the Cathars were a bunch of homosexuals.

What the Hell???

The End of the Cathars

The greatest city of the Languedoc was Toulouse, yet the crusade had not yet taken it. Simon de Montfort sought to remedy this disgrace not long after Innocent's death.

He attacked the city, but could not break it. He finally offered to meet Toulouse's leading citizens to discuss peace terms. Just like the "peace negotiations" at Carcassone, however, the whole thing was a ruse. After the town leaders came out from behind their fortifications, he took all of them prisoner and threatened to kill them if Toulouse did not yield to him. Rather than see hundreds of people put to death, the townspeople backed down. Simon imposed terms of surrender that reduced the once-vibrant city to poverty. Satisfied that he had crushed Toulouse, Simon took off for Provence where there were few heretics, but lots of opportunities for him to plunder more wealth for himself. While he was away, Count Raymond rode back onto the scene. He had been forced to watch helplessly as the crusade tore apart his domain, and he had reached his breaking point. When he made it clear he would tolerate the crusade no longer, he was hailed as a savior by the people of Toulouse. Rebellion then broke out once again.

When de Montfort got the news of the uprising he quickly wheeled his forces back around to Toulouse. There would be no mercy this time as he gave orders to kill every man and woman in the city. The people knew what fate awaited them if they lost the coming battle, so they threw everything they had into staving off the crusaders once again. Men, women, boys, and girls manned the city's defenses in an all-or-nothing battle. The crusaders attacked repeatedly, but were repulsed again and again. Finally, a lucky shot from a catapult nailed de Montfort in the head, killing him instantly. Without their leader, the crusaders quickly lost their will to fight and broke off the attack. Toulouse had been saved.

The smaller town of Marmande was less fortunate. Pope Honorius II decided that it was necessary to prove the crusade was still a force to be feared, so he chose the town seemingly at random for a demonstration of his strength. The unsuspecting town was overrun, and its 7,000 inhabitants were mercilessly put to death.

In 1222 Count Raymond died—incredibly—of natural causes. As an excommunicant, he was refused a Christian burial. His son, Raymond VII succeeded him.

Four years later, a fresh crusade was launched against the Cathars. This time the French King Louis VIII was brought in to run the show. This was a huge opportunity for Louis to expand the borders of France, and he took full advantage of it. He marched his army south and laid waste to the Languedoc. He burned crops, chopped down orchards, poisoned wells and did whatever else he needed to in order to force the surrender of the entire area.

Raymond VII was imprisoned and taken to Paris where he was treated to the same punishment his father had received. He was paraded out in front of Notre Dame, stripped, scourged and forced to swear he would spare no effort in persecuting heretics.

With the crusade now over, Pope Gregory IX (who was Innocent's nephew) launched an inquisition to finish off the Cathars once and for all. Gregory apparently believed the Cathars partook in wild sex orgies. The babies conceived in these fantastical shindigs were killed, burned, and their ashes were mingled with dung to make a horrific sort of communion wafer. The story was beyond ridiculous, but perhaps the anus-kissing story had grown stale by that time. At any rate, the Inquisition would prove to be just as horrible as the Crusade had been.

The Inquisition was conducted by Dominican monks who were the spiritual successors of St. Dominic, whose efforts to convert the same heretics had met with failure years earlier. The monks were relentless in their pursuit of the Cathars and anyone who tolerated them. People were dragged before the Inquisition on the thinnest of evidence. They were put under relentless pressure to confess and to give up the names of others who could be put through the same process. Anyone found guilty not only faced the prospect of being burned to death, but also of having all their possessions seized and their surviving family members turned out into the streets. The confiscation of property made the Inquisition a very profitable venture for the Church and increased the incentive to widen the Inquisition.

The Inquisition allowed no appeals, and anyone who dared to represent a defendant before the tribunals could be charged with the same crimes as the defendant. This assured that the accused would not be lawyering up for the proceedings.

Many of the accused hit upon the ploy naming dead people as having associated with heretics, thereby sparing their living friends and family members. The Church responded to these charges by exhuming the corpses of the accused and burning them for their crimes. They then seized the property of their descendants. Somewhere, Pope Stephen VI had to be smiling at all these exhumations.

But the inquisition was not satisfied to merely to roast the dead. They executed people *en masse* and held book burnings in their zeal to wipe out the heresy. At Montésgur, 200 Cathar perfects were captured and given the choice to recant or die. They all chose death. They were tied together and set aflame. Twenty-one more Cathars volunteered to be burned with them. In one particularly chilling episode of the Inquisition, a bishop pretending to be a perfect tricked an elderly, delirious lady on her deathbed into betraying her true faith. Upon hearing her confession, the bishop ordered the dying wretch to be tied to her mattress. The bedding was then dragged out of her house and into a field where it was placed atop a pile of kindling and burned with her still strapped to it.

The Inquisition dragged on for years and years. In 1252 Pope Innocent IV turned up the energy of the Inquisition by approving the use of torture to extract confessions from the accused. In 1321 the last known perfect was burned. With that, the faith was gone forever.

Gregory IX had an eventful papacy that went well beyond the genocide of the Cathars. But despite all the intrigues and battles he was behind, it was his attitude about cats for which he is best remembered. Gregory was not what you might call a "cat fancier." He was convinced the critters were diabolical and consorted with the devil, so he condemned the animals. A massive cat slaughter ensued. As the cat population crashed, the rat population exploded. Those rats carried the fleas that are usually credited with eventually spreading the Black Death throughout Europe. The resulting plague left millions upon millions of people dead.

Pope Boniface VIII

In 1293 a tiny college of cardinals met to elect a new pope. Torn between the Orsini and Colonna families who each desperately wanted to enrich themselves by getting their own candidates crowned, the cardinals were hopelessly deadlocked and remained so for months on end. As the standoff dragged on and on, a letter to the cardinals arrived from a priest named Peter of Morone. He was a hermit who dedicated his every moment to veneration of the Holy Spirit. His letter chastised the cardinals for leaving the Church adrift as they failed in their duty to elect a new pope.

The college was unmoved by the tongue-lashing they received from Peter. One of the cardinals even sarcastically suggested that they should elect Peter pope. As the stalemate went on *ad nauseam*, however, the joke began to be taken seriously. Finally, the cardinals settled on Peter as a compromise candidate that would not threaten the interests of either family since he was as removed from Roman politics as a person could be. The fact that Peter had never sought the office nor dreamed he would be considered as a candidate was of no concern to the cardinals.

The first course of action after the election of Peter was to tell him. This was no easy task because Peter was hidden away in a small cave high in the mountains not far from Naples. A Church procession made its way up the slopes looking for him. It took five days to find him, and when they did, they found an utterly bewildered man in his 80s who shunned human contact. It took considerable persuasion to get him to agree to serve as pope and leave his cherished solitude, but Peter did eventually take the job. He moved down to Naples and took the name of Celestine V.

It quickly became clear, however, that Celestine was *way* out his league in the office of the papacy. He was a simple man who sought little in life other than solitude, yet the opulence of the court of King Charles of Naples now surrounded him. He spoke little Latin, knew nothing of Church or state politics, did not understand the power or wealth he commanded as pope, and did not know that he could not trust the people who swarmed around him. To the consternation of the cardinals, he refused to move to Rome. He opted instead to stay in Naples in a castle belonging to King Charles. He built a small cell for himself inside the castle in which he tried to live like a hermit again. All the while, the King Charles and the cardinals tried to exploit his naïveté by manipulating him to their own advantage.

No one was better at this than Cardinal Benedict Gaetani who posed as a friend to the bewildered pope while all the while coveting his position. At some point, Gaetani must have pointed out to the unhappy Celestine that he could walk away from it all if he wanted to. Gaetani was a master of the law, and he was more than willing to help Celestine through the process of abdication.

Gaetani got everything in order for Celestine. After a mere fifteen weeks as pope, Celestine did the take-this-job-and-shove-it routine and abdicated. A new conclave was convened, and this time they were able to agree on a new pope. Needless to say, they elected Gaetani who took the name Boniface VIII.

Celestine may have been kooky, but he was undeniably devout in his faith. Boniface was another matter. He openly sought the pleasures of the flesh and made no apology for it. He defended as "natural" his fornication with women and sodomizing of boys. He once remarked while eating dinner that man had as much chance of life after death as the bird he feasted upon.

The top priority for the newly elected pope was to get the hell out of Naples. As soon as he could, he packed up for Rome and notified Celestine that he would be expected to make the trip with him. Celestine was horrified at the thought of moving to Rome, as the city was the antitheses of the simple solitude he craved. But Boniface would not risk having a popular religious figure out in the world where he could possibly threaten his rule. So he ordered the ex-pope to come with him to the Vatican where he could keep him under his constant watch. Celestine, however, was able to sneak away from the procession while on route to Rome. He was long gone before anyone noticed.

When his absence was discovered, Boniface ordered a massive manhunt to track down and arrest the pope-on-the-loose. Celestine had gone back to his old mountain hideout, but it quickly became obvious that this would not be safe. When word came that papal officials were headed that way, Celestine took off. He left a monk behind to notify the pursuers that Celestine was gone for good. When the papal search party met up with the monk, they murdered him on the spot.

Celestine abandoned the mountains and caught a boat to Greece. A storm arose at sea, however, which forced the ship back to Italy. Once he was back ashore, Celestine was inundated by admirers. This made him stick out like a sore thumb. He was promptly arrested by King Charles' men and turned over to Boniface, who imprisoned him. Celestine reputedly said to Boniface "You entered like a fox, you will reign like a lion, and you will die like a dog." Celestine died ten months after Boniface locked him up.

With his main "rival" out of the way, Boniface had more time to concentrate on the things that really mattered, like diverting as much Church money as possible into enhancing the position of his family. He adorned his relatives with enormous gifts of land. That property often came at the expense of the Colonna family, who were pissed off to no end by this divine land grab.

It wasn't long before this resentment broke out into open warfare between the Colonna and the pope. Boniface excommunicated everyone in the family to the fourth generation and launched a crusade against the Colonna. This allowed him to raise money all over Europe to wage his family feud. The crusaders who came to Italy killed and enslaved not only Colonna family members, but also any peasants who were unfortunate enough to live on Colonna property.

The Colonna had little chance of competing against a pope who could command such resources. They suffered several military losses until they were left with a single stronghold: the city of Palestrina. Palestrina would be no pushover, however, as the city's defenses were formidable. Boniface offered a truce to the Colonna to avoid the costly battle that lie ahead. The Colonna agreed to surrender the city in return for clemency. Boniface made good on his promise not to slaughter the remaining Colonna, but he hadn't promised to treat the town of Palestrina well. He exacted a horrible vengeance on the city that had supported his enemies. He destroyed every single structure in the city except for its basilica, and he salted the earth for good measure. Needless to say, Palestrina never recovered from the devastation. The Colonna objected to Boniface's sadistic treatment of Palestrina and were excommunicated again as a result.

The remaining Colonna escaped to France where they would be out of Boniface's reach, as the French King, Philip IV, wasn't a big admirer of the pontiff. Philip's problem with Boniface centered on the issue of taxes. The standard practice of the day was that the state would collect taxes and forward a cut to the Church. Philip decided that he needed all the taxes he collected to fight with England, however, so he could spare none for the Church. The enraged Boniface then tried to exert himself as the ruler of all of Europe, both holy and temporal, just as Innocent III had. He decreed that no king ruled without his approval. But Philip would have none of this. He sent an army to Italy to confront the pope. The Colonna and numerous others of Boniface's enemies augmented the king's forces. They quickly captured Boniface in the town of Anagni as the stunned townspeople put up no defense on Boniface's behalf. This was a town that owed its prosperity to the favor that Boniface had shown it, however. After three days, the good people of Anagni came to their senses and realized that Boniface was their meal ticket. If he went down, they would go with him. So they rose up and freed the pope who then escaped to Rome.

But things had changed. Philip's defiance of Boniface had ruined Boniface's aura of invincibility. As their fear of the pope melted away, people found the courage to openly oppose him. Boniface, for his part, became consumed with paranoia and trusted no one. He died one miserable month after his rescue.

The effort the French had put into toppling Boniface continued to pay off for them when his replacement was selected. A series of French popes would follow Boniface. They relocated the papacy from Rome to Avignon, France for the next seventy years.

The French King Phillip IV was to play another significant role in the history of the Church. In 1307 he decided that he could enrich himself by claiming the treasure of the Knights Templar for himself. The Templars were a sort of holy-warrior sect that had fought for generations in the Holy Land and had been forced back into Europe after the Crusades had run aground. They had reaped lots of money from special Church collections over the years and had also captured a great deal of swag for themselves in the Middle East. The Templars were also pioneers in the area of banking and had established branches for that purpose around Europe.

Phillip accused the Templars of every crime against God that he could think of. He was able to browbeat Pope Clement V into going along with him on the issue. In Church law, the Templars answered to no one but the pope, but the political situation of the day meant that Clement was little more than a vassal of the French King. Philip ordered the arrest of all the Templars in France and then forced Clement to expand that order to all Catholic lands.

The Templars were tortured into confessing innumerable offenses including killing babies, having sex with demons, urinating on the cross, worshiping an idol called "Baphomet," and practicing homosexuality. The knights withdrew their confessions after the torture was stopped, but to no avail. Scores of Templars were burned at the stake. In 1311 Clement dissolved the order for good. In 1314 the last Templar grand master was burned to death outside of Notre Dame, crying out his protestations of innocence until the end.

In the year 1300 Boniface initiated the first-ever Jubilee. These are holy years in which the faithful get a chance to gain forgiveness for their sins by making a pilgrimage to Rome. The tradition continues to this day.

What the Hell???

Lost and Found

The Catholic Church is awash in holy relics; in fact, all Catholic churches own at least one such object. Churches in other faiths also collect holy relics. In the vast majority of cases the relics are objects that belonged to—or supposedly belonged to—one saint or another. But there have been an awful lot of saints, and while I don't want to call these relics a dime a dozen, I will say that there is no shortage of such items. If you're in the market for something a bit more exclusive, however, what could be better than something that once belonged to Jesus himself? But surely none of Jesus' stuff is still floating around, right? You would think that all his former possessions would have been discarded or lost over the millennia, but there are lots of folks who claim it is still with us today.

You may be skeptical as to whether any of this stuff genuinely belonged to the big guy. That would be with good reason too, as there is no evidence that any of these objects ever came in contact with Jesus. And it's worth remembering that the huge demand for holy relics in the Middle Ages created a cottage industry for unscrupulous relic merchants who gleefully produced whatever artifacts were being sought. Add to this the churches whose success often depended upon the quality of the relics they could obtain, and you had buyers who were not very motivated to cast too critical an eye on the objects they acquired.

Here is a rundown on some of the most celebrated of the divine artifacts.

The Cross

As the very symbol of Christianity, the cross Jesus is said to have been crucified upon takes a special place in the hearts of the faithful. Perhaps then, it is not surprising that pieces of the "True Cross" (as it is called by Christians) can be found from one end of Europe to the other. There are so many churches displaying fragments of the True Cross that it has been cynically suggested that if they were all put together, there would be enough wood to build Noah's Ark. This is doubtlessly an exaggeration, but it does illustrate the point rather well.

So where did the True Cross come from in the first place? According to Christian tradition, Roman Emperor Constantine the Great's mother, St. Helena, discovered it in the year 333. She went on a holy archeological dig in the Middle East with the goal of unearthing objects mentioned in the Bible, and the cross was at the top of her most-wanted list. There are numerous different stories describing how she found the True Cross. My favorite of these involves her torturing a Jewish leader by starving him until his hunger forced him to reveal the secret location of the cross to her. He had been concealing the cross because he knew it would prove that Jesus really was God, or something along those lines (Hey, I didn't promise that this story was going to make any sense). How he knew where it was in the first place is unknown, but once the hiding place was revealed, a hitch arose, for there were three crosses found there. To determine which one was the True Cross, a dead person was touched with each cross. When the True Cross came in contact with the corpse, he immediately rose from the dead. St. Helena then brought back part of the True Cross to Europe where it was broken up and distributed to churches far and wide.

Are these pieces of the True Cross real? We don't know if the various splinters even come from the same piece of wood, let alone from a cross. Even if you are inclined to believe the tale of St. Helena, there is a three-hundred-year gap between her time and that of Jesus. This massive break in provenance should be a bit worrisome to someone trying to authenticate such objects.

The Nails

You didn't think Helena was going to find the cross without also coming up with the nails did you?

Helena did supposedly find the nails, although we don't know if she found three nails or four. Legend says that on her return voyage from the Holy Land, a storm came up and threatened her ship, so she tossed one of the nails into the sea to calm the tempest. Another nail was made into a bridle bit for

Constantine's horse. I find it strange that Helena would undertake such an arduous journey to bring back a revered holy relic only to see it shoved into a horse's mouth, but that's the story. The remaining nail, or nails, were incorporated into a crown for her son. The nails have allegedly been preserved and are on display in various churches today. The problem is that there are at least thirty different churches that now claim to have the nails used to crucify Jesus. It's safe to say that at least most of them are mistaken.

The Crown of Thorns

The Crown of Thorns on the other hand is a singular item, which is kept in Notre Dame in Paris along with a chunk of the True Cross and one of the aforementioned nails.

The Crown of Thorns came to France in 1239 when the king acquired it after the Byzantine emperor, who had previously owned the crown, had been forced to sell it to pay off his debts. We know the crown had been in Byzantine hands for a few centuries by then, but the trail gets murkier the further back in time you go, and there is no evidence that places the crown in the time of Jesus—let alone on his head. As the Notre Dame website itself puts it, "Despite numerous studies and historical and scientific research efforts, its authenticity cannot be certified. **It has been the object of more than sixteen centuries of fervent prayer**" (bolding theirs). In other words, it's not the real crown, **but feel free to venerate it anyway** (bolding mine).

The Crown of Thorns is encased in an overly ornate, golden sheath (this is France after all). If you peer beyond all the decoration, however, you can see something unusual about it. It turns out that the Crown of Thorns has no thorns on it! It used to have thorns, but they were cut off by French kings and handed out to reward people who had done them favors.

The Gifts of the Magi

Did you ever wonder what Jesus did with the gold, frankincense, and myrrh that he was given by the Magi? The Bible says nothing about it; in fact three of the four gospels make no mention of the Magi themselves. Legends have arisen to fill the void, however, including one tale that claims the two thieves executed alongside Jesus stole them from him.

But it turns out that Jesus' birthday swag was not stolen, lost or spent. It was saved and passed down through the ages until it landed in an Orthodox monastery named St. Paul's, which sits atop Mt. Athos in Greece. If you should be lucky enough to get to see the gifts in person, prepare to be underwhelmed. In artistic depictions of the adoration of the Magi, the gifts are usually depicted as treasure chests filled with goodies for the baby Jesus, but the collection at St. Paul's is more bust than bling. The set consists of three small trinkets of woven metal with a few frankincense and myrrh beads sown onto the pieces. The beads are dried out and brownish, so they resemble animal droppings. It doesn't look much like a set fit for a king, but maybe the Magi had good cause to be a bit stingy. After all, they were the first Christmas shoppers in history to have to buy presents for someone they didn't even know.

The Holy Grail

It's the mother of all holy relics, the cup from which Jesus drank at the Last Supper—or at least that's the common perception today. The legend of the Holy Grail actually has a long and convoluted history. In the beginning, it wasn't even thought to be a cup. It was a term used to describe a platter or even a stone that could work miracles. The idea that the grail was the cup from which Jesus drank at the Last Supper gradually gained currency, however, and the Monty Python and Indiana Jones movies have settled the matter in the public imagination.

As everyone knows, the Holy Grail is also the ultimate archeological find imaginable. So you might be surprised to learn that it has already been found—*twice*! You can see it in Spain at the Valencia Cathedral or you can see it at the Cathedral of San Lorenzo in Italy. The Italian grail, which is more of a bowl than a cup, was captured during the crusades and carried back to Italy as a great trophy, but it lost a lot of its panache when it was accidentally broken into pieces in the nineteenth century. This grail was claimed to be made of emerald, but when it broke it proved to be made of ordinary green glass. The Spanish grail is the more respected of the two. Several popes, including Benedict XVI, have used it during mass. The object is very old, and is perhaps the only object in this section of the book that actually dates back two thousand years. It is made of carved agate, and guesses about where it was made range from Egypt to Turkey. Nonetheless, there is no evidence the cup was ever in Jerusalem, let alone on Jesus' table. Furthermore, the fine quality of the vessel casts doubt upon it. Vatican art expert Umberto Utro told the *Catholic News*, "It's impossible Jesus drank from it; that there were such rich and fine vessels used at the Last Supper was nonsensical." He asserted that Jesus "most probably used a cup made from glass like everybody else."

Jesus' Blood

According to tradition, a man named Joseph of Arimathea wiped blood from the body of Jesus after his death. Naturally, the cloth he used is still with us. It mysteriously turned up in Constantinople in the Middle Ages where it remained until crusaders captured it when they looted the city in 1204. Today it can be found in Bruges, Belgium, where it is housed in the Basilica of the Holy Blood. The cloth with the blood on it is kept in a glass cylinder that is brought out and paraded through the streets every year on Ascension Thursday. This tradition is several centuries old although the path of the procession had to be changed in 1578 due to religious warfare that was then raging around Bruges. It is this altered route that remains in use today.

Jesus' Burial Shroud

Joseph of Arimathia also was supposed to have provided the burial shrouds in which Jesus was laid to rest. Through the centuries, dozens of such shrouds have turned up and been venerated, but today all of them are pretty much forgotten except for one shroud in Italy. The Shroud of Turin, as it is known, is the most famous holy relic in all of Christendom. The reason for its renown probably stems from the image of the face on the cloth that looks like a faint, blurry portrait of a man. Though the image may be vague, it provides believers with the opportunity to imagine they are gazing upon the face of God.

The shroud turned up out of nowhere in the 1350s in the city of Lirey, France, and it didn't take long for suspicions about its authenticity to arise. In 1389 Bishop Pierre d'Arcis wrote a letter to Pope Clement VII (there will be more about him in the next chapter) expressing his concern over the object. In his letter, he declared the shroud to be "cunningly painted" and "a work of human skill and not miraculously wrought or bestowed." He added that the forger who created the shroud had admitted to his deceit. But people still wanted to believe in the shroud, and as the years went by it became more and more revered. In 1506 Pope Julius II called it "that most famous shroud in which our Savior was wrapped when he lay in the tomb." He also reminisced that his predecessor, Pope Sixtus IV said of the shroud, "men may look upon the true blood and portrait of Jesus Christ himself."

Notwithstanding its miraculous status, the shroud was sold and moved around several times. In 1532 the shroud's holy derivation wasn't enough to prevent it from being damaged in a fire that burned holes through it and left it singed. The shroud eventually ended up in Turin, Italy, where it remains today. In 1898 it was photographed for the first time, and the images of the face garnered widespread attention for the shroud. In 1988 the scientific community was allowed to take bits of the shroud to test its age. Three groups working independently at Oxford University, the University of Arizona and the Swiss Federal Institute of Technology ran carbon dating tests on the shroud, and they all arrived at the same conclusion; the shroud dated back to about 1350. In an amazing coincidence, this is the same time it first showed up in France! Furthermore, textile experts have claimed that the type of weave used in the cloth is of a medieval style that was not seen in Jerusalem two thousand years ago. In 2009 an Italian scientist created a shroud very similar to the Shroud of Turin using only technology that would have been available in the fourteenth century.

Nevertheless, the faithful continue to believe that the shroud is a tangible link to Jesus. In 2010 Pope Benedict XVI visited the shroud and called it "an icon written in blood" and "a burial cloth that wrapped the remains of a crucified man in full correspondence with what the Gospels tell us of Jesus."

Jesus' Foreskin

As a Jewish boy, Jesus would have been circumcised shortly after his birth. And what became of the foreskin from this procedure? One would think that it would have simply been thrown away at the time, but in fact, at least eighteen different relics claiming to be the foreskin (or "Holy Prepuce") appeared in Europe during the middle ages.

One alleged foreskin in particular is worth our attention here. This particular bit of Jesus was presented as a gift to Pope Leo III in the year 800 by the legendary King Charlemagne, who in turn claimed it was given to him by an angel. St. Bridget of Sweden had a vision about the foreskin which was taken as verification of its authenticity. When Rome was looted in 1527 the relic disappeared. Thirty years later the foreskin—or another one claiming to be the original item—reappeared in the town of Calcata, Italy. The foreskin was credited with a number of miracles such as creating a perfumed fog that settled upon the town, and pilgrims flocked to the city to see it. The church offered a ten-year indulgence to those who venerated it. The faithful queued up to see it in lines so long they reached clear outside the city walls. A tradition arose in which the foreskin was proudly paraded through the streets each year on the day of the celebration of Jesus' circumcision.

But as the years went by, the whole foreskin concept lost some of its charm. The various other foreskins said to be from Jesus were lost or destroyed, and the one remaining in Calcata started to seem a bit unsavory to some people. In 1900 the Catholic Church decided that it had heard enough about the foreskin and declared that anyone who wrote about or discussed the matter would be excommunicated. In 1954 the sanction against talking about the foreskin was strengthened to include shunning in addition to excommunication. The Church took this action even as it continued to support the notion of the relic's authenticity. The edict of 1954 inspired the local priest in Calcata to remove the foreskin from the Church. He took it home where he kept it in a shoebox in the back of his closet. In 1983 the foreskin was stolen, and it has not been seen since. The thief was never apprehended, but suspicion in the incident has focused on the Vatican itself on the theory that the foreskin was too great an embarrassment for the Church to endure any longer.

But if you think this is the all there is to say about the foreskin of Jesus, allow me to disabuse you of that illusion, for this is one body part with an endlessly colorful history.

Take for instance, the case of the thirteenth century Austrian nun, Agnes Blannbekin. By all accounts Blannbekin was a devout woman—a devout woman who claimed that she ate Jesus' foreskin. She said the foreskin simply appeared in her mouth one day, and she swallowed it. Then it was resurrected just as Jesus had been resurrected after he died on the cross, only this time it was just the foreskin that was resurrected, and the event took place inside her mouth. She swallowed the foreskin again, and it came back again. This happened over and over again until she had consumed it about a hundred times. How she knew that the flesh was from that particular part of Jesus' anatomy, I cannot say. After this, Blannbekin never ate meat again saying that the flesh of Jesus was all the meat she would ever need. St. Bridget also claimed to have magically eaten the foreskin of Jesus. Both women reported that it tasted incredibly sweet.

Another high point in the history of the foreskin occurred about four hundred years later, when Galileo turned his telescope on the planet Saturn and observed its rings. Papal librarian and scholar Leo Allatius published a document with the snappy title *De Praeputio Nostri Jesu Christi Diatriba* in which he advanced the theory that the foreskin had ascended from Earth with Jesus after his resurrection and had been deposited around Saturn, thereby forming its rings.

And then there is the story of St. Catherine of Siena. Catherine was an extraordinarily pious nun of the fourteenth century who took her role as a bride of Christ literally. She said she had a vision in which she was married to Jesus, and he sealed the deal by presenting her with a wedding ring made of—you guessed it—his foreskin. Catherine believed the ring was actually on her finger and claimed that she could see it there for the rest of her life. As you might imagine, the ring was invisible to everyone else in the world.

I think it's fair to say Catherine was a very troubled young woman. She lived to suffer and went out of her way to do so. She wore hair shirts and chains, she flogged herself every day, she slept on a hard bench with a rock for a pillow, and she drank pus from the sores of the sick. She ate little else though, as she had a serious eating disorder, probably anorexia. Given all this it's little surprise she died at the age of thirty-three. Despite her odd behavior, she was not only canonized as a saint, but she was also named a Doctor of the Church and is now the co-patron saint of Italy—along with St. Francis of Assisi.

> After Catherine died her body became a holy relic itself, or more accurately, it became holy relics. She was laid to rest in Rome, but it wasn't long before her head and the finger that wore the invisible ring were clandestinely cut off and carried away to Siena where they are venerated to this day. Her emaciated head is covered in shriveled flesh, and her teeth protrude from her open mouth, so it looks like something from a horror movie, but it is proudly placed on display nonetheless. Catherine's left foot was also lopped off and is now housed in a church in Venice. What's left of her corpse still resides in Rome.

Pope Urban VI

In April of 1378 the College of Cardinals convened in Rome to go about the business of selecting a new pope. It was a tense time in the eternal city. The cardinals were divided into French and Italian factions in what was a bitter power struggle. The Roman populace—wary that another French pope would once again take the Holy See to France—clamored for a Roman pope. Things got ugly as the Roman throngs grew more and more insistent. With the prospect of a full-scale riot hanging over their heads, the cardinals elected Bartolomeo Prignano as pope. Prignano was an inauspicious bishop and the last non-cardinal who would ever be elected pope. Prignano was an Italian—though not a Roman—and he had been educated in Avignon, so he seemed like a promising compromise candidate. Furthermore, he seemed to be an unassuming milquetoast from an inauspicious family who would be easily pliable to the will of the cardinals. He was unanimously elected, but before he could be notified of his election, the mob in the streets made it past the papal guards and burst in on the cardinals. In fear for their lives, the cardinals propped up an old Roman cardinal on the throne and presented him to the rabble as the new pope. The cardinals then ran out of town before the rioters could learn that they had been hoodwinked.

Prignano eventually did get crowned pope, however, and he took the name Urban VI. Instead of the calming, compromise candidate the cardinals had hoped for, however, he turned out to be a cruel, arrogant hothead who damaged the Roman Catholic Church almost beyond repair.

Once crowned pope, Urban quickly let his newfound power go to his head. He showed himself to be an angry, raving tyrant who turned out to have no interest in compromise with the French faction of the Church. Instead, he vehemently insulted the French cardinals and threatened to overwhelm the Church with new Italian cardinals unless they acquiesced to him. In fairness to Urban, it should be pointed out that the French faction was likely plotting against him from day one, and some of the insults he hurled at the cardinals were reasonable demands that they stop living like kings on the backs of the people. It should also be mentioned that he went out of his way to offend the Italian cardinals as well, but no matter. The French cardinals slipped away from Rome, met in Avignon and decided that since the election of Urban had been carried out under threat of mob violence, the whole thing didn't count. They elected their own pope, Clement VII, thereby touching off the Great Western Schism. This crisis would consume the Church for almost forty years.

Popes Urban and Clement excommunicated each other. Clement went the extra mile and declared Urban to be the Antichrist. The Church was thrown into civil war. Both popes raised armies, and the kingdoms of Europe allied themselves with one pope or the other. Urban's army defeated Clement's at the battle of Morino, but that victory accomplished nothing more than securing Rome for Urban. After the battle, Clement retreated to Avignon where he lived in a sort of alternate Vatican, which was awash in splendor.

Urban then completely took his eye off the ball by concentrating less on his rivalry with Clement and more on enriching his family's land holdings. Specifically, Urban coveted the Kingdom of Naples, which was ruled by Queen Joanna, a supporter of Clement. Her support of Clement gave Urban an excuse to get rid of her. He excommunicated her and set out to depose her. Her cousin Charles overthrew her and supported Urban's papacy, though Charles himself was ethnically French. In return for Urban's support, Charles was supposed to turn over the kingdom of Naples to the pope's worthless nephew. This would be the same nephew who once abducted a noblewoman from a convent and raped her repeatedly in a house that was under papal guard. When Urban heard of the abduction and rape he refused to punish his kinsman. He dismissed the whole thing as a foible of youth, though his nephew was thirty-nine years old at the time.

Once in charge of Naples, Charles had his cousin Joanna put to death. He also made it clear that he had no intention whatsoever of sharing the fruits of his victory with the pope's sleazy, moronic nephew. Military setbacks elsewhere had made Urban more reliant than ever on Charles, but he still could not resist publicly lashing out against his supposed ally at seemingly every chance he got. The situation came to a head when Charles' main political rival dropped dead, leaving him with no need for an alliance with Urban any longer. Yet Urban was blissfully unaware of the changing political landscape. He took a small army to Naples to throw his weight around only to discover that Charles now outweighed him. The trip was disastrous. Urban's party was imprisoned for five days when they were captured en route to Naples. Charles ignored them when they finally did arrive. The cardinals who were forced to accompany Urban on this trek gradually came to realize that they were on a futile, endless quest lead by a tyrannical loon, so they started to make awkward plans to replace him. Pope Urban found out about their plot—if it could even be called that—and had six of the cardinals arrested.

In his rage, he ordered the cardinals to be tortured. One portly cardinal was repeatedly hoisted up to a ceiling and dropped to the floor while the pope's nephew looked on and laughed. Urban complained to his torturers that the cardinal was not screaming loudly enough, and he threatened them with torture themselves if they did not start getting better results. The head of the torturers decided he had had enough of Urban. He risked his own life by sneaking away from him. The torturing continued without him.

Meanwhile, the relationship between Charles and Urban deteriorated to the point of open warfare. Charles marched against Urban's army and besieged him at the city of Nocera. The trapped Urban reacted with his typical diplomacy and restraint. He appeared on the town's fortress ramparts numerous times a day to shout his excommunications and insults at the forces arrayed against him. Since he did this every day, the enemy troops waited for his shows and greeted his predictable tirades with a deluge of arrows that somehow never managed to hit His Holiness while he went through the entire bell, book, and candle excommunication ceremony. This routine went on for almost five months.

Then Urban caught a break. Forces that supported him broke the siege, and he was able to escape. His party headed for Naples once again where he expected to be rescued by ships from Genoa. Along the way, he murdered one of the forlorn cardinals he was still dragging along with him and left his body to rot on the roadside. Incredibly, it seems no one stopped to think that since Naples was under the control of Charles, it might not be the best idea to go there. When it became clear that the ships could never pick him up there, Urban lead his exhausted entourage to the other side of Italy, where the ships could dock. When Urban arrived in Genoa he undertook the task of appalling the Genoese by murdering five more cardinals, possibly by burying them alive.

The day after the divine homicides, he left for the city of Perugia where he was assembling an army for another attack on Naples. The force set out on its quest with Urban in command, but they abandoned the pope along the way when he ran out of money with which to pay them. This left him with no choice but to fall back to Rome.

In Rome, Urban declared a jubilee for the next year for the purpose of raising cash for another war by shaking down the faithful who would make pilgrimages to Rome in celebration of the blessed event. Alas, Urban would not be able to make use of these ill-gotten gains as he died before the jubilee even got started. Urban's death was widely rumored to have been from poisoning, but we will likely never know the true cause of his demise.

The Great Western Schism did not end with the Urban's death. When both Urban and Clement died, their respective colleges of cardinals elected separate successors to their thrones. The Italian college—as you might imagine—was not large at the time, thanks to Urban's thinning of their ranks.

The dual papacies lasted for decades until the competing cardinals got together in an attempt to end the disgrace. They opted to depose both the Roman and French popes and elected a compromise pope to replace both of them. The problem with the cardinals' plan quickly became apparent when the popes in Rome and Avignon both refused to step down after the new pope was elected, thereby leaving the Church with an even more ridiculous trio of popes.

In 1415 the kingdoms of Europe decided that if the Church could not end this farce they would. Six kingdoms met at the Council of Constance, forced all three popes from their perches and selected one man to replace them all. The pope they selected was Baldassare Cossa who took the name John XXIII. Incredibly, John was a former pirate who apparently realized that he could score more plunder in the Church than he could through larceny on the high seas. He was also a famous womanizer who was said to have had 200 sexual conquests (including many nuns) before becoming pope. He had been a priest for one whole day when he was elected pope.

Infuriated by secular kingdoms taking over their holy duties, the cardinals finally united as one, deposed John and elected Pope Martin V to replace him. Martin was a member of the Colonna family that Pope Boniface VIII had attempted to wipe out years earlier. Martin's election finally put an end to the Schism. His papacy is otherwise notable for his attempt to exterminate the followers of Jan Hus and John Wycliffe. He is also remembered for having owned ten African slaves.

For the record, The Roman popes (including Urban) are considered to be the legitimate popes by the Church today. The French popes and the pirate-turned-pope John XXIII are all now considered antipopes.

Torquemada

In the 1470s Queen Isabella of Castile was under pressure to initiate an inquisition in her kingdom. Her husband King Ferdinand of Aragon—looking forward to all the treasure he would be able to rake in from the Inquisition's victims—had already approved it in his lands. Various religious leaders also urged the queen to move. She wanted a unified kingdom didn't she? How could that happen when Jews who had converted to Christianity were secretly still practicing their old faith? How could she, a devout Catholic, tolerate such an outrage in her own territory? Yet Isabella—perhaps fearful of the injustice an inquisition could bring with it—resisted. Finally her longtime confessor, a Dominican prior named Tomás de Torquemada lent his trusted voice to the debate. He argued in no uncertain terms that there must be an inquisition in Spain. Isabella relented. When the Spanish Inquisition was set up, Torquemada's reward was to be named as one of eight inquisitors sanctioned for the ghastly proceedings. A few years later, Pope Sixtus IV made him the Grand Inquisitor of Castile at the request of the King and Queen.

It's not as though the Spanish Jews had been sailing along blissfully up until this point anyway. In 1391 a spate of rioting in what would eventually become Spain had left thousands of them dead. Nearly one hundred years later, the land was still rife with anti-Semitism. Jews were forced to live in ghettos and to wear identifying badges on their clothes. It was also forbidden for Jews to associate with Christians. Naturally, it occurred to some Jews that if they were to convert to Christianity their prospects in life would brighten considerably. The converts, known as *conversos*, were always viewed with some suspicion, however. Were they genuine converts or were they just opportunists who were still practicing Judaism behind closed doors? Torquemada was determined to cure this cancer that he imagined to be infecting the Church. The Inquisition was the tool he needed to do it.

The Spanish Inquisition kicked off in the city of Seville. It started with a semi-reasonable sounding offer called the Edict of Grace, which promised amnesty to any *converso* who came forward and confessed to his apostasy. At least 20,000 people in Seville took advantage of the deal. It turned out that there was a catch, however. Only sincere penitents would be given amnesty, and the only way one could demonstrate his sincerity was to give the Inquisition the names of other *conversos* who were still practicing Judaism. To refuse to give up the names of others could mean death, so the penitents were highly motivated to talk. A huge wave of arrests broke out over the city in the wake of these confessions.

Those accused of apostasy, heresy, bigamy, sodomy or other "crimes" would find themselves before a terrifying tribunal that followed strict rules laid out by Torquemada. The accused would not be permitted to face their accusers or to even know what exactly they were charged with. They would be provided with a defense, but if the defenders decided their client was guilty they were obligated to abandon the case, leaving the defendant on his own. Anyone could testify against the accused, even heretics and excommunicants, but such people were prohibited from testifying on behalf of the accused. Additionally, anyone who did testify on behalf of a defendant would come under suspicion himself and could easily face his own charges. This discouraged all but the bravest of people from standing up for the accused. The Inquisition also employed tricks to get convictions. They sometimes used people fluent in Hebrew who would visit the accused in the guise of rabbis to coerce confessions. One commonly used ploy was to promise full forgiveness to defendants if they would confess. It wasn't until after the confessions that the defendants were informed that this forgiveness would occur only in heaven.

But of course, not everyone was willing to confess. In such cases, the inquisitors would be forced to "employ the question." This was a euphemism for torture. In torture—as with everything else—the inquisitors followed strict instructions laid down by Torquemada. They were not allowed to freelance things by merely torturing anyone in any manner they wished. For the most part, they followed set procedure.

First off, the man or woman would be made to fast for several hours before employing the question. This was to prevent the accused from chocking to death on their own vomit before they could confess to anything. Then the victim would be stripped naked, shown the instruments they were to be tortured with and given another chance to confess. The torturers were instructed to act sad as they stripped and prepared their victims for torture to impress upon them that they really didn't want to do this, and all of it could be brought to a stop if they would only confess. Stenographers were always on hand to record any confession or other self-incriminating comment that might spill out of the accused.

The torture itself normally fell into one of three favorite techniques. The first of these was the rack, a device so famous it scarcely needs description. It involved a person secured to a machine while lying down with arms extended upwards. The victim was then slowly stretched as his muscles and tendons tore, and his joints became dislocated.

Another common torture was the hoist. This involved a rope and pulley attached to a high ceiling. The victim was tied up with his arms behind his back, and then he was slowly lifted off the floor by a rope connected to his arm shackles. This left the victim's entire body weight to fall on his shoulders as he was raised higher and higher. Occasionally, the torturers would let the victim drop and then catch him with a jerk to increase the agony. If the victim still wouldn't talk, he would be lowered to the ground where weights were attached to his body, and then the process would be repeated.

Lastly, there was the water torture. Here, the victim was tightly strapped to a board with her nostrils plugged. Her mouth was forced open and held in place by a metal apparatus. A linen cloth was held over her mouth, and water was slowly poured onto the fabric. The weight of the water forced the cloth to descend into the victim's mouth and then down her throat. The victim would feel as though she were drowning and would fight for air. The torturers were careful to use just enough water not to actually drown the victim. After a period of this cruelty, the rough cloth was dragged out of the victim's throat, and the gagging man or woman was given another chance to confess. If they refused, the process would be repeated. As if this weren't enough, a tourniquet could be applied to the victim somewhere about the mid-section. This would be turned tighter and tighter while the water was being poured into her. Sometimes the tourniquet would cut the victim all the way to the bone.

Torquemada's rules for torture did include some lenient measures. It was forbidden to employ the question twice to the same person, and torturers were not allowed to kill their victims. Even these directions were cynical ploys though. While people could not be tortured twice, the torture could be "suspended," and then continued later. When a person passed out or seemed close to death, the torturer could simply suspend the torture and then continue it a second or third day. If a person were tortured to death the inquisitor would need to seek forgiveness for killing him, but he could get that from a fellow inquisitor. As such mutual forgiveness was assured, there was no real penalty for such murders.

And yet all this suffering was only part of the trial. The actual punishment phase of the proceedings still awaited those who were convicted—and nearly everyone was convicted. If a person was willing to confess and to name others they could be spared the worst penalties. Such a person would often be sentenced to life imprisonment, his property would be confiscated (with the Inquisition pocketing one third of the swag,) and his children and grandchildren would be shamed. This meant they would have to wear special clothing showing their infamy, they would be forbidden from traveling, and they would be barred from ever holding any type of honorable employment.

If the person was convicted without confessing their horrible deeds then the Church would be left with no choice but to wash their hands of the miscreant and turn them over to the secular arm. This meant that the victim was sentenced to death, but the Church—in it's merciful way—was not about to lower itself to the level of killing people. So they turned people over to the state to be murdered in exactly the manner the Church prescribed.

The Church was not about to do this without a big ritual, of course, and this process was called the *Auto de Fe*, or "Act of Faith." First, the victims had their heads shaved, and they were forced to wear a special outfit of shame that often included a tall, cone-shaped hat. They were stripped to the waist and led barefoot (no matter the weather) on a parade of the doomed through public so that everyone in town would know of their infamy. Since the ladies were forced to go topless as well as the men, this was a chance for the town pervs to get a Church-approved eyeful of the female anatomy. The damned carried unlit candles with them, which symbolized the darkness of their souls. The Dominican inquisitors, dressed in spooky black and white robes with large hoods, led the procession. The victims were marched into church where a special mass was recited for their damned souls. After the mass, they were taken out to the stakes to be burned. Even now, they were extolled to confess. A priest would stay by their side even after the victims had been tied to the stake, and the fires had been lit. He would implore the victim to make amends as there was still time left to receive the mercy of the Church. Many people feeling the heat of the flames undoubtedly did confess at this point, but the only "mercy" they received was to be strangled to death at the stake rather than being burned alive.

As the Inquisition spread throughout Spain, Torquemada's power continued to grow. In 1484 he took charge of the Inquisition in Aragon in addition to Castile. He no longer answered to the King and Queen by this time. Only the pope could bring the grand inquisitor to heel, and that wasn't happening. Torquemada's cruel decrees kept right on coming. In 1485 he updated the rules of the Inquisition. From then on, all people who knew of heretics were required to report them or they would be considered heretics themselves. Even worse, he ruled that rabbis who were aware of converts who had gone back to Judaism must report those people to the Holy Office. This was the first time the Inquisition was extended beyond it's original mandate to only punish relapsed converts. Rabbis who failed to report relapsed converts faced death, of course. Torquemada also ruled that people who committed fraud should be branded in the face.

As you might imagine, all the money being forfeited by convicts was making Torquemada a rich man. What might surprise you is that he wasn't living it up on all the blood money he was reaping. Torquemada appears to have been a true believer in the hateful brand of religion he preached. He lived a spartan life, dedicating his fortune to the Church. He personally financed the construction of a new Church in the city of Avila, but it came with a telling stipulation; no Jews or Moors were allowed to enter the building.

Torquemada could arrest, torture, and kill the Jews who had converted to Christianity, but those who remained Jews were largely beyond his reach. This was driving him nuts. He decided the only solution to Spain's Jewish problem was to get rid of them all. He petitioned the monarchs constantly to expel them from their lands.

A bizarre case would help his cause. An urban legend emerged concerning the kidnapping of an amazingly devout Christian boy by Jews. The boy, who came to be known as "Santo Niño," was said to have been spirited away from his blind mother by Jews who crucified him on a cross. They tore his heart out in an attempt to cast a dark spell that was supposed to have rid Spain of all Christians. After the lad was put to death, he naturally was said to have performed any number of miracles. Never mind that this story was completely ludicrous; several Jews were arrested, tortured, and executed for the made-up homicide. The phony incident also helped to fuel popular opposition to the continuing Jewish presence in Spain.

But the monarchs were conflicted on the issue. The Jews had been loyal subjects to the crown. They had contributed greatly to the *Reconquista* of Spain from the Moors, and they served a crucial role in the Spanish economy. What's more, the Jewish community offered the monarchs a rumored 30,000 ducats to forget the whole concept of expulsion. Torquemada was infuriated by the proposition. In what must have been a spectacular audience with Ferdinand and Isabella he reminded his sovereigns that Judas had betrayed Christ for thirty pieces of silver, and the Jewish offer of thirty thousand ducats could be no coincidence. In reality, the Jews had probably offered much more than 30,000 ducats, but no matter. He took a crucifix, threw it down before the monarchs and said he would have no part in such a deal. The Jews were ordered out Spain soon afterward.

The order of expulsion, called the Alhambra Decree, also affected Muslims living in Spain. This was in direct violation of the recently signed peace treaty that sealed the re-conquest of Spain, but this treachery didn't bother the crown or the Church. The crucial matter was that Spain was doing right in the eyes of God.

Spain's Jews and Muslims were given three months to either convert to Christianity or leave. To convert meant that—in addition to abandoning one's faith—one would also be eligible for the Inquisition. So leaving seemed like the better plan to most people confronted with this bleak choice.

But leaving was no picnic either. These were families that had been in Spain for as far back as could be remembered. To leave meant starting over in a new kingdom where the welcome mat was not likely to be rolled out for Jews. Additionally, the new exiles would not be able to bring much with them when they left. They were forced to sell off most of their possessions to people who knew they were desperate to sell. They were therefore offered only a pittance in return for their worldly goods. The exiles were not allowed to bring gold out of the kingdom with them either. Many Jews were robbed upon arriving in their new lands. Jewish women were sometimes raped. Rumors circulated that Jews were swallowing their gold to smuggle it out of Spain, so some Jews had their guts slit open by bandits to see if there was gold inside them. Beaten, destitute, and humiliated, many Jews saw no choice but to return to Spain, convert to Christianity, and pray the Inquisition would not take them.

Torquemada had an insatiable appetite for more and more victims. Emboldened by his virtually unchallenged power, he went after bigger and bigger fish. He brashly tried to destroy two bishops, charging that they were descendants of apostates. Both of the bishops appealed to Rome and won the support of Pope Alexander VI (see the later chapter about him) who didn't share Torquemada's fiery religious zeal. The pope's medaling in his Inquisition infuriated Torquemada. He had one of the bishops arrested and charged him with being a *converso* himself. The bishop garnered a hundred witnesses for his defense, but the Inquisition convicted him anyway. Not daring to execute a bishop, the Inquisition striped him of his vestments, stole all his wealth, and sentenced him to life in prison.

Complaints about Torquemada were now streaming into Rome. The pope realized that he had to curb the inquisitor who had gotten too big for his britches, but Torquemada still had the support of Ferdinand, Isabella, and much of the Spanish population. Alexander's solution to the dilemma was to appoint several other inquisitors to positions with just as much clout as Torquemada's. This diluted Torquemada's power so much that he could no longer act as a dictator over the Inquisition.

Torquemada didn't live long after that slap down. He died in 1498. His Inquisition, however, continued on. Following the basic framework he laid out, it outlasted him by about 300 years. Many years after his death, Torquemada's bones were stolen from his church in Avila and burned. The man who had caused untold numbers of men and women to be sent to the pyres would himself be consumed by fire, but not until it was far too late to stop his reign of terror.

And a further insult has been visited upon Torquemada. A number of modern historians have concluded that the Inquisitor was himself the grandson of Jewish converts to Christianity. If this had been exposed during his life it would have been deeply embarrassing at best.

There was no way to avoid the Inquisition. If you decided to skip town when the Inquisition started setting up shop in your area, the fact that you left would be all the evidence needed to convict you in absentia. If you were later brought back, you would then face your punishment.

Since you couldn't risk criticizing the Inquisition, running away wasn't likely to work, and you had little chance of emerging victorious from its courts, it's not surprising that some people got it in their heads to fight back. When the Inquisition spread to the city of Saragossa, a group of conspirators led by a man named Juan Pedro Sanchez assembled to do just that. Their desperate plan was simple; they would stop the Inquisition by assassinating the inquisitors themselves. Their first target was the dreaded inquisitor Pedro Arubés who was second only to Torquemada in Aragon.

The plotters sneaked into the Cathedral of Saragossa where Arubés was stationed and waited in the shadows for him. When Arubés appeared he was both armed and decked out in armor. This was an odd outfit for reciting prayers in a cathedral, but Arubés had figured he might become a target of retaliation against the Inquisition, and he was not willing to become a martyr for his faith. When he set down his weapon, the attackers leapt out of their hiding places and beat and stabbed him to death.

The retribution for the slaying was predictably ruthless. One conspirator was captured and tortured into confessing his role in the affair. He gave up the names of the other attackers after he was promised mercy for doing so. He was then hanged and drawn and quartered. The "mercy" he received was that his hands were not cut off first. This was a generosity the other conspirators were not shown. Those first arrests were followed by more and more arrests. Eventually hundreds of people were accused of participating in the crime, which in reality had only a handful of participants. Sanchez himself was somehow able to sneak away.

The killing was a total failure for the plotters. Not only did it fail to stop the Inquisition, but it also inflamed public opinion further against the Jews.

Then there is the matter of Pedro Arubés himself. No sooner was he dead, than reports of miracles he performed began streaming in. In fact, his blood on the cathedral floor was even credited with performing miracles. He was quickly declared a martyr and became widely revered in Spain. In the nineteenth century Pope Pius IX (see later chapter on him) canonized the inquisitor as a saint. If you feel like celebrating him, you should know that his feast day is September 17th.

What the Hell???

Human Sacrifice in the Aztec Faith

When the Spanish arrived in what is now Mexico, they were greeted by sights they could have scarcely imagined. In 1521 they entered the Aztec's capitol city of Tenochtitlan, a city that was larger than any in Spain at the time. In the center of the city stood a massive temple that the Spanish called Templo *Mayor*. The temple loomed high above the citizens whose homes radiated out from it. The temple was taller than the spires on Spain's great Seville Cathedral.

The Aztecs were the inheritors of Central America's religious traditions that reached back more than a thousand years. One of the long-standing traditions in Mesoamerica was the need for human sacrifice. The Aztecs not only continued this practice, but also greatly expanded it.

To the Aztecs, the gods required a variety of blood sacrifices including human sacrifice in order for the world to run smoothly. The Aztecs' intricate calendar was rife with holy days and religious feasts that required human sacrifice. They believed that the human body held essential forces that needed to be released to replenish the universe. They truly believed that the world would come to an end if the sacrifices were to stop.

There were lots of different ways in which people's essential forces could be released. Some ceremonies called for the victims to be shot with arrows as if they were deer being hunted, while others required the victim to fight gladiator-style to his death. Unlike Roman gladiatorial combat, however, the victim was armed only with a faux weapon, was tied to an immovable object and was outnumbered four to one, so there was no hope of survival for the sacrificial combatant. Victims might also be drowned, burned, thrown from high places, decapitated or strangled depending upon which feast was being celebrated.

The most common style of sacrifice, however, was the removal of the heart. A typical sacrifice involved the victim (who would usually be adorned in a special costume to make him look like a god) being led up the steps of the temple. When he arrived at the top he would have to perform a dance and would then be laid out upon a stone where four men would hold down his limbs while a priest would take a stone knife and plunge it into his chest below the ribs. The priest then reached in through the gaping wound and pushed his hand up through the victim's chest cavity until he got hold of his heart. He would tear out the still-beating heart and hold it up in front of the quickly fading victim. He would then hold up the heart to the sky and praise a god before placing the heart into a special jar. The victim's blood was often wiped over the temple walls to increase the divine energy being released. And yet this wasn't the end of it. The victim's corpse (which was now called an "Eagle Man") was given a swift kick by the priest and would go rolling down the great length of the temple steps with arms and legs flailing wildly all the way down. When the corpse got to the ground, the arms, legs, and head would all be cut off. Often times the skull was emptied out and put onto a rack with innumerable other heads. The racks were prominently displayed and served as an ominous warning to the Aztecs' potential enemies. As the victims for these sacrifices were often prisoners of war taken by the Aztecs, the warning was clear: resist the Aztecs, and this could be your fate.

Not that this should be seen as a desecration of the corpse; in fact it was the reverse. This was all done in accordance with strict, sacred protocols. There is evidence that even the victims thought that human sacrifice was what made the world go around.

Not all victims of sacrifice were prisoners either. Slaves were commonly put to death as well. States allied with the Aztecs were expected to produce victims to be sacrificed by the Empire, and they usually sent slaves. The constant demand the Aztecs had for sacrifice victims from both friend and foe helped to stoke resentment of their empire throughout Mesoamerica. It also helps to explain how the invading Spanish were able to find so many native allies, without whom they could not have beaten the Aztecs so easily.

Special holy days called for special manners of sacrifice. One feast day, called *Tlacaxlpeualiztli*, was also known as the Feast the Flaying Men. This feast had strong militaristic overtones. The victims for this celebration were prisoners captured in battle. They were put on display for forty days to allow everyone enough time to admire the war trophies and the warriors who had captured them. They were sacrificed in the mock combat style, but that was only the beginning of the ritual. The family of the warrior who had captured the victim would cannibalize parts of him in a special meal. The victim would also be skinned, and the proud warrior would wear the skin like it was clothing. He would proudly parade around town adorned in this grizzly attire. The bones of the dead man were presented to the warrior as well, and he would erect a pole on his property upon which he would display the thighbone of his victim. After twenty days the victim's skin was taken to the temple where it would be buried. Needless to say, this had the effect of discouraging people from surrendering to the Aztecs during battle.

Another manner of sacrifice involving prisoners of war was the *Toxcatl*. For this sacrifice, the prisoners were closely inspected to find the most perfect man among them. The lucky man would then be treated as if he were a living god for a year. He would be adorned in the finest clothing and was showered in gifts. People who encountered him would call him "lord." Near the end of year he would be given four wives. When his year was up he marched up the temple steps, stopping to smash a flute along the way. When he arrived at the top, his heart was ripped out.

The biggest and most important holy event in the Aztec world was the New Fire ceremony which occurred only once in every fifty-two years. In the Aztec faith, this was the ceremony that kept the sun moving in the sky. They believed that if this ceremony failed, an endless, demon-filled night would descend upon the world. People were put to death as part of the New Fire celebration of course, but since the stakes were so high for this sacrifice everyone was expected to do his part. A fire was set on the temple, and then the fire was taken down via torches that were sent throughout the Empire in a manner similar to the Olympic torch relays of today. When the torch arrived in various Aztec communities, it would be used to set hearth fires for households. People would flock to the sacred fires and hold themselves over them until they blistered from the heat. Everyone would gash their ears, catch the flowing blood on their fingers and flick it into the fires. Even babies' ears were sliced open for this event.

The majority of the victims of Aztec sacrifices were men, but some holy days called for the sacrifice of women. In fact, women made up about one third of the sacrifice victims. Women were associated with the growth of crops, and their sacrifice was thought necessary to feed the Empire.

One such ceremony required the sacrificial woman to have sex with the king before she was taken to the temple and killed. After her death she was skinned, and the tallest, strongest male then got the privilege of wearing her skin in what has to be the most extreme example of cross-dressing in world history. As long as he wore the skin he would pretend to be a woman, and everyone would play along with the charade by referring to him as "she." Four slaves would be brought before this "goddess," and he, er she, would kill all of them. A man would then tear the thigh from the skin the man/woman was wearing and make it into a mask. A warrior would wear this mask to the border of an unfriendly tribe and plant it there. Fighting with the targeted tribe would often erupt over this provocation.

Even kids were required to be sacrificed in this religion. Child sacrifice victims were known as "human paper streamers." The ceremonies that took their lives must have been especially grim. First off, the victims appear to have not been slaves; they came from Aztec families in good standing. Furthermore, the purpose of their sacrifice was to elicit emotion from onlookers, as it was their tears that were thought to bring the rains that watered the crops. Though the priests were experienced killers, it must have tested the mettle of even these men to put children to death. There were serious consequences for priests who were unable to carry out their duties regarding the killing of kids.

Naturally, the Spanish were appalled at all of this when they encountered the Aztecs. They considered the practice primitive and barbaric. Naturally, they used it as justification for their conquest of Mesoamerica. This was no primitive society, however. They had a faith with a long history, an intricate calendar filled with elaborate feast days, a powerful priest class and a religious infrastructure as impressive as anything else in the world. In all these respects they were similar to the Spanish. Was human sacrifice barbaric? Hell yes! Not even the most determined apologist could morally justify the horrific bloodletting the Aztecs performed on a regular basis. But this was going on at the same time that the Spanish were engaged in the Inquisition, the Spaniard Alexander VI was serving his catastrophic term as pope, and the Spanish King Charles V led his army to Rome where they raped and murdered their way through the city. If the Spanish wanted to find barbarism they needn't have bothered with building ships.

Besides, what would the Aztecs have thought if they could have seen Spanish churches? In addition to the possible spectacle of seeing people being burned alive near the churches, they would have seen an image of a man-god being sacrificed, and people eating his flesh and drinking his blood. They would probably have been at a loss to understand why their religious practices were so vilified.

The Aztec religion is long gone, but traces of its emphasis on sacrifice and death remain today. Take for instance the worship of La Santa Muerte. Santa Muerte ("Saint Death" in Spanish) is a fairly new religion that has gained millions of followers in Mexico and is spreading through the Americas. The central figure of the faith is the titular Santa Muerte who is usually depicted as a skeleton in robes carrying a scythe. She looks very much like a cross between the Virgin Mary and the grim reaper. The faith seems to be born out of the old pre-Columbian practices described above, mixed with Catholicism. This is not to say the Catholic Church approves of Santa Muerte; in fact, the opposite is true as the Church condemns the practice as devil worship.

Santa Muerte is willing to overlook a lot of faults in her worshippers. As long as you stay loyal to her, she will forgive any other transgression you may have committed. This makes Santa Muerte an especially attractive figure to those involved in Mexico's brutal drug wars, though the faith has many adherents who are not involved in criminal enterprises.

Santa Muerte is also willing to grant favors that cannot be asked of traditional saints. You can pray to her for the deaths of your enemies for instance. When asking for favors, it is expected that worshippers will make sacrifices to Santa Muerte called *La Santisima*. The greater the favor requested, the greater the sacrifice that is expected. It has been rumored that such sacrifices can involve blood or even human sacrifice, but this has not been substantiated.

Pope Alexander VI

In 1492—in addition to Columbus sailing the ocean blue—a papal conclave convened to elect a replacement for Pope Innocent VIII. The election turned into an orgy of bribery, which eventually saw a Spanish cardinal outspend his rivals to gain the Holy See. There were reports that he had four mules loaded with silver marched to the conclave to pay off one of the cardinals, but this claim is widely scoffed at by historians. Votes in the College of Cardinals were a lot more expensive than that. The four mules could have been no more than a down payment.

The Spanish Cardinal was Roderic de Borja. Italians corrupted "Borja" to "Borgia"—a name whose infamy lives on to this day. Borgia took the name Alexander VI. Then he and his family set off on a course that would disgrace the Church, lay waste to a big chunk of Italy, and ruin countless thousands of lives.

Shortly after Alexander's election, a stampede of Borgias took lofty positions in the Church. One envoy complained, "Ten papacies would not be enough to satisfy this swarm of relatives." No less than five of the pope's kin were ordained as cardinals including his son, Cesare, who had no interest whatsoever in religious affairs. Then again, his dad didn't either.

Alexander also took advantage of his papal power to maneuver his daughter Lucretia into a favorable marriage. He married her off to Giovanni Sforza to cement his alliance with the groom's powerful family. Lucretia was at the ripe old age of twelve at the time. Notwithstanding her youth, Giovanni was actually the *third* guy her dad had arranged for her to marry. The first two engagements fell through before the lovebirds could make it to the alter. The wedding to Giovanni was a predictably lavish affair. The pope attended it with his mistress.

Then things started going from bad to worse. France invaded Italy with devastating results to the local population. Rather than condemning the unprovoked attack, Alexander took advantage of the situation by forging new alliances to strengthen his political position. As a result, he no longer needed the support of the Sforzas who had been instrumental in getting him elected pope. And since he didn't need the Sforzas anymore, it was a waste to have his daughter married to one of them. Giovanni Sforza saw the writing on the wall and fled Lucretia and Rome before Alexander could get his hands on him. Nevertheless, Alexander was still able to force Giovanni to publicly admit that he was impotent and that he had never consummated his relationship with Lucretia so the marriage could be dissolved. This lie humiliated Lucretia who took to a convent in her shame. Alexander later excommunicated Giovanni.

Alexander poured treasure on his sons, especially his favorite son, Juan, whom he seemed to be grooming for bigger and better things, although Juan's only detectable talent was womanizing. That favoritism ended, however, when Juan disappeared. A few days later, his murdered body was found in the watery highway of death known as the Tiber River. A grief-stricken Alexander swore to find his killer. He also decided that it was time for him to straighten up and fly right, so he concocted a series of badly needed reforms for the Church.

At first, the general suspicion in the killing of Juan was that an enemy of the Borgias or a cuckolded husband was behind the slaying, but rumors soon began to circulate that the killer was none other than Juan's brother, Cardinal Cesare Borgia. The whispers grew into a cacophony until hardly anyone doubted that Cesare was behind the whole thing, though there was no proof against him. Alexander then decided to dispense with the murder investigation and began to look upon Cesare as the son that was destined for greatness. He also permanently set aside all the reforms he had planned to introduce to the Church.

Meanwhile, back at the convent, Lucretia had gotten pregnant. Rumors swirled that the child belonged to her incestuous father. I'm not one to cut Alexander a lot of slack, but it is doubtful that he actually had sex with his own daughter. She did have a lover, however, who was murdered (undoubtedly by her family) and thrown into the Tiber. Lucretia's love child did not survive.

But hey, she was single again! Which presented another opportunity for Alexander to marry her off to his advantage. This time the lucky bachelor would be the seventeen-year-old Don Alfonso di Bisceglie who came from another wealthy family. Perhaps surprisingly, Lucretia really hit it off with her new husband. Alas, their love was star-crossed from the start.

Don Alfonso was attacked and stabbed repeatedly one day as he was leaving the Vatican. He barely survived the attack and took to bed to try and recover. Suspicion for the attack immediately fell on Cesare who was said to be jealous of his brother-in-law. While Cesare was taking a walk near the room in which Alfonso was recovering from the stabbing, he was nearly struck by an arrow. Cesare wasted no time in retaliating. He sent his assassins to Alfonso's room where they asked Lucretia and the women with her to leave before they strangled him.

But enough with maters of the heart; the Borgias were about business, and there was business to be done. In France, King Louis XII had just taken the throne, and he needed a favor. He had his eye on a young lady he wished to marry, but he was already married to a woman he wished to dump. The pope saw a chance to shake down the French king in return for the annulment he desired. At first, he tried to get the king to give up his daughter, Princess Carlotta, to marry Cesare. Alexander had Cesare resign his position as cardinal so he would be eligible to marry. Carlotta was able to resist that overture, however, and instead the king found another French noblewoman for Cesare to marry. This sealed an alliance between France and Alexander, and they immediately drew up plans to join forces for war in Italy. Huge amounts of Church money went into financing the effort, and the resulting campaign was a humanitarian catastrophe, but it did enrich the pope and his family. By the way, King Louis' scorned first wife would later be canonized St. Joan of Valois.

Cesare led the ensuing military campaign. He rolled up impressive territorial gains and captured (and allegedly raped) one of the Sforza women for good measure. He returned to Rome in 1500 to an enormous victory celebration thrown by the pope.

By now the Borgias were mad with power and were spinning out of control. Alexander excommunicated and murdered powerful people and seized whatever assets they held. The Borgias were said to have killed four cardinals, though only one of those cases was definitely a Borgia homicide. Cardinals who were fortunate enough to have died without assistance from the Borgias also had their property confiscated. Alexander also sold cardinal positions to raise cash and made other heads of state pay bribes for annulments.

Cesare threw a banquet for his dad and sister in which fifty courtesans danced nude while naked prostitutes crawled under the tables gathering chestnuts off the floor. One attendee wrote in his journal that he prostitutes later copulated with servants, and that the pope awarded prizes to the most vigorous performers. Such lewdness was not unprecedented in Alexander's life. While he was a cardinal, he had hosted a sex orgy of such legendary wildness that he outraged the seemingly unshockable Italian people who were well accustomed to debauched Church officials.

When Cesare returned to the battlefield, he continued to pile up victories. When he captured the city of Faenza, he promised its leader, Astorre Manfedi, safe passage. Cesare then betrayed him, imprisoned him, had him put to death and tossed his corpse into—where else?—the Tiber River.

Alexander left Rome to go about the business of dividing the spoils of the newly conquered territories. While he was gone, he left Lucretia in charge. This was the last time that a woman ran the Catholic Church. Lucretia's tenure as regent of the Church didn't last too long, however, as she was soon married off again by her dad in yet another political alliance. The wedding proceeded despite the objections of the groom who probably preferred to stay amongst the living.

The populace of Rome despised and feared Alexander, and even more so, Cesare. Their rule came to be known as "The Time of the Antichrist." Borgia spies watched the city like a secret police force listening for dissention. One man who spoke critically of the family had his hand cut off and his tongue cut out. A Venetian ambassador who disparaged the Borgias was strangled and tossed into the Tiber.

But all good things must come to an end. In 1503 Alexander died. His bloated corpse was too fat to fit into its coffin, and no one troubled to make a bigger one for him, so the pontiff had to be punched and stomped into the box. No priest bothered to attend the body while it lay in repose. His successor, Pope Pius

III, refused to say a mass for Alexander saying, "It is blasphemous to pray for the damned."

Without Alexander around to lend him the Vatican ATM card, Cesare found himself on hard times. As his power inexorably slipped away, he was forced into increasingly desperate and humiliating positions. He was imprisoned twice, exiled once, and he lost all his lands. To make matters worse, his face had become so disfigured by syphilis that he had to wear a mask. By 1507 he was little more than a mercenary. The circumstances surrounding his death are debated, but it seems that he met his end when he led his troops into battle at a place called Viana. Hilariously, his men decided not to charge when the order came, leaving Cesare to unwittingly go it alone. Cesare was immediately killed, and his body was robbed of its armor and clothing. His naked corpse was stuffed under a rock. Cesare was only thirty-one years old at the time of his death.

He received a better burial then he deserved, but in the seventeenth century he was exhumed, and his remains were scattered. His monument was torn down, and his epitaph was obliterated.

Lucretia fared a bit better. Her final husband turned out to be an indifferent, syphilitic whoremonger, but she was able to hold her position after her dad died, and she even became an object of affection to many people. She too died young after a complicated childbirth.

> In one of the rare moments when Alexander was attending to Church business, he made the decision to divide the non-European world into spheres of influence between Spain and Portugal. The two Kingdoms were bitter rivals in the Age of Exploration; the decision was designed to keep them from tearing each other apart so they could concentrate on tearing apart heathen indigenous people instead. The dividing line went through the eastern part of South America. This is why Brazilians speak Portuguese today rather than Spanish.

Savonarola

It is one of history's great coincidences that at the same time Pope Alexander VI was leading the Church in his breathtakingly immoral manner, a preacher named Girolamo Savonarola was only a few miles away, guiding the city of Florence in quite a different fashion. Savonarola was as devout and pious a man as Alexander was decadent and vile. Ultimately, however, Savonarola's piety was almost as pathetic as Alexander's lasciviousness.

Savonarola grew up in the Italian city of Ferrara, which was in the midst of a golden age brought about by its crafty leaders who had the good sense to stay out of the wars that were endemic to Italy in those days. But Ferrara's good fortune disgusted Savonarola who, even as a boy, was so stern and dour that he expected people should concern themselves almost exclusively with religious matters and avoid the trappings of the secular world.

When he was twenty years old, Savonarola fell for the daughter of a noble family who lived near him. He declared his love to her only to have his proposal soundly rejected by the lady who informed him that there was no way a man like him could ever hope to attain someone as far above him in society as she. After this humiliation, Savonarola appears to have given up hope of finding any earthly happiness. He dedicated the rest of his life to the Church, entering the Dominican order not long afterward.

In 1481 Savonarola was sent to Florence for his first assignment. This was at the time of the Italian Renaissance, when Florence was the epicenter of the explosion of art and thought that was revitalizing Europe after the interminable sleep of the medieval era. The art and philosophy of the classical era were being rediscovered. A tidal wave of new learning was sweeping over society, and a new idea, humanism, was catching on.

None of this was to Savonarola's liking. He was aghast at the things he saw in Florence. He detested humanism, and he resented the renewed study of the ancient gods of Greece and Rome. Of course, no one in Florence was actually worshipping Zeus or Apollo, but that mattered little to Savonarola.

It was in the arts where Savonarola's disapproval was perhaps most keenly focused. He held strong opinions about all of the arts. In fact, he dabbled extensively in art himself having composed numerous morose songs and poems. Savonarola was a fan of simplicity in art. He felt verse should be in common language, free of any decoration. He was even opposed to the use of meter in poetry. He was mortified that classical poets such as Ovid, whom he considered to be obscene, were being rediscovered. He believed the visual arts should be equally spartan. Any hint of elegance or flair met with his disapproval. He felt painting should be used to create simple objects such as humble portraits of Mary and the saints. These portraits were supposed to encourage pious veneration of their subjects. He lashed out against Renaissance painters telling them, "You artists, if you only knew as I know, what scandal (your paintings) cause, you would desist. But you place all these vanities in the churches! Do you believe the Virgin Mary went about dressed as you have painted her?"

Savonarola made his debut in the Florentine pulpit in 1482. In accordance with his philosophy, his sermon was constructed in as plain a style as he could manage. This was the opposite of the eloquent style of preaching that was popular in Florence at the time. Savonarola's sparsely attended mass was a flop. After a few more years of spinning his wheels in front of a city that wasn't responding to him, Savonarola was sent to the village of San Gimignano. His ministry in Florence appeared to be permanently over.

But life in the little town rejuvenated Savonarola. He still kept his sermons as barren as he could, but he found he could get a response from the people by throwing a healthy dose of fire and brimstone into them. Furthermore, he now claimed he was hearing voices and seeing visions from God. He became convinced he was a prophet comparable to Old Testament figures such as Jeremiah. He started making all sorts of predictions, some of which panned out, some of which did not, and many of which were so vague they really couldn't fail. Savonarola was no longer a boring priest, and his star was on the rise.

He made his return to Florence in 1489 with an impassioned sermon. Now he was a hit. His fame grew as he continued to give fiery, fist-pounding sermons. He preached of reconstructing all of society, of his supposed prophetic visions, and of his disapproval of humanism. In 1491 the Florentine leader Lorenzo de Medici threatened him with exile unless he cooled it with his bashing of the Medici family, but Savonarola felt confident enough to ignore him. His subsequent election as prior of the San Marko monastery helped to strengthen his position in the city.

In 1492 Lorenzo was on his deathbed, filled with the fear of being sent to hell. He summoned Savonarola to hear his confession and give him absolution. Savonarola heard the confession, but refused to pardon the de-facto king of Florence, leaving him thinking he would go to hell. Lorenzo died soon afterward, but Savonarola's battles with the Medici were far from over.

Two years later, a French army led by King Charles VIII swept into Italy and conquered Florence. Savonarola was overjoyed. He saw the invasion as God's retribution against wicked, humanist Florence. He compared the invasion to God's cleansing of the Earth with Noah's flood. He also saw it as the fulfillment of his prophesies. He never actually prophesied a French invasion, mind you, but self-proclaimed prophets have a long history of giving themselves credit where it is not due.

Savonarola was apparently the only man in Europe who didn't know Charles' invasion of Italy was not motivated by altruistic virtue. He spared no compliment when it came to the French king. He gushed over him, "Oh most Christian king, you are an instrument in the hand of the Lord. You have been sent by him to relieve the woes of Italy, and this I have been predicting for many years. The Lord has sent you to reform the Church." He went on to warn Charles that he must honor the Lord's wishes. Charles paid no attention to that caution, however, and abused Florence to no end. Savonarola never held it against him though.

Others did. Fearing they would suffer the same fate as Florence, a collection of city-states combined into an alliance against France and succeeded in pushing Charles out of Italy. Savonarola hated the Italian alliance and refused to support them against

Charles. After the French abandoned Florence, Savonarola formed the heart of a Florentine resistance to the Italian alliance and essentially became the leader of city. His followers, derisively called *Piagnoni* or "Weepers" because they often cried at his bombastic sermons, formed something resembling a militia that kept the Medici out of Florence and the monk in power.

In Savonarola's Florence, there would be some spectacular changes made. If you think of Florence as the Eden of the Renaissance, then you can think of Savonarola as the serpent intent on destroying it. His ranting about art and the study of the classics had force behind them now. All artists and thinkers had to follow his dictates. Some of them were swept up in his fanaticism as well. It is quite possible that master painter Sandro Botticelli burned some of his own works after falling under Savonarola's sway. Homosexuals (who had been tolerated before Savonarola's rise to power) were now put to death. Gangs of Weepers beat prostitutes and ransacked bars.

In Rome, Pope Alexander VI watched the developments in Florence with alarm. He had his own designs on Florence, but Savonarola was thwarting his attempts to broaden his influence in Italy. He decided that the monk would have to be dealt with. In 1496 he offered Savonarola a cardinal's hat in an attempt to get him out of Florentine politics, but Savonarola rejected the promotion. Furthermore, he stated that he would only obey the pope when he agreed with his rulings. He even hurled numerous thinly disguised invectives at him.

In 1497 Savonarola gave a sermon in which he lashed out at his enemies after his opponents had tried to vandalize his pulpit. The mass turned into a riot. His comments from the sermon were transcribed, printed, and distributed far and wide. Alexander had taken all he was willing to tolerate from Savonarola and excommunicated him. Savonarola responded to his excommunication by going on the attack against the pope.

When Alexander's son was murdered, Savonarola sent him a condolence letter that was really a holier-than-thou missive in which he rubbed in the pope's loss. He continued preaching as well, despite the fact that this was clearly forbidden since he was an excommunicant. He told his audience that anyone who agreed with the pope was a heretic. He called the pope a "broken tool" in a widely published tract.

Most famously, the Weepers broke into people's homes and stole the objects that offended Savonarola. Wigs, dice, cards, mirrors, veils, perfume, masks, makeup, books that contained "dangerous" thinking, and "indecent" paintings and sculptures were all confiscated. An enormous fire was set in the city piazza, and all the objects were thrown in (though not until after the pile had been sprinkled with holy water). Many of the townsfolk under the influence of the fanatical preacher tossed in their worldly goods as well. This event came to be known as the Bonfire of the Vanities. It has echoed throughout history as a cautionary example of religious fervor gone insane.

But this was the peak of Savonarola's glory. The people of Florence were starting to turn against him. His ongoing battle with the pope was draining his popular support, and he had no powerful supporters to fall back upon. In desperation, he sent letters to five kingdoms in which he accused Alexander of buying the papacy and of leading an immoral life. He asked the monarchs of these kingdoms to support him in a bid to depose Alexander. Unfortunately for Savonarola, papal agents intercepted all the letters before they ever left Italy. When confronted with this attack against him, Alexander ordered Savonarola's arrest.

The attempt to take Savonarola turned into a mob scene. A battle broke out in the church in which Savonarola was staying. His defenders fought with crosses and whatever else they could find against those who had come for their leader. One man in the scrum had his eye poked out with a crucifix wielded by a monk before Savonarola gave himself up.

Savonarola was imprisoned by the Church and tortured with the hoist. Under the duress of torture, his faith wavered. He admitted that he was in the wrong, but he recanted his confession when he recovered. On May 23, 1498, he and two of his fellow monks were hanged in the same piazza where the Bonfire of the Vanities had occurred. While their bodies were still dangling in the air, a new bonfire was set below to consume them. Youths, many of them probably the same thugs who had worked on behalf of Savonarola in the past, threw stones at the corpses while they burned. Cheers went up as bits of the bodies broke off and fell into the fire. Savonarola's remains and all of his possessions were thrown into the Arno River (the Tiber does not flow through Florence) in order to prevent them from being venerated in the future.

Years later, the German author Johann Goethe may have summed up the fanatical monk's life best when he called Savonarola, "A fantastic and ridiculous monster, who in an ungrateful, obstinate, and terrible manner opposes himself to the grandiose, lovely, serene life of Florence."

> In case you were thinking to yourself, "my goodness, this man should be wearing a halo," you are not alone. Since not long after Savonarola died, there has been pressure on the Church to see him canonized as a saint. Leading this charge has always been the Dominican order to which he belonged. In the 1990s a commission was formed by the Church to look into his life in what could be a first step on the road to sainthood. Additionally, the Vatican newspaper praised him as a "tireless preacher for moral reform."
>
> There is one problem with Savonarola's candidacy for sainthood, however. The book burnings? The art burnings? The homosexual killings? No. The real hitch is that he openly defied the pope. Everyone agrees the pope was a jackass, but he was still the pope. So it would seem that this matter will most likely get batted around for a few more centuries before it finally gets resolved.

Pope Leo X

Pope Pius III died almost immediately after succeeding Pope Alexander VI. The stern Julius II succeeded him. Julius' modest ways brought a stop to the Church's hemorrhaging of money, and he restored its treasury to its former glory. He also called upon the cardinals to curtail their lascivious behavior.

The cardinals considered Julius' buzz-killing papacy to be an unmitigated disaster. When he died in 1513, they looked for someone who could put the fun back into their church gigs. Giovanni de' Medici looked like a promising candidate to revive the good old days. There was trepidation about letting a Medici on the papal throne, however, as the family was a huge force in Italian politics, and no one was anxious to make them even stronger. Another problem was that Giovanni was still a young man. He had been made cardinal at Medici insistence at the tender age of fourteen. Though decades had passed since then, he was still youthful, and the prospect of a pope who could rule for forty or fifty years was not something the cardinals wanted. They feared such a long rule would allow Giovanni to stamp the Medici imprint on Italy in an indelible fashion. But Giovanni was a portly, wreck of a man who seemed to be in constant medical distress. The cardinals bet he wouldn't live too long and elected him pope.

Giovanni took the name Leo X and wasted no time in getting about the business of partying down. His coronation parade was such an elaborate affair that it cost one-seventh of the entire church treasury. Leo rode through the parade perched atop a magnificent white elephant named Hanno. A boy covered in gold paint danced as part of the entertainment. The paint turned out to be toxic, and the boy died soon afterward. After the coronation, Leo continued to live the good life. No expense was spared in his pursuit of opulence. In the space of one year, he had completely depleted the Church's savings

This is not to say that Leo was nothing but a party boy, however. He had an appetite for power that was fitting for a Medici. In 1516 Leo purged the Papal States of any rulers who were not dependent upon him. He deposed Fransico Maria della Rovere, the Duke of Umbria in the process, even though the Duke was his nephew. Della Rovere had murdered a cardinal earlier in his life, but he had been given a papal dispensation for the crime. Leo used it as grounds to oust him anyway, and he excommunicated him for good measure. Pushed into a corner by Leo, Della Rovere felt he was left with no choice but to fight. Leo brought French troops into Italy to bolster his side, and he was victorious. The hopeless Della Rovere sent a challenge to Leo to face him in a duel. The offer so infuriated the pope that he had the messenger who brought the request arrested and tortured to death despite a guarantee of safe conduct the pope had made to him.

By this time, some of the cardinals had come to regret their choice of Leo as pope because he was aggrandizing the Medici as much as had been feared. A plot was hatched by some of the cardinals to kill him off by poisoning the salve he used to treat an ulcer on his anus. The plotters had decided that a cardinal named Petrucci would be elected pope after Leo's death. The assassination attempt failed, however, when Leo proved to be too shy to let an unfamiliar doctor see his butt. Leo eventually found out about the plot, but Cardinal Petrucci was able to make a getaway before being arrested. Leo offered Petrucci a deal. He would allow him to come back to Rome with a guarantee of safe passage in return for very little from Petrucci. Amazingly, Petrucci was dumb enough to fall for this ploy, and he returned only to be arrested and tortured by Leo. Under the duress of the torture he gave up the names of other cardinals involved in the plot who were also arrested. Leo had Petrucci put to death, and the other plotters were stripped of their positions.

Leo's decadent lifestyle, and the wars he was fighting put a staggering burden on the Church money box. The Church's income was immense, but it was not nearly enough to cover his expenses. Adding to the financial crunch was the construction of the new St. Peter's Basilica, which was underway at the same time. He started to sell everything he could think of to raise funds. Church positions were sold left and right. Thirty-one men paid to become cardinals at tremendous cost. The pope pawned off plates and other items from the Vatican. He borrowed heavily from Europe's banking families. Most famously, indulgences were sold to keep the money coming in. Indulgences were official papal forgiveness of sins, and the sale of them was blatantly unseemly. This, of course, was the impetus for Martin Luther's Protestant uprising in 1517.

The challenge Luther posed to the church was grave, and Leo was absolutely not up to the task of dealing with it. His lifestyle was such a grotesque moral example that his mere existence strengthened Luther's case against the Catholic Church. Furthermore, Leo was too distracted by Italian politics to be bothered much by Luther anyway. At first, he just ignored him. By the time he started taking him more seriously, the Lutheran movement had already taken root. He excommunicated Luther, but he never made any attempt to win over the hearts and minds of the people who were leaving the Church in droves.

Leo died in 1521 at the age of forty-six. He left behind massive debts that ruined his creditors. The cardinals who had gambled on him dying young when they elected him pope had been proven correct, but no one foresaw the permanent damage he would do to the Church.

I know what you're thinking; what ever happened to Hanno the elephant? Well, it's a sad story really. Leo loved Hanno as a boy loves his dog; yet only two years after receiving Hanno, the beast became seriously ill with constipation. One suspects that Vatican officials might not have known what elephants were supposed to eat. In a desperate bid to keep him alive, Hanno was fed some sort of cure that was infused with gold. Alas, prayer and insanely expensive quackery were not enough to save poor Hanno. The mighty beast died with Leo at his side. Leo personally wrote a rather terrible poem as a memorial to Hanno, part of which pleaded with the gods to give the years stolen from Hanno's young life to extend the life of Leo.

Of course, that didn't work out either.

Part II

The Battle for Souls

Martin Luther

In 1517 a German monk named Martin Luther compiled a list of ninety-five theses attacking the immorality of the Catholic Church's money-grubbing sale of indulgences. Luther may or may not have nailed the theses to the door of the Castle Church in Wittenberg, but even if that legend is untrue, he definitely made his grievances widely known. He even sent a copy of his theses to the pope!

In so doing, Luther touched off a chain of events that would result in the Protestant Reformation, changing the nature of Christianity for all time. Luther did this at no small risk to himself, as the potential punishment for heresy included torture and death. But Luther was in the right place at the right time. He was able to find protectors, especially Prince Frederick III of Saxony, who shielded him from the rage of the Church. This gave him and his new religion the chance to flourish.

Luther translated the Bible into German, and with the aid of the recently invented printing press, made the book available to literate people everywhere. The Church forbade the publication of the Bible in the common languages of Europe as a way to keep its members from adopting any ideas about the scriptures that ran contrary to its teachings. When the Bible was in Latin, only those who had been educated (by the Church) to read Latin could understand it. By publishing the Bible in a commonly spoken language, Luther made it possible for ordinary people to make their own judgments about scripture for the first time.

Given this, it's not hard to see how Luther has come to be a hero in the eyes of many Protestant people. He has been portrayed in print and on screen as a larger-than-life religious superstar of burning virtue. But such accounts leave out much of the true Luther, a man who was filled with stunning faults.

Luther was born in the German town of Eisblen in 1483 to what could be fairly called middle-class parents. He got a good education with a concentration in law, although he seems to have always preferred theology. In 1505 he was nearly struck by lightning while riding his horse. He took his escape from that close call as a sign that he must become a monk. He did become a monk and then a priest, but he fostered a growing disillusionment with the Church in which he served. In 1517 he unleashed his legendary ninety-five theses, and all hell broke lose. The Church and Emperor Charles V both condemned him; it was only by the protection of the like-minded Prince Frederick that Luther was able to avoid being burned at the stake.

Yet Luther was a hot-tempered and vulgar man. No one was safe from his outbursts and criticism, including Prince Frederick to whom he owed his security. He also had a seemingly inexhaustible affection for scatological references. He frequently used such terms even in formal situations.

So he had a potty mouth. The fact that he helped lift the veil of the middle ages off Europe surely makes up for that, right?

The truth is, that while Luther is often depicted as a central figure in leading Europe out of the dark ages, he was emphatically *not* a figure of the age of enlightenment. In fact, he would have abhorred the very idea of such a thing. Luther believed that rationalism was the path to ruin, as he thought the world was literally crawling with demons and devils that were waiting to pounce upon anyone who dared to employ critical thinking. He called reason the "devil's bride" and a "pretty whore." He is quoted as saying "Reason must be deluded, blinded, and destroyed. Faith must trample underfoot all reason, sense, and understanding, and whatever it sees must be put out of sight and... know nothing but the word of God."

If that wasn't strong enough for you, there is also this, "Reason is the Devil's greatest whore; by nature and manner of being she is a noxious whore; she is a prostitute, the Devil's appointed whore; whore eaten by scab and leprosy who ought to be trodden under foot and destroyed, she and her wisdom ... Throw dung in her face to make her ugly. She ought to be drowned in baptism... She would deserve, the wretch, to be banished to the filthiest place in the house, to the closets."

Then there was the matter of the Peasants' War of 1524 to 1525.

The peasantry of sixteenth century central Europe lived dreadful lives filled with misery. The peasants paid the dire weight of the crushing taxes established by the princes of the day who paid no taxes themselves. As if that weren't enough, they were also forced to tithe to the Church. Peasants were considered the property of their lords and were often forced into what was essentially slavery. When they died, their lords took their best possessions for themselves, thus denying their families of their meager inheritance.

The Catholic Church exploited the peasantry just as the nobility did. When Luther, a man who often boasted about having descended from peasants, threw the Church on its backside, many thought the time for social justice had finally come. Insurrections against the rich and powerful erupted across Germany, and to a lesser extent, in Switzerland and Austria. As hostilities escalated, the peasants sometimes brutally murdered their masters in what was turning into a full-blown revolution. The rebels expected Luther to endorse their campaign, but they were in for a big surprise. Luther condemned the peasant's movement in no uncertain terms. He admonished the rioters to lay down their weapons and to "give unto Caesar what is Caesar's" as Jesus had commanded. This was effectively an order to the peasants to accept their lot in life as being hopelessly stuck at the bottom of society.

His orders may not have been high on economic justice, but he was reaching for a higher virtue, namely that murder and warfare could not be justified no matter the circumstances, right? Unfortunately, that rationale holds no water, thanks to the instructions Luther gave the nobility. For them, he skipped the live-and-let-live sermon of pacifism, and he didn't bring up the part of the Bible about how it's easier for a camel to pass through the eye of a needle than it is for a rich man to enter heaven. No, to the upper classes he preached that baptism does not make men free, and he demanded that they "smite, slay, and stab" the rebels. But Luther was preaching to the choir in this case. The nobility were determined to crush the peasants with or without Luther's blessing. They organized powerful armies to put down the rebellion. The peasants, on the other hand, were disorganized and lightly armed. When Luther condemned their cause many lost hope and abandoned the movement. When the battle was joined the peasants were slaughtered. When all was said and done, the peasants were made to live in conditions even worse than before the uprising.

But the most disturbing aspect of Martin Luther must be his attitude toward the Jews. Luther initially expected his new faith would sweep up massive numbers of Jewish converts. Luther was convinced that once the Jews were free from the oppression of the Antichrist in Rome (as he referred to the Catholic Church) and shown the undeniable truth of the Gospels, they would flock to his brand of Christianity. When that didn't happen, the dark side of his nature exploded.

He unleashed a campaign of hatred against the Jews that was nothing short of breathtaking. He wrote two pamphlets that dealt extensively with Judaism, *On the Holy Name and the Lineage of Christ* and the quaintly titled *Of the Jews and Their Lies*. In them, he states the Jews are no longer God's chosen people, rather they are a "base, whoring people, that is, no people of God, and their boast of lineage, circumcision, and law must be accounted as filth." He calls the synagogue a "whore" and an "evil slut" full of the devil's shit in which the Jews wallow like swine.

I must admit I'm a little confused by this metaphor. Why would a slut be full of Satan's excrement? Nevertheless, it did give Luther another chance to use the salty language he was so fond of, and—as I have pointed out—he was no fan of reason anyway.

Luther wasn't content to merely hurl insults at the Jews, however. He laid out excruciatingly diabolical steps instructing the faithful on how Jews must be dealt with.

Firstly, that their synagogues and schools should be burned down and what will not burn should be razed and covered with earth, that no man will ever see a stone or cinder of it again...

Next, that their houses should be broken and destroyed in the same way...

Third, that all their prayer books and Talmuds, in which such idolatrous lies, curses and blasphemies are taught, should be taken from them...

Fourth, that their rabbis should be forbidden, at risk of life and limb, to teach from now on...

Fifth, that escort and road should be completely prohibited to the Jews. For they have no reason to be in the country...

Sixth, that they should be prohibited from usury and that all their cash and fortunes in silver and gold should be taken from them...

Seventh, that young, strong Jewish men and women should be given flail, axe, hoe, spade, distaff, spindle, and be left to earn their bread by the sweat of their brows...

For, as all can see, God's wrath over them is so great that gentle mercy will only make them worse and worse, and harshness little better. So away with them at all costs.

We read this screed with the hindsight of history. It doesn't take much imagination to connect Luther's raving hatred of the Jews with Adolf Hitler's "final solution." The actual connection is harder to establish, however. Luther at least thought the Jews were eligible for salvation if they only would accept Christianity. The Nazis on the other hand, thought that the even most sincere conversion from Judaism to Christianity could not erase the stain of Judaism. Furthermore, Luther's anti-Semitic writings had largely fallen out of public consciousness before the Nazis revived them. Nevertheless, "away with them at all costs" is a phrase that will retain its haunting power for generations to come, and it's impossible to deny that Luther's teaching was an important milestone in the progression of anti-Semitism in Germany.

Luther took his anti-Jewish campaign a step further by pleading with local rulers to have Jews expelled from their territories. He eventually succeeded in getting the Jews driven out of the German provinces of Saxony, Brandenburg, and Silesia.

In 1546 Luther returned to his birthplace in Eisleben to give his final sermon. It was another rant against the Jews.

He died three days later.

Luther, inadvertently, did do the Jews one favor. In 1510 thirty-nine German Jews were burned to death for desecrating a sacred communion wafer. When Luther later preached that the wafer was merely a symbol rather than the actual flesh of Jesus, the theological justification for such murders greatly diminished in the German states that converted to his new faith. This was not so in neighboring Poland, which remained Catholic. The thinking was that Jews so hated Jesus that they yearned to punish him. They would hammer on or stab at the communion host until it would miraculously bleed. Of course, if Jews actually believed the host miraculously transformed into the actual flesh of the Lord, they probably would have become Christians rather than remaining Jews. Nevertheless, loads of Jews were burned and drowned in Poland for this nonsensical offense. In one case, after the accused wafer-abusing Jew had been put to death, the surviving Jews of his community were forced to pay annual reparations as a penalty for his imagined crime. They were graciously allowed to stop making these payments 373 years later.

I mentioned earlier that Luther had a potty mouth. Well, it turns out that is more literally true than you might have imagined. In her book *The Big Necessity: The Unmentionable World of Human Waste and Why It Matters* author Rose George asserts that Luther ate a spoonful of his own feces every day because he thought it had medicinal properties. He also praised the benevolent God who would make such a wonderful cure-all so widely available.

What the Hell???

The Fall of Rome

The second Pope of the Medici clan was Clement VII, who was the half brother of Pope Leo X. Clement was also one of the most incompetent diplomats in the history of the world. He had trouble making up his mind and changed his allegiances without any apparent regard for who he was offending or how he was weakening his own position. As a result, his diplomatic dealings nearly always met with disaster.

This ineptitude led him into war with Charles V, who, as both the King of Spain and the Holy Roman Emperor, commanded forces vastly superior to anything the pope could muster. As if that weren't bad enough, Clement made enemies close to home too, so Italians were willing to go to war with him as well. In 1526 the first blow was struck. A force under the command of a cardinal attacked Rome and looted various churches including St. Peter's. As bad as that was, things were to get much, much worse.

Armies arrived from Spain and Germany to attack Rome in 1527. The pope's forces were quickly defeated leaving the city defenseless. The victorious troops were offered a pittance in pay for their victory, and they rebelled by descending upon Rome to plunder the eternal city. The Spanish and Italian troops stole whatever they could carry and kidnapped men for obscene ransoms, killing those whose families could not pay. The Lutheran troops from Germany (who had themselves been Catholics not more than ten years earlier) added a measure of religious hatred to their pillaging. Priests were slaughtered *en masse*. Nuns were raped and then killed. Some nuns were raped and then sold repeatedly to fresh rapists. When they were inevitably exhausted by this, they were deemed worthless and put to death. The enraged marauders destroyed ancient relics of Rome along with contemporary Renaissance masterpieces. More than two thousand corpses were dumped into the Tiber River. Yet that was only a small fraction of the dead.

Throughout this orgy of death, Clement hid in the unassailable castle of St. Angelo, helpless to stop the massacre outside that his foolishness had brought about. He eventually was able to sneak away from Rome in the disguise of a humble commoner and continued his papacy. He still had no clue as to what he was doing, however, as would later be evidenced by his inept handling of King Henry VIII's request for an annulment of his marriage.

John Calvin

When Martin Luther launched the Protestant Reformation, he pulled the cork out of the genie bottle. Other reformers quickly appeared who had their own opinions about Christian theology, and they didn't hesitate to promote them.

One such man was John Calvin. Calvin was born in France in 1509 under the name of Jean Cauvin. The name "John Calvin" is merely an anglicized version of his name, but as that is the one everyone uses, it is what we will stick with here.

When he was twelve years old, Calvin's dad was able to set him up with a lucrative, undemanding position in the Catholic Church. As he grew older, his father decided that law would be more profitable for his son than the God business, so he steered him in that direction. Calvin studied law as his father had ordered, but he never lost his zeal for things religious, and though Calvin never took holy orders, he made preaching his life's calling.

He first began to get noticed in 1533 while he was living in Paris. He helped to write a radical speech for his friend Nicolas Cop that was warmly received by Catholic officials. And by "warmly", I mean it got them burning mad. Calvin was linked to the speech by widespread rumor and was thus forced to flee France. At the invitation of a friend, he ended up in Geneva, Switzerland.

Calvin wasn't shy about sharing his theological opinions. Perhaps the one he is most famous for is the concept of predestination. Contrary to popular perception, Calvin did not invent predestination. He certainly promoted it, however. This concept holds that humans are vile creatures because of original sin, and as such, there is nothing we can do to earn our way into heaven. Only the mercy of God can bring salvation. Since God is omniscient, he knows if he will save a person before he or she is even born. So your fate is sealed before birth. This may not sound like the most uplifting or inspirational idea, but it did catch on. It spread across what would become puritanical northern Europe and eventually made its way to America with the Pilgrims.

But I'm getting ahead of myself. Calvin's message won him admirers in Geneva, but it didn't sit well with everyone. In 1537 Calvin proposed the creation of a Reformed Confession of Faith, a religious governing body that would have control over all Genevans. This body would ensure that everyone was adhering to strict puritanical principles and would wield the power of excommunication to deal with any moral slackers. The potential for abuse in such a body was obvious; many people took exception to it, and Calvin ended up being chased out of town in 1538. He retreated to Strasbourg, France. While he was there, the situation in Geneva gradually changed as city council members favoring him got the upper hand. They invited him to return to the city in 1541. He came back more powerful than before, because this time around he had been asked to lead the city's faithful.

Calvin's notion of an ecclesiastical government now came into fruition. Geneva became a moral police state in which the citizens were obliged to live their lives in a holy fashion as defined by Calvin. But Calvin still did not hold absolute power. There was still opposition to him within the city, most notably in the form of Ami Perrin, who was one of the city fathers. Perrin had once been a supporter of Calvin, but he thought the preacher had overstepped his bounds this time. When Perrin was out of town on city business, his wife was arrested for the crime of dancing, a practice which Calvin forbade. When Mr. Perrin got back, he was infuriated by the news and later tried to overthrow Calvin. He failed and was exiled for his trouble.

Exile was a pretty soft punishment compared to what Jacques Gruet got. Gruet was not the type of fellow who took to Calvin's theocratic rule with ease. He frequented bars and did little to hold back his non-puritanical thoughts. He said, "If I want to dance, leap, lead a joyful life, what business is it of the law?" This was a dangerous sentiment in Geneva, however, and when a placard with a message offending Calvin was posted in a church, suspicion for the deed fell upon Gruet. Calvin had him arrested and tortured into confessing the crime. The authorities raided Gruet's house and found a treasure trove of evidence against him in the form of his writings. In them Gruet not only complained about Calvin's running roughshod over Geneva, but he had also written a good deal that was critical of Christianity itself. He even went so far as to call the whole thing a "fairy tale." The concept of atheism was virtually inconceivable in those days, and it removed any chance of mercy for Gruet. He was quickly put to death, and his writings were burned.

And then there is the whole affair surrounding Michael Servetus. Servetus was a brilliant Spaniard, a definitive example of the Renaissance man. He is thought to have been the first European to discover pulmonary circulation, beating his closest competition to the punch by about one hundred years. He also liked to dabble in theology. In 1531 he wrote a book called *On the Errors of the Trinity*, which caused something of a stir. In the book, he argued that there was no scriptural basis for the belief that there was one God in three persons. He used the writings of many Church fathers to buttress his argument. The book's reception was as violent as you might expect, and Servetus was forced to write a second book apologizing for the blasphemy of his first book. This second book, however, ended up merely reiterating the arguments of the first. After this, he laid low for several years and largely stuck to practicing medicine.

He still thought he was right about the Trinity, however. In 1545 he started up a correspondence with Calvin on the issue. Calvin had little use for Servetus' ideas and sent him a copy of one his own books in the hope that the blasphemer might learn something from it. Servetus responded to Calvin's gesture by correcting all the errors he felt Calvin had made in his book and then sending it back to him along with a draft for another book he was preparing on theology. Calvin blew a screw over this. In a letter to an associate, Calvin wrote "Servetus wrote to me lately and coupled his letter with a long volume of delirious fantasies… I am unwilling to pledge for his safety, for if he shall come (to Geneva) I will never permit him to leave alive."

Servetus' book came out in 1553, and for the cherry on top of the insult sundae he had scooped up for Calvin; he included his letters to him in the book's appendix. Servetus published the book anonymously, but the authorship was quickly discovered (it was probably Calvin himself who blew the whistle on him.) He soon found himself under arrest in France. The Catholic Church charged Servetus with heresy and tossed him into jail. Servetus made a daring escape by climbing the prison wall before he could be tried, however, so he was sentenced to death in absentia.

Then Servetus got stupid. Instead of running off to safety he decided to look up his old pen pal, John Calvin, in Geneva. Historians are at a loss to explain why he would do such a thing; perhaps he was still trying to press his trinity argument on Calvin. At any rate, Calvin was looking out over his congregation while giving his sermon one Sunday when he was dumbfounded to see Servetus' face looking back at him. Calvin immediately notified the authorities and had Servetus arrested. Calvin wrote of the incident, "We have now business in hand with Servetus. He intended perhaps passing through this city; for it is not yet known with what design he came. But after he had been recognized, I thought he should be detained... I hope that sentence of death will at least be passed upon him."

Servetus was brought before the city council to be tried. The council was divided between pro and anti-Calvin factions, and Servetus' conviction was not guaranteed. The council appealed to Churches throughout Switzerland for their opinion on the matter. When those responses came back they unanimously called for death, so Servetus was immediately burned at the stake. His books were thrown into the fire for good measure. Servetus' dying words, "Jesu, thou Son of the eternal God, have compassion on me!" were fodder to be ridiculed in the mind of Calvin who declared that he should have said "eternal Son of God" rather than "Son of the eternal God." This anti-Trinitarian remark further cemented the case for Servetus' death in Calvin's eyes.

The case caused a sensation in Europe. It demonstrated that the new Protestant Churches would have little tolerance for dissenting opinions in their realms. Calvin, for his part, tried to soften his role in the affair a bit by claiming he had asked that Servetus be beheaded rather than suffer the horrors of immolation, but he never wavered in his belief that the execution was proper. Years later he advised "do not fail to rid the country of those scoundrels who stir up the people to revolt against us. Such monsters should be exterminated, as I have exterminated Michael Servetus the Spaniard."

After the Servetus debacle, the city council members who had been opposing Calvin were rousted from office, and a solidly pro-Calvin council took charge. This essentially obliterated whatever separation between church and state remained in Geneva and left Calvin as the undisputed authority in town. Several other people were put to death for heresy in Calvin's theocratic state, but none of these cases would be as infamous as the killing of Servetus.

In 1903 a small monument was put up in Geneva commemorating Servetus. There is also a street named after him there. A much larger monument to Calvin (and other religious leaders) was erected a few years later.

Calvin is one of the most beloved of Protestant reformers today. He is credited with a vast array of accomplishments ranging from pioneering the concept of individual freedom to inventing capitalism. The fact that these claims are rather dubious rarely gets in the way of the praise.

> Calvin wasn't the only person who was glad to see Servetus put to death. As we have seen, the Catholic Church had already sentenced him to death. The Scottish Protestant reformer John Knox wasn't losing any sleep over the killing either. He lashed out at those who questioned the burning of Servetus in a lengthy diatribe in which he said, "the sentence of death executed against him was not cruelty" and "the judges who justly pronounced that sentence were neither murderers nor persecutors." He also used the occasion to take a few shots at the "multitude of the Jews, who judged, and to this day do judge, the death of Christ Jesus, his blessed ordinance, the public preaching of his Evangel, and the administration of his Sacraments, to be nothing necessary to our salvation."

King Henry VIII

When one contemplates the founders of Protestantism one thinks of men like Martin Luther, John Calvin, Huldyrch Zwingly, and John Knox. These were men who, for better or worse, were consumed with theological passion and dedicated their lives to it. But one cannot leave King Henry VIII of England off the list, though his passion was more for a piece of ass than a rethinking of Christianity.

Henry was born in 1491, but he was not born to be king. He had an older brother named Arthur who was the heir to the thrown. Henry was merely the spare prince who would always play second fiddle to Arthur. And so it was when the Spanish Princess Catherine of Aragon (the daughter of the legendary Ferdinand and Isabella) entered the marriage market. She was married off to Arthur to seal an alliance between England and Spain. Henry was a mere spectator at the wedding.

But the honeymoon was a short one. Arthur became ill and died not long after the wedding leaving Catherine a widow in a strange land. King Henry VII also passed away, and young Henry claimed the thrown he had not counted on having.

One of the first moves Henry VIII made as king was to claim his brother's widow as his wife. For the wedding, Henry received special papal dispensations making sure there would be no moral hang-ups about marring his former sister in-law. Things went along swimmingly at first. Henry even had enough confidence in Catherine to leave her in charge of fighting with Scotland while he was off waging war in France. All that needed to be done was for Catherine to produce a son to take his place in the line of Tudor kings. Catherine did have a son, but he died after living only a few days. When Catherine finally had a healthy baby, it was a girl, whom the royal couple named Mary. Catherine got pregnant a total of seven times, but Mary would be the only survivor.

Henry took this bitterly. He wondered if God was punishing him. He remembered the warning of Leviticus 20:21 stating that it is an impurity for a man to take his brother's wife. The Bible warns that such a couple will be childless. Henry and Catherine weren't childless of course, but Mary hardly counted in Henry's mind since she was a girl. By the way, the book of Deuteronomy requires that a man marry his widowed sister-in-law, but Henry chose to ignore that bit of scripture.

It probably didn't help that Catherine had grown remarkably fat after all her pregnancies. It was even said that she was as wide as she was tall. Henry's heart hardened against her, and he began casting his eye elsewhere. He went through mistresses as he pleased, until he came up against Anne Boleyn, a woman who insisted on being more than the King's flavor of the month.

Boleyn was like nothing Henry had encountered before. Henry had already been knocking boots with Anne's sister Mary, but Anne was more skillful in the art of manipulation than her sister (who, by the way, was married). She insisted on marriage before consenting to Henry's carnal wishes. She would make Henry wait for it. And wait, and wait…

The problem was that Catherine was not going to go quietly into that good night. She was the aunt of the Emperor Charles V, so Henry couldn't just rub her out; he would have to play nice—or at least non-violent—with her. At first it was hoped she would listen to reason. The Vatican, eager to avoid a nasty fight, sent a legate to Catherine who offered her the exciting opportunity to go off to a nunnery for the rest of her life so Henry could chase tail as he pleased. Amazingly, Catherine rejected that tantalizing offer. Instead, she looked at Boleyn as a vile home wrecker and vowed to fight for her marriage to the bitter end.

The ensuing battle dragged out for years and years. Henry applied all the pressure he could to Pope Clement VII for an annulment, but Charles pressured Clement just as hard to refuse Henry's request. Charles' armies had recently reduced Rome to ruins, so Clement needed no reminder of the Emperor's strength. On top of all that, Clement was—as we have seen—an indecisive fool who had trouble making up his mind even in the best of times. He opted to drag the case out for as long as he could without resolution.

Henry fought hard in the legal arena. He had at his disposal his minister, Cardinal Wolsey, a clever man with extensive legal knowledge and an endless amount of cunning. Wolsey tried his best to wrest a divorce from the pope, but he couldn't do it. Eventually, his failure on this front brought about his downfall. Henry seized all of Wolsey's property and ordered him to London to face the King's displeasure, but Wolsey lucked out and died before he got there.

Henry had his case tried in debates at the finest Universities across Europe and won judgment after judgment that his marriage to Catherine was invalid. Yet the Church was unmoved. This further infuriated Henry because he had spent a lot of good money bribing the juries at all those universities to see the case his way.

In 1534 Henry had had enough. He split with the Roman Catholic Church, declared that he, and not the pope, was ultimate authority on religious matters in England and confiscated the property of the Catholic Church. With Henry now in charge of his new Church he had no trouble procuring a quick invalidation of his marriage to Catherine. He then promptly married Anne Boleyn. After this, the Catholic Church finally ruled in Catherine's favor on the divorce issue, but of course it no longer mattered. It was a case of too little, too late as far as Catherine was concerned.

This sudden religious conversion imposed upon England was not without its bumps in the road. After all, there was a vast network of Catholic clergy in the kingdom that was loyal to Rome. Why should they just abandon their faith and change their allegiance to Henry, a man they felt was under the influence of a woman many of them saw as a radical whore?

Henry had ways to deal with this problem. The Act of Treason, which made it a capitol offense to suggest that the King was a heretic, was passed into law. Priests were required to pray for Henry and to reject the "Bishop of Rome" as the Pope was now to be called. Those in the Church who had supported Catherine's side during the divorce were arrested and executed. This included Sir Thomas Moore (today known to Catholics as St. Thomas Moore) who was easily the most well known religious figure in England. Moore had been Henry's friend since childhood and had often counseled him, but that meant little to Henry.

But Moore was fortunate. As such a prominent person he was merely beheaded for his crimes. Others suffered much worse fates. Henry had four monks paraded through the streets and then slowly hanged. They were cut down while still conscious and then castrated. After this, their abdomens were sliced open and their intestines pulled out and lit on fire before the eyes of the doomed victims. They were then quartered and beheaded. Their heads were put on spikes, and their dismembered body parts were sent around the kingdom as an example of what would happen to anyone who opposed the new religious order. The clergy fell into line behind Henry pretty quickly after that. Henry ordered that all monasteries be dissolved. He confiscated all the Church money he could get his hands on. He even looted St. Thomas Becket's tomb of five thousand ounces of gold and had the saint's bones destroyed. He continued the Catholic practice of making new bishops pay enormous fees before they could take office, but the money generated by these bribes now found its way into his pocket rather than the pope's.

In fact, Henry kept most of the Catholic traditions and practices in his new Church. It's not that he wasn't aware of the Protestant Reformation going on elsewhere in Europe, as he was—perhaps surprisingly—very interested in theology. Henry's problem was that he viewed reformers with considerable distrust. It was okay for him to throw over the Pope, but in general, reformation seemed anti-authoritarian and threatening to the king. Supporting radical Protestant reform would be just as dangerous as adhering to Catholicism in his England.

Yet his new queen was a devoted Protestant. This in and of itself wasn't too terrible a thing to Henry, but Anne didn't know when to keep her mouth shut, which as Henry's wife was supposed to be nearly all the time. As a result, Henry started getting sick of her fast. To make matters worse she bore him a daughter, Elizabeth. This came in addition to a pair of miscarriages. Anne's inability to produce a son meant that she could no longer be trusted in Henry's mind. Besides, Henry was already in love with another woman, Jane Seymore.

So Anne, the cause of all the years of battling with the Catholic Church, the spilt with Rome, and countless executions, had to go. Getting rid of her would be a lot easier than dispensing with Catherine had been. Anne was an Englishwoman with no foreign monarch to come to her aid. She was completely at Henry's mercy, and she would get none.

A musician named Mark Smeaton was arrested and tortured into confessing an affair with Anne. This alone was enough to make Anne a traitor, but Henry wanted more. Eventually five men, one of them her own brother, were accused of being Anne's lovers. A show trial was held in which all the plainly innocent defendants were sentenced to death. Anne was murdered after spending less than three years as queen. Henry then quickly married Jane Seymore.

Jane was sympathetic to Catholic loyalists, but she was also wise enough to know that Henry was the boss in their marriage, so she kept her opinions to herself. This proved difficult in 1536 when a religiously motivated uprising against Henry broke out in northern England. The rebellion had some teeth to it, and an army was formed against Henry that was strong enough to possibly defeat Henry's forces in battle. Having little other option, Henry invited the rebel leader Robert Aske to join him for dinner to hash out their differences. At the splendid banquet, Henry surprised Aske by giving into him on issue after issue. He promised to pardon all the rebels and to shower northern England with favors. A delighted Aske returned north, and the rebellion died down when the people heard of Henry's pledges. But Henry had lied. He waited for the uprising to cool off, and then he attacked. He arrested all the leaders of the rebellion had them put to death. Aske was draped in heavy chains and then suspended for hours on the side of a building until he finally perished.

Whatever pressure Jane put on Henry in support of these people must have been slight, but even that could be deadly where Henry was concerned. It mattered not, however, because Jane gave Henry what he wanted most in the world, a son. As the mother of Prince Edward, Jane's position with the king was now rock solid, but she didn't get to enjoy it for long, as she died a few days after giving birth.

This put Henry back on the marriage market, and that sent sensible women across Europe scurrying for cover. Finally, Henry's minister, Thomas Cromwell, found him a woman who would agree to marry him. But when Anne of Cleves arrived from Germany, Henry was repulsed by the sight of her. He could find no way out of the marriage, so he plugged his nose and went through with it only to dump her shortly thereafter. In a bizarre move, he had her declared to be his "sister" instead of his wife. Cromwell was convicted of treason and executed as payment for his matchmaking efforts.

While Henry was still married to his wife-cum-sister he eyed a young lady at his court who captured his heart straight away. This was Catherine Howard, a vivacious teenager who made friends easily. Henry was old enough to be her father; in fact, his daughter Mary was four years older than Catherine. What's more, his conquests at the dinner table had rendered him obese. The *pièce de résistance* of Henry's sex appeal was a wound on his leg that refused to heal and made it hard for him to walk. What girl could say no to that? Not one whose family had designs on royal power.

The adorable couple was married straight away. Unsurprisingly, it didn't take too long for things to turn sour. Henry found out that Catherine had once had a lover named Francis Dereham, though the relationship ended before she had met the King. Even worse, there were rumors going around that Catherine was involved in a flirtatious relationship with a man at court named Thomas Culpeper. Henry blew his top over this news and had everyone involved arrested. Culpeper and Catherine's lady in waiting were beheaded. Dereham, who was of lower social rank, got the whole burning entrails treatment as his punishment for having consensual sex with an unmarried girl he couldn't have known would go on to be queen. Catherine was also sentenced to death. In a macabre scene, she asked that the executioner's block be brought to her cell so she could practice placing her head upon it the day before her slaughter.

After Catherine Howard's murder, Henry was single again; but he was too much of a stud to stay that way for long. The next object of his affection was Catherine Parr. Catherine was a deeply religious, Protestant reformer who saw Henry as being a larger-than-life man of God. She said he was "our Moses" who had "delivered us out of the captivity and spiritual bondage of the Pharaoh." She prattled on and on like this. Nevertheless, she didn't want to marry Henry, perhaps because of the fates of his first five wives or maybe because he was larger-than-life in a pretty literal sense by this time. She retreated into prayer to seek God's answer to how she should reply to Henry's proposal. God apparently didn't like Catherine much as he instructed her to marry Henry.

Henry's health had deteriorated to the point where he was often an invalid by this time, and Catherine was his nurse as much as she was his wife. She took a special interest in his daughter Elizabeth and helped to immerse her in a strong Protestant upbringing. Unfortunately for Catherine, Henry was having another of his mood swings, and he was cracking down on religious reformers again. Most religious books were banned, and the English-language version of the Bible was prohibited to all Englishmen with the exception of upper-class males. Most importantly, lots of reformers were rounded up and burned alive. Yet Henry was married to just such a reformer. Henry realized this, and never one to let sentiment get in his way, ordered Catherine's arrest and imprisonment in the Tower of London.

Catherine caught wind of the punishment Henry had in store for her, and she went into full contrition mode with her husband. She made herself out to be nothing but a silly and rather stupid woman who knew little of the great matters of religion, and she promised her utter submission to Henry. That must have been what he wanted to hear as he then dropped the whole matter. He died shortly thereafter.

In the ensuing centuries, Britain would see purges of both Protestants and Catholics, a devastating civil war, sectarian strife in Ireland, and other humanitarian catastrophes that could ultimately trace their genesis to the fact that King Henry wanted to hop into bed with Anne Boleyn.

Henry's son Edward succeeded him to the throne. Edward defied his father's wishes by jumping into full-fledged Protestant reformation, but he died when he was only fifteen years old leaving his very Catholic sister, Mary, as the next in line for the crown. A Protestant coup was staged to prevent Mary's rise to power. The plotters put Edward's teenaged cousin, Lady Jane Grey, on the throne. She lasted all of nine days as queen before she was overthrown by Mary, who then had her put to death. Mary returned England to Catholicism and had about 300 Protestant leaders burned as heretics in the process. She never succeeded in having children, however, so when she died the crown passed to Elizabeth who threw England back to Protestantism and had Catholic leaders rounded up, tortured, and killed. She too failed to produce an heir. When she died, the Tudor dynasty died with her.

What the Hell???

The Battle for Souls

The Protestant Reformation left Western Europe divided into Catholic and Protestant regions. The two groups could have agreed to respect each other as brothers under the same God, or they could have torn each other apart in years of horrific warfare. Guess which option they went for.

Among the worst of the fighting were the French Wars of Religion, which were actually a series of nine wars that sprawled across the second half of the sixteenth century. The trouble started before that, however. In 1521 the great minds at the University of Paris decided that Luther was a heretic and banned all Protestant books, but this didn't stop John Calvin from training missionaries in Geneva to infiltrate France and spread his theology. A few years later a statue of Mary was trashed in Paris; the first of what would turn out to be a great many such acts of vandalism against the Catholic Church carried out by Protestants. In 1534 Protestant placards appeared around Paris that touched off a panic amongst Parisians who thought a massacre of Catholics was imminent. A few people were put to death over the incident, and that calmed nerves for the time being.

But the relationship between French Catholics and Protestants was an uneasy one at best. After King Henry II died and left his fifteen-year-old son Francis II in charge, the tenuous peace fell apart. Francis and his domineering mother, Catherine de Medici (the niece of Popes Leo X and Clement VII, both of whom we previously met,) were overbearing Catholics who saw religious unity as essential to preserving the kingdom. So Francis enacted new policies that were designed to crush the heretics. He had Protestants rounded up, tortured, and executed. One group of thirty Protestants meeting secretly in a forest to plot against Francis were ambushed by the king's men, executed, and left to rot in the streets of the city of Amboise. The putrefying corpses rendered the city unlivable for some time. After this the Protestants began to assemble their own armies.

123

King Francis died young, and his little brother, Charles IX, took over. King Chuck was all of ten years old at the time, so Catherine de Medici's power over the throne was unaltered by her elder son's death. It was at this time that the Protestants (known as Huguenots in France) went on a rampage. In an effort to show their total contempt for Catholicism they looted and vandalized churches wherever they existed in numbers great enough to get away with it. They destroyed sacred objects, fed communion wafers to dogs, burned crucifixes, and defecated on altars. This all went over with Catholics as well as you would expect. They became convinced that Calvin was the Antichrist and had thirty Huguenots killed in the town of Vassy in retaliation for the church seizures.

When a Huguenot army occupied Orléans, it meant war. The Catholics outnumbered the Huguenots in France, but several German principalities and England intervened on the Protestant side to even things out a bit. The Battle of Dreux was the first big contest of the war. The battle was long, close, and bitter. By the time it was over the royalist side had won a nominal victory, and the battlefield was littered with thousands of corpses. A peace plan halted the war not long afterward, but it pleased no one and was condemned by both Calvin and Pope Pius VI.

This was to set a pattern for the wars: Fighting would erupt, foreign powers would intervene, people would be horrified by the devastation, the cost was too much to bear for both sides, and then a peace accord would be reached. Catholics were upset that Huguenots would be permitted to exist; Huguenots were upset that they were not given full equality under the law. Mistrust ruled on both sides, and then fighting would erupt again. Gradually, the wars got worse as cavalier slaughter became more common. After a while both sides stopped bothering with taking prisoners, opting to kill their captives instead.

It's not like the King wasn't trying to keep the peace. During one of the breaks in the wars, a massacre broke out in Rouen when Huguenots failed to remove their hats in respect when a priest carrying a communion host walked by. The outrage over this disrespect led to mob violence that left forty people dead. In order to get a grip on the situation, the crown had an additional sixty-six people executed over the incident, but such efforts were all for naught as a new war invariably would break out.

In 1572, during one of the peaceful interludes, Admiral Coligny, a Huguenot leader in Paris, was shot in an assassination attempt but survived. King Charles rushed guards to his sickbed to protect him from further harm. The King and his mother even visited him to wish him well. Then the king had a remarkable change of heart. He ordered his men to kill Coligny. They did so, and then they decapitated him and tossed him out of a window. The headless corpse was then set upon by a mob in the street below. Why Charles did this is a matter of great conjecture. It may have been that he (or his mom) decided that enough was enough, and this was the time to get rid of the Huguenot leadership once and for all.

In the wake of Coligny's murder, the floodgates of hate broke wide open. Unchecked violence swept through Paris, and Huguenots were slaughtered in huge numbers. As news of what became known as the St. Bartholomew's Day Massacre spread throughout France it was met with new massacres. Huguenots were put to death all around France. It seems that everywhere this happened people thought they were carrying out the king's wishes, but in fact, Charles had ordered no such massacres. Not that this was bothering people much, however. When word of the slaughter got to Rome, Pope Gregory XIII was so overjoyed to hear it that he held a special service blessing the massacre, and he had a medal struck that commemorated the event.

The Protestant reaction to the massacre was rather curious. Many people could not come to terms with what they saw as God's abandonment of their cause. They came to doubt the validity of their movement, and many of them gave up went back to Catholicism. The Huguenots' numbers never recovered from the massacre and the following exodus away from the faith.

But there were still enough Huguenots left to fight a war, and at the city of La Rochelle they delivered a spectacular defeat to Charles' troops, preventing him from turning the massacres into a military gain. This led to another uneasy peace.

King Charles didn't get to enjoy this tenuous peace long, however, as he died in 1574 leaving Henry III as the new king. There were two problems with this: Henry was a hardcore Catholic who would be even less tolerant of Huguenots than his predecessors, and the next in line for the throne was a Protestant, Henri de Navarre. The thought of a Protestant King of France was more than a bit unsettling to Catholics. A Catholic League was set up in Paris to prevent his possible ascension, and Pope Sixtus V issued a bull, which forbade Navarre from ever taking the crown.

To make matters worse, King Henry was an incompetent ruler. He ordered a series of assassinations of popular Catholic nobles that led to an outcry against him. As his political position deteriorated he was forced to make an alliance with Henri de Navarre to keep himself in power. This led to charges from Catholics that he was an atheist and an agent of Satan. A Dominican friar took matters into his own hands and fatally stabbed the king. Paris erupted in celebration at the news of his death, and the murderer was informally branded a "saint."

But that meant Navarre was first in line for the throne now. Catholics hustled another contender, Cardinal de Bourbon, into the picture and declared him to be King Charles X in an effort to keep the Kingdom in Catholic hands. Bourbon's claim to the throne was weak, however, and he was also being held prisoner by Henri de Navarre, so his prospects of collecting his crown and scepter were bleak.

Henri de Navarre was crowned King Henry IV, and he went to war to grab Paris from the Catholic League. Unable to take the city outright, he laid siege to it. This turned into an unmitigated nightmare for Parisians as starvation gripped the city. There are reports from this time of children being chased through the streets by men intending to cannibalize them. Someone got the bright idea of exhuming skeletons from a cemetery and grinding their bones into a powder that was used to bake bread for the poor. This bone-bread turned out to be highly toxic. As people were dying left and right, clergymen delivered sermons urging the populace to believe that death was preferable to Protestant rule. Anyone who even breached the subject of negotiating with Henry was put to death and thrown into the Seine.

Relief for Paris came in the form of King Philip II of Spain. Philip could not bear the thought of a Protestant France, so he sent an army into France to go after Henry. The Spanish saved Paris, but they could not defeat Henry. This led to battle after battle with no end to the fighting in sight. Finally, Henry agreed that he would take Catholic instruction whenever he could find the time for it in return for his undisputed rule in France. This led to another peace agreement although the pope, infuriated by the accord, excommunicated Henry and all of his followers anyway. I'm not sure how a Protestant could be excommunicated from the Catholic Church, but let's not let logic ruin our fun.

In 1593 Henry did opt to become a Catholic. His opponents saw this as nothing but a disingenuous ploy to consolidate his power, but in public at least Henry was always Catholic from this time forward, and he began to take steps to slowly rid France of Protestants. His Edict of Nantes of 1598 severely limited the worshipping rights of Protestants, but some Catholic clergy members publicly protested against it anyway.

At least twenty attempts were made on the life of King Henry IV. Most of them were carried out by Catholic extremists who doubted the validity of his conversion. Finally, in 1610 a man who was angry that the Huguenots had not been forced to convert to Catholicism successfully murdered the King. King Louis XIII succeeded Henry, and he eventually renewed the religious wars. In 1629, with the Huguenots' political and military power smashed to pieces, the fighting finally ended. In 1685 King Louis XIV stripped the remaining Huguenots of all their rights.

But if you thought the French wars were as bad as warfare between Catholics and Protestants could get, you were dead wrong. For just as the fighting in France was winding down, the Thirty Years War was cranking up.

This massive war began in 1618 in Prague when a meeting between Catholics and Protestants resulted in three Catholics being thrown out of windows more than fifty feet high. Amazingly, none of the victims of this ambush were killed by the fall. Catholics claimed that the Virgin Mary had interceded on behalf of the men by saving them while Protestants claimed their landing had been softened by a large dung heap. In the aftermath of the assault, the Protestants of Bohemia expelled all Jesuits and seized the property of the Catholic Church. They also chose their own King in open defiance against the Hapsburg Empire, of which they were a part.

Needless to say, this didn't sit well with the Hapsburg Emperor Ferdinand. He sent an army to Bohemia that crushed the challenge to his rule. He also violently reinstated Catholicism in Bohemia, but this aggravated other Protestants and widened the war. In 1625 Denmark became the first foreign power to throw itself into the fight by intervening on the Protestant side. The Danish military adventure was a massive failure, however.

Everything was rolling Ferdinand's way, and he started getting cocky. In 1629 he decided it was time to strictly enforce the Peace of Augsburg, a treaty that had been signed years earlier, but which had not been enforced much. The treaty dispossessed thousands of Lutherans from their lands, and for Calvinists the consequences were even worse. Since Calvinism didn't exist when the treaty was originally drawn up, there was no provision in it for the faith. Therefore Calvinism was outlawed in the Holy Roman Empire, which included the completely Calvinist city of Geneva.

All of this was more than Protestants could stand, and previously neutral principalities around Germany rose up in revolt. Even worse, Sweden invaded the Holy Roman Empire, and its forces, led by the military legend Gustavus Adolphus, racked up victory after victory against Catholic forces. The Swedish effort was financially subsidized by Cardinal Richelieu of France. Though France was vehemently Catholic, there was no reason to let that get in the way of an opportunity to weaken a Catholic neighbor. After Ferdinand's forces obliterated the city of Magdeburg and left 20,000 dead in their wake, even more princes joined on the Protestant side. It looked like a Protestant victory was at hand. But then Gustavus Adolphus was killed in battle, and the Swedish war effort faltered. This gave Ferdinand the chance to get back on top, but he was jealous of his best military commander, so he had him murdered.

Both sides in the war were now in turmoil due to the loss of their most capable commanders. It was at this time that a Spanish force entered the war on the Catholic side and went on a rampage against the Protestant territories. In 1635 the Peace of Prague was agreed upon to finally end the war, but it was scuttled only days later when France entered the war on the *Protestant* side. As if that weren't enough, Sweden attacked their fellow Protestants by invading Denmark, which meant that Denmark fought for both sides during the war. Don't you just hate it when political matters get in the way of a good, old-fashioned holy war?

The war ebbed and flowed across what is now Germany until 1648 when, with all sides fairly well exhausted, a lasting peace was finally reached.

So what did all this accomplish? Spain was pretty much a spent force and would never be a great power again, while France had become the greatest power on the continent. The Holy Roman Empire was broken up, and it was left utterly devastated since most of the war had been fought on its territory. In Germany alone, thousands of castles were destroyed in the conflict. The death toll of the war was beyond anything that had ever been seen before. Somewhere in the neighborhood of seven to ten million people had been killed in the struggle; a number that would not be equaled until World War I two hundred years later. And oh yes, the borders between the Protestant and Catholic areas of Europe had not changed in any meaningful way.

Conflict between Catholics and Protestants did not end with the Thirty Years War. The last conflict between the groups was settled with the "Good Friday" agreement of 1998, which officially brought an end to the fighting between Catholics and Protestants in Northern Ireland after centuries of hostility. The treaty appears to be holding despite periodic violence that persists to this day.

Pope Urban VIII

The battle of science vs. religion seems like it's as old as time itself, but it isn't. This is because science as we know it today with methodological experimentation didn't exist for most of human history. Before the advent of science, religions could create virtually any mythology they wished, and no one could argue against it with anything resembling evidence-based reason. That began to change in the seventeenth century, however, and when it did Pope Urban VIII found himself in the middle of the scrum over whether the Earth revolves around the Sun or vice-versa. He dealt with the issue in a way that was both forceful and decisive. It was also dead wrong, so his efforts ended up saddling the Church with an embarrassment that would endure for centuries to come.

The notion that the Earth moved around the Sun was first proposed by Nicolaus Copernicus in his book *De Revolutionibus*, which was published in 1543 when he was on his deathbed. Copernicus offered no evidence to support his heliocentric system, but he saw that a Sun-centered world was cleaner and simpler than an Earth-centered one in that it eliminated the bizarre contrivances that were needed to explain why planets occasionally seemed to be moving backward through the night sky.

The idea kicked around Europe for a few decades without really taking off until the Italian genius Galileo Galilei got hold of it. By 1597 Galileo had come to realize the Copernican model was "much more likely than that other view of Aristotle and Ptolemy." He had taken the telescope (which he did not invent, but which he vastly improved) and pointed it at the sky. Through it, he saw four moons orbiting Jupiter. This upset the Church-endorsed view of the ancient stargazer Ptolemy who decreed that everything in the heavens revolved around the Earth. Clearly, this was not the case. He also observed that Venus had phases like the Moon did. This could only mean that Venus was circling the Sun and not the Earth.

As Galileo made his discoveries known he immediately attracted opposition. In 1612 a Dominican priest wrote, "that opinion of Ipernicus, or whatever his name is, appears to be against Holy

Scripture." And in 1614 another priest condemned Galileo and his followers as being "practitioners of diabolical arts... enemies of true religion."

The problem with the Copernican system was that the Bible seemed to be at odds with it. The Book of Psalms says, " O Lord my God, Thou art great indeed... Thou fixed the Earth upon its foundation, not to be moved forever." In the Book of Joshua, God orders the Sun to stand still in the sky for a day to give the Hebrews enough time to finish slaughtering their enemies, thus implying that the Sun was moving rather than the Earth. Galileo took these passages to be symbolic rather than literal, so he didn't think the heliocentric model posed any threat to Christendom.

The Church saw things differently. An edict was handed down in 1616 that condemned the Copernican model as "false and contrary to Holy Scripture." Furthermore, Copernicus' book was suspended until the necessary "corrections" could be made to it. But Galileo saw a silver lining to the ruling because he understood the decree to allow for the discussion of the Copernican model as long as it was only treated hypothetically.

In 1623 Maffeo Barberini was selected to be pope and took the name of Urban VIII. Galileo saw this as being a terrific stroke of good fortune as he had a long and positive relationship with the new pope. At a dinner party in 1611 he had been engaged in an argument concerning why ice floats. The pro-Aristotle contingent at the party asserted that it was the smooth shape of the ice that failed to break the surface tension of the water and thus held it afloat. Galileo countered that ice would float no matter what its shape. He even submerged ice to demonstrate that it invariably rose back to the surface when he released it. Such experimentation was a novel way of understanding the world. It had long been held that the way to unlock the mysteries of the world was for smart people to contemplate them. Galileo, with his hands-on experiments, rejected that method and in so doing was on the cusp of introducing true science to the world. Among the guests at the party was Barberini. The future pope enthusiastically took Galileo's side in the dispute saying, "I pray the Lord God to preserve you, because men of great value like you deserve to live a long time to the benefit of the public." In 1620 Barberini had written a fawning poem about Galileo called

Dangerous Adulation. Four years later he referred to Galileo as his "brother."

In 1624 Galileo made several visits to the pope, and on one of those occasions he read to Urban a letter he had written to a Monsignor Ignoli, who had argued against the Copernican model. The pope made no objections to Galileo's impassioned defense of the heliocentric model, so Galileo took this as the pope's tacit approval of his argument. Soon afterward, he began work on a new book about the relationship of the Earth and Sun.

The book was called *The Dialogue*, and it took him six years to write. It was set up as a conversation between three men debating the merits of the Copernican and Ptolemaic models of the world. The characters were Salviati (who argued for Galileo's own views,) Sagredo (a wise man who usually took Salviati's side in the debate,) and Simplicio (an arrogant fool who clung to the Earth as the center of things). Galileo used numerous arguments to show the Earth was moving around the Sun. In addition to those already mentioned, he used his study of sunspots to show that the Sun itself was rotating, and the Earth was tipping on its axis as it made its way around it. He also erroneously argued that the tides were the result of the Earth's rotation.

Before he could publish his book, Galileo had to submit it to Church censors. He was forced by the censors to revise the beginning and ending of the story to reflect the pope's view that all complexity in nature came from God and to reinforce the edict of 1616, which held that the Earth was the immovable center of the world and that the argument against the Earth-centered universe was merely hypothetical.

While Galileo was at work on his book, things were not going well for Urban. The Thirty Years War was dragging on, and it was taking a toll on the pope. The war had descended into a fight between two Catholic kingdoms: France and Spain. The smart move would have been for the pope to try to mediate the conflict to prevent the world's most important Catholic powers from tearing each other apart and to spare a war-weary land from even more death and destruction, but Urban had good friends in the French royal family, and he threw his support behind them. This infuriated Spain and led to accusations that

Urban had failed to defend the faith. Urban also developed a raging paranoia of Spanish revenge against him. He imagined that Spanish spies surrounded him, and he expected a Spanish invasion fleet to come for him at any time. The stress caused him to become increasingly unglued. He had an astrologer imprisoned after he predicted his death, and he had all the birds in his gardens put to death because their songs disturbed him.

It was in this atmosphere that *The Dialogue* hit the shelves. The book was an instant hit, and it caused an instant scandal. Urban was told the book was a personal insult to him, and he ordered a commission to review it. They reported back to him, "We think Galileo may have overstepped his instructions by asserting absolutely the Earth's motion and the Sun's immobility, thus deviating from hypothesis…One must consider how to proceed, both against the person and concerning the printed book." In September 1632 Galileo was ordered to appear before the Office of the Inquisition. An incensed Urban remarked, "May God forgive Signor Galilei for having meddled with these subjects."

But Galileo was sixty-eight years old by this time. He claimed he was too sick to travel to Rome from Florence. Three doctors signed an affidavit affirming this, but the Inquisition told him to get moving anyway. They threatened to drag him to Rome in chains if he did not come on his own. He did make the trip and was then kept waiting for months as the Inquisition was in no hurry to start his trial.

When the proceedings finally got underway, Galileo tried to defend himself by claiming that he had only argued the heliocentric case hypothetically, as he was allowed to do. The Inquisitors countered that the Church had ruled that the Copernican system could not be taught in any way at all. Galileo tried to object to this, but the matter was resolved.

With his main defense thus taken from him, Galileo fell back to a secondary strategy that could fairly be called "lying his ass off." He claimed his book was intended to show the *weakness* of the Copernican argument rather than to promote it. He did admit, however, that upon rereading *The Dialogue* he did see how someone might get the impression that he had been endorsing the "false" argument that the Earth moved around the Sun, but that was not his intent. He offered to lengthen the book so that the Church-endorsed version of reality could be argued more forcefully. Such a ploy may seem farcical in retrospect, but Galileo was a desperate man. He feared his book would be banned and that his freedom and well-being were in danger as well. One witness, upon seeing him return from a day of testimony remarked, "The poor man has come back more dead than alive."

Urban called a meeting of the inquisitors. He told them the book should be banned and Galileo should be imprisoned. He also demanded that the jurors question Galileo over the intent he had in writing *The Dialogue*. He authorized the use of torture if necessary. Galileo was told he was in danger of torture, but he stuck to his phony guns. He claimed he had once been unsure of which system was correct, but he had held the Earth-centered view since the 1616 ruling on the subject.

When the verdict came down, Galileo was "vehemently suspected of heresy, namely of having held and believed the doctrine that the Sun is the center of the world and does not move from east to west, and that the Earth moves and is not the center of the world." *The Dialogue* was banned, and Galileo was imprisoned. He was forced to kneel before the inquisitors and read an apology written for him by the tribunal. He swore he would believe the Earth was the unmoving center of the world, and he would never say otherwise in the future. Urban ordered the news of Galileo's punishment to be posted far and wide to dissuade anyone else from repeating his heresy. He rejected the numerous appeals he received to pardon Galileo.

Galileo was imprisoned in Siena at first and then moved to house arrest in Arcetri. He was forbidden to have any visitors who might discuss scientific matters with him. Urban forbade all of Galileo's books from being reprinted, which effectively banned his entire body of work. Nonetheless, Galileo set to work on a new book while he was incarcerated. In this book he wrote out the rules of motion as he had come to understand them. The book, known as *Two New Sciences*, was to form the foundation of physics. But there was no chance the Church would allow anything he wrote to be published. So a copy of the manuscript was smuggled out of Italy, and the book was printed in the Netherlands. Galileo pretended he had no idea as to how the book ever found its way out of his house.

When Galileo died in 1642, Urban squelched all attempts to honor him posthumously as he considered any commemoration of Galileo to be an assault on his papal authority. When Urban himself died two years later, Roman crowds celebrating his demise smashed a sculpture of the pope to bits. Urban had engaged in military scheming that had left the Church in an astonishing amount of debt that would haunt the institution for years to come, but today he is remembered for little other than his furious opposition to Galileo, the first person who ever looked into the night sky and understood what he was seeing.

Notwithstanding the Roman Catholic Church's eventual acceptance of a sun-centered solar system, there are still some Catholics who refute the idea today. These are members of the archconservative Catholic group called the Society of St. Pius X. To be clear: this group does not reflect the official position of the Catholic Church; in fact Pope John Paul II excommunicated them in 1988 (although those excommunications were remitted in 2009). The Society was created by the French archbishop, Marcel Lefebvre, who held the modern Catholic Church in contempt because they have committed such atrocities as saying mass in languages other than Latin. The society promotes an extremely conservative social agenda and supports far-right political figures, especially in France.

There are a number of people in this group who reject the notion that the Earth revolves around the Sun. Robert Sungenis, who is at the forefront of the movement to get the Church to reconsider the subject of heliocentrism, was quoted by the *Los Angeles Times* in 2011 saying, " Heliocentrism becomes dangerous if it is being propped up as the true system when, in fact, it is a false system. False information leads to false ideas, and false ideas lead to illicit and immoral actions—thus the state of the world today… Prior to Galileo, the Church was in full command of the world, and governments and academia were subservient to her." That same year a conference called "Galileo Was Wrong. The Church Was Right" was held in Indiana near the campus of Notre Dame University. The point was not only to promote this profoundly unscientific worldview, but also to pressure the Church by putting the event on the doorstep of America's most prominent Catholic University.

In 1757 the Catholic Church finally dropped its objection to the Copernican model, but *The Dialogue* remained a banned book. It wasn't until 1835, nearly two hundred years after Galileo's trial, that the Church's Index of Forbidden Books was published without *The Dialogue* on it. In 1966 when the Church could no longer keep up with the number of titles being released, it abandoned the Index altogether. In case you were wondering, Adolf Hitler's *Mein Kampf* was never placed on the list.

In 1851 Léon Foucault proved the Earth was rotating with the use of a pendulum, but by that time the debate had long been settled. The logical case Galileo made was so superior to the Church's argument from authority that the notion of an immovable Earth at the center of the universe crumbled entirely despite the best efforts of the Church to enforce its belief.

In 1992 Pope John Paul II admitted that the Church had erred in the Galileo case due to what he called "tragic mutual incomprehension." I doubt Galileo would have agreed with the "mutual" part.

What the Hell???

This is Turning into a Witch-Hunt!

Being an American, I cannot think of witch trials without thinking of the Salem debacle of 1692 in which twenty people were put to death for the crime of practicing witchcraft. The Salem trials and Arthur Miller's 1953 play *The Crucible* (which was actually inspired by Sen. Joseph McCarthy's hunt for communists) are standard fare for American high school students, so it's understandable that this event has come to define witch hunting in the United States. The truth of the matter, however, is that the Salem trials were little more than a sideshow compared to the full-blown slaughter that was witch-hunting in Europe. It is impossible to say exactly how many people were killed for being witches, but an estimate of 100,000 could well be on the conservative side.

What might be surprising about witch-hunts is how recently they took place. One might think witch trials were artifacts of the darkest of the dark ages, and in fact there were people who were put to death for witchcraft in those days. But there were no widespread witch-hunts going on in the 700s. The systematic search for witches started out in the late Middle Ages and picked up steam as time went by. The Renaissance did not diminish the fervor for witch-hunts, and the Protestant Reformation and the Catholic Counter-Reformation in no way eroded the practice either.

The big moment that transformed witch-hunting from a scattershot practice in Medieval Europe into a big-time enterprise was when two Dominican inquisitors from what is now Germany, who were meeting resistance from local populations to their witch trials, appealed to Pope Innocent VIII for help. He responded to their pleas by issuing a bull, which granted them permission to proceed with their work in no uncertain terms. From this bull flowed the publication of the *Malleus*, written by the same two men with Innocent's bull serving as a preface. This document was essentially a handbook into how to conduct witch-hunts. It also assembled various witchcraft traditions together for the first time. Perhaps most chillingly, it also condemned as heretics anyone who denied the reality of witchcraft. Heresy, of course, was punishable by death; this assured that there weren't going to be many objections to the trials. The *Malleus* was reprinted repeatedly throughout the years, and it spawned many imitators, both Catholic and Protestant, over the ensuing centuries.

So-called "witches" were tried in both ecclesiastical and secular courts, although there wasn't much difference between the two in the end as priests routinely brought suspects to the attention of secular courts, and secular officials often participated in Church trials.

Torture, euphemistically referred to as "The Ordeal," was allowed in both types of courts. The most common types of torture used were the hoist, the rack (both described in the chapter on Torquemada,) and various types of clamps such as thumbscrews and head vices. Unlike the Spanish Inquisition, however, there was little central authority overseeing the witch trials, so there was a lot of room for various courts to freelance with the types of torture they wished to employ. Additionally, many judges at the witch trials believed that Satan gave witches magical abilities to resist pain. They tried to overcome this imagined advantage held by the defendants by ramping up level of torture. They subjected the victims to fire, they tore out their fingernails with pliers, they stabbed out their eyes, chopped off their ears, crushed their testicles, and so on, *ad nauseam*. Tellingly, the overall conviction rate for defendants at European witch trials was about fifty percent, but in cases where torture was used the conviction rate rose to ninety-five percent. It was the confessions of the tortured that made the difference. Once you had confessed to witchcraft, even under such obviously unfair circumstances, there was no doubt as to the verdict of the case.

And the accused would also be tortured into giving up the names of other witches. When those people were arrested, tortured and forced to name even more witches, a routine witch arrest could blossom into a full-blown panic in which scores of people, possibly even hundreds, could be arrested. There were infamous witch-hunts in which hundreds of people were put to death. One witch scare in Spain's Basque country produced 1,800 confessed witches of which 1,300 were children. And it's not like the huge number of witches that were being rounded up and murdered were causing Church leaders to pause and contemplate the legitimacy of the convictions. In fact, just the reverse was true. They were more worried about the number of witches they weren't catching than they were about the number of victims they had roasted.

They believed that staggering numbers of witches were active in Europe. The witches were "known" to attend witch Sabbaths, which could draw as many as 100,000 witches at a time. These Sabbaths were mockeries of the Catholic mass and featured naked dancing, communion made either of dung or the flesh of dead babies, intentionally awful singing, and Catholic liturgy read backward. Witches supposedly arrived at these Sabbaths by flying to them. The fact that no one ever actually witnessed such a Sabbath nor the thousands of witches sailing through the air to attend them didn't cause the slightest bit of skepticism as to the veracity of the claims that these things were real.

In 1517 Martin Luther came out with his ninety-five theses attacking the Catholic Church. Not one of these theses objected to executing people for witchcraft. In fact, Luther was in agreement with the Catholics on this point. It may even be said that he was more prone to supporting witch-hunts than the Catholics, as he envisioned the world as a place that was practically overrun with demons and in which Satan had a genuine physical presence. John Calvin also had no objections to witch-hunting. Moreover, Protestants promoted the Bible and published it in the languages of the common people, so the command of Exodus 22:18, *Thou shalt not suffer a witch to live* rang unambiguously in Protestant ears.

The role of the devil in the witch trials was an important one for religious authorities. For the witch-hunts were not just about people practicing black magic, but more importantly they were about the pacts that witches supposedly made with the devil to obtain their dark powers in the first place. This pact was the greater crime and was the reason that so many witches had to be put to death rather than letting them off with lighter sentences. Especially in Protestant areas, it was believed that the devil left a mark upon the witch's body when the diabolical pact was sealed. Therefore a physical inspection of the victim could provide irrefutable "evidence" of the person's guilt. A birthmark or a mole could be enough to damn the defendant. As if that weren't enough, a cottage industry of witch hunters sprang up to provide evidence of the pact—for a reasonable reward of course. These people employed tricks such as the use of sleight of hand to appear to prick a person with a pin. When the site of the prick didn't bleed that would be proof that the victim was a witch.

While practically everyone in Europe believed in black magic and sorcery in those days, the idea of satanic pacts was mostly limited to the elite classes. Monks, landlords, and nobles read up on the danger that these unholy alliances posed to society and their privileged place in it. It was these people who drove the witch-hunts. Many peasants probably never even heard of the concept of witches dealing with the devil until charges of such were read against them at their trials.

Witch-hunting mania reached what you might call its "golden age" in the late sixteenth and early seventeenth centuries. Witches were arrested and murdered everywhere in Europe, but some places saw a lot more witch-hunting than others. The hardest hit areas were Germany, Switzerland, Austria, Poland, Scotland, and France. In most of these areas there was a great deal of religious turbulence caused by the Protestant Reformation. Wherever religious strife between Protestants and Catholics or between Protestants of different denominations occurred, the greatest witch hysteria could be found. And it was not Protestants killing Catholics or vice-versa that accounted for the huge body counts. In nearly all cases, the alleged witches were of the same faith as their accusers. On both sides, the need to purify society was paramount.

So who were the witches? In theory anyone could be a witch, and people of every stripe were accused of witchcraft, but there were definitely themes amongst the victims of the hunts. First off, the so-called witches were overwhelmingly female. Two German towns that were overrun with witch hysteria lost so many ladies that when the panics finally ended each of them was left with only a single woman resident. Women and girls were thought to be intellectually and physically inferior to men and therefore less resistant to the charms of Satan. They were also seen as being horny temptresses, which provided a way for the devil to approach them. Furthermore, women's work included tasks that made them more likely to be hit with witchcraft charges. Cooks were often around the sorts of things that supposedly could be used to make potions. Midwives invariably would be present at stillbirths, which could lead to charges that they had cast spells to kill the children for use in their satanic Sabbaths.

Witches were also old. Most were over the age of fifty. Senility doubtlessly played a part in this. People given to babbling about things that were not real were likely to be considered as sorcerers and were also more likely to confess to charges they didn't comprehend. Poverty also played a big role. Most witches were poor and therefore less able to defend themselves from the charges against them. Rich people got accused too, but when that happened it often signaled the end of the witch-hunt, as the powers-that-were would call a halt to further prosecutions for witchcraft in that particular time and place.

There was no "typical witch," but if you were an unpopular, widowed peasant who worked as a midwife in Germany you might have had a hard time getting affordable life insurance.

The accusers could be almost anyone. It was the clergy who most often presented the accused to authorities, but it was regular people who most often brought the accusations in the first place. If someone couldn't bear children, or lost a child or a farm animal, it was common to look for someone to blame for it. Did some old woman look at you funny? That could well be the evil eye. Did a hailstorm wreck your crops? Surely a witch summoned it. Accusers could also be motivated by revenge for old grievances or any number of other motives. No matter the cause of the accusation, once the trial began all advantages belonged to the accuser and none to the defendant. A 1661 a witch-hunt in the German town of Lindheim serves as an illustrative example. The hunt erupted after a child died at his birth. It was said that witches murdered the child and made his flesh into a wretched salve. The baby was exhumed, and his corpse was shown to be unmolested, but the court paid no attention to either such conclusive evidence or to the total lack of evidence against the accused. The midwife and the child's parent's were arrested and tortured into giving up more witches. The father escaped from jail and won a decision in another town to stop the proceedings. When he got home, however, he found that his wife, the midwife, and twenty-eight other people had already been put to death.

After the mid 1600s witch-hunting went into a gradual decline, but it took a very long time to go away. There was some nervousness about the theological grounding for the whole idea of witches being in league with the devil, which made it seem like God and Satan were more or less equally powerful. This smacked of the dualist heresy for which the Cathars had been condemned. The notion of satanic pacts slowly started to ebb as well. Just as importantly, the use of torture in witch trials was gradually discontinued, and without it confessions dropped off sharply. But people didn't stop believing in witches. Witch trials continued throughout Christendom for decades to come. The last legal witch execution in Europe took place in Switzerland in 1782, but extra-legal mob killings continued well after that. An Irish woman was murdered for witchcraft in 1894, but that wasn't even close to the last killing of a witch. An alleged witch's house was burned down in Germany in 1976. She was injured and her pets were killed, but she survived. A man was killed in France for sorcery the very next year, and in 1981 a Mexican woman was stoned to death for practicing witchcraft. Two people were executed in Saudi Arabia in 2011 for the same crime.

In developing nations, murders of witches are more common. In 2013 a young woman in Papua New Guinea was accused of witchcraft after a small boy died. She was grabbed by a mob of vigilantes who then stripped her clothes off, tortured her with a hot iron, doused her with gasoline and set her alight in front of hundreds of onlookers.

The Agence France press agency reported shortly thereafter that an estimated 70,000 to 80,000 people worldwide have been put to death for witchcraft since the end of World War II.

Let's face it; witches were a dime a dozen in the old days. If you really wanted to stand out as a badass, you could be convicted of being a werewolf. That's right, they were hunting werewolves too. Though theologically dubious, (the Gospels are rather short on mentions of werewolves) a surprisingly large number of people were tried and convicted of being shape-shifters. Coincidentally, these people usually lived in areas that were heavily forested. The arid region of central Spain seems to have been remarkably werewolf-free for some reason.

Oliver Cromwell

Oliver Cromwell was not a religious leader in the strictest sense, as he held no position in any church. But his leadership of England was so saturated with his fervently held religious passions that to see him as any kind of a secular figure is practically impossible.

Actually, it was nearly impossible to see Cromwell as any kind of a leader at all for most of his life. Cromwell was born in 1599 to a family that was in the upper class, but just barely. As Cromwell grew into adulthood, his financial condition worsened and worsened. Still, he had a respectable family name and was able to get himself briefly appointed to parliament in 1628. He seems to have impressed no one during his first stint in government.

When Cromwell was about thirty years old, he underwent a major religious awakening that would be called a "born-again" experience today. His limited surviving writings from this era burn with a religious zeal that would never leave him. He worried that the reformation had not gone far enough, and he was concerned that there was still a scent of Catholicism in the Church of England. He also seems to have come to believe that God had selected him for greatness and would eventually present him with his special calling. Any trace of a special calling was hard to see at this time, however, because in 1631 he was forced to sell most of his lands and take the humiliating position of a tenant farmer. Five years later Cromwell caught a break when his uncle died, and the resulting inheritance was enough to push him back in to the lower ranks of the gentry.

Cromwell was able to parlay his newfound position into another term in parliament in 1640. Cromwell was part of what came to be known as the Long Parliament, a tumultuous period in which King Charles I and the parliament fought increasingly nasty battles with one another until the entire process collapsed into the English Civil War in 1642. Cromwell was still a small fish in parliament at the time. When the war broke out he gathered together a local militia that enjoyed a small amount of success, so he was given a middling military rank by parliament. Cromwell was in a good position in the sense that the area he was stationed in was heavily pro-parliamentarian, and he faced weak royalist opposition, which he defeated on numerous occasions. Cromwell saw this as proof-positive that God was intervening in his life. Even more fortuitously, as he was piling up victories the Parliamentarians were getting beaten up elsewhere in the war, so he was able to move up steadily in the ranks.

Cromwell made the most of this opportunity by chalking up victories, which he attributed to God in no uncertain terms. After he won the Battle of Marston Moore he rejoiced, "We never charged, but we routed the enemy... God made them as stubble to our swords... Give glory, all the glory to God."

God apparently was in a charitable mood at the Battle of Basing House as well. This battle was a turning point in the story of Cromwell, however. Whereas he was normally fairly quick to accept surrender from royalist troops, he made an exception here, seemingly because the defenders were mainly Catholics. In fact, Cromwell was reputed to have called the place a "nest of Romanists." Most of the defenders at Basing House were put to death. Cromwell's raving hatred of Catholicism would guide him in this manner for the rest of his life.

The war dragged on to its conclusion with the Parliamentarians victorious and King Charles imprisoned, but no sooner had the King's forces been defeated than the Parliamentarians fell into fighting amongst themselves. On one side were the Presbyterians, who favored a central Church and a restored monarchy. They were opposed by the Independents (including Cromwell) who thought that idea sounded too Catholic even though both the Church and the monarchy were Protestant. Cromwell's argument eventually won the day. The key point in the debate came when he left parliament, gathered up the army, marched on London and forced the Presbyterians to see things his way.

Not long after, King Charles escaped from prison, royalist uprisings broke out, and Scotland attacked England from the north. Cromwell rode against the Scotts, defeated them and gave glory to God for this "unspeakable mercy." Charles was quickly recaptured and put on trial where he would encounter this same unspeakable mercy. Cromwell was one of the judges at the king's trial and signed the order for him to be beheaded. Fed up with people who didn't see things his way, Cromwell then removed all the Presbyterians from parliament.

But Cromwell was just getting started. In 1649, with the Parliamentarian position in Great Britain shored up, the Protestants were able to turn their attention to Ireland, which had been roiled by horrendous religious infighting for several years prior to this. A force thousands of men strong was dispatched to the Emerald Isle to put down what Cromwell called the "barbarous and bloodthirsty" Irish. Because, you know, the English had been such models of civility and pacifism. Prayers were said before lots were cast to determine which units would be sent to invade Ireland. Upon his arrival, Cromwell gave thanks to God for bringing him to the island.

The Irish would have less reason to thank God for Cromwell's visit as the campaign took a nasty turn in a short order with massacres occurring in two battles in which Cromwell was in command.

When the city of Drogheda fell to Cromwell he ordered all who had defended the town, all who had assisted them and the town's Catholic clergy to be slaughtered. Thousands of people were thus put to death after the battle including a thousand or so who had taken refuge in a church, which Cromwell ordered to be burned while it was packed with people. Cromwell called the massacre at Drogheda "a righteous judgment of God upon these barbarous wretches who have imbued their hands in so much innocent blood."

Next up was Wexford. The situation here was murkier. Again thousands of townsfolk were massacred following the battle, but Cromwell did not actually order the carnage this time. Instead his troops, who had been fed a steady diet of Cromwell's anti-Catholic viewpoints, broke through the town's defenses while Cromwell was still negotiating its surrender. Once inside they wiped out everyone they could get their swords upon, and burned the town down for good measure. Cromwell was taken by surprise by the development, but he was none too distressed about it. He called the blood-soaked killing field his men created "God's righteous judgment."

The massacres get the most attention of the English campaign in Ireland, but in reality the worst was yet to come. The Irish populace was subjected to brutal policies after the war that today would likely be considered ethnic cleansing, if not worse.

Tens of thousands of Irishmen were sent to the Caribbean to spend the rest of their lives as slaves. Countless thousands more were encouraged to emigrate from Ireland. The Puritans tried to parlay the military victories into an abolition of Catholicism in Ireland. This included a campaign to rid the island of all its priests. Internment camps were created for the Catholic clergy, and large rewards were offered for the capture of any priest trying to hide from the English. Most of the priests were eventually deported from the island.

Irish landowners were also targeted by the new regime. They surrendered vast amounts of property to pay the wages of the English troops who had invaded them. Both Irish Catholics and Protestants forfeited their holdings, but Catholics were made to surrender much more. Those displaced by the forfeitures were sent to Connaught, the most unlivable part of Ireland where they were dumped with no shelter and no prospects. Eventually all Irishmen and Catholics were ordered out of every walled city in the country and were made to stay at least two miles away. It is estimated that Ireland lost a staggering five sixths of its population by the end of the Cromwellian period.

In 1653 Cromwell looked back at his demolition of Ireland with pride. "It had pleased God... to reduce Ireland," he crowed.

But all this happened after Cromwell had left Ireland. He couldn't hang around for all the fun there as Scotland was in revolt again. The Scotts proved to be extremely difficult foes this time around, and Cromwell's army was severely challenged by them. The massive causalities and general misery he suffered didn't dim his conviction that God was on his side, however, as he blathered on constantly about it. He once even ordered his troops to stop fighting once in mid-battle so they could recite a Psalm.

Given this, it's perhaps surprising that Cromwell emerged victorious in Scotland once again and returned to parliament in triumph. When parliament took up debate on a constitution that he did not approve of, he reached out to the army again, this time to disperse parliament entirely. This stunt left Cromwell as the only real power in England. Uncomfortable with this totalitarian position, he arranged for a new parliament to be created, one made up entirely of people who were judged to be of sufficient godliness. This "Parliament of Saints", as it came to be known, didn't work out too well as the "saints" didn't get along with each other as well as Cromwell had hoped. When the Parliament of Saints collapsed, Cromwell was left once again as the de facto dictator.

Bear in mind that this was little more than twenty years after he had been a lowly tenant farmer. Now he was literally living like a king. He resided in palaces that had belonged to King Charles only a few years before. And he wielded the power of king as well. Whereas the parliaments Charles had to deal with were thorns in his side, the parliaments Cromwell dealt with were created at his wish mostly for the sake of showing the world that he was not a dictator. Nonetheless, Cromwell dissolved all the parliaments that were created during the time he ruled England. It seems that he actually wanted to create a British republic of some sort, but when contentious issues arose he had to have his way on them. Compromise was just not in his nature.

And as the unchallenged ruler, he got to call the shots. This included waging war against Spain. But when English forces were defeated by the Spanish at Hispaniola, he fretted that he had provoked God by not living humbly enough. It never occurred to him that God was on the side of Catholic Spain, though he always saw his own victories as proof of God's partisanship. After his forces later scored a success against the Spanish at the Canary Islands he was back in form, thanking "the goodness and loving kindness of the Lord" for the triumph.

In 1658 Cromwell shuffled off this mortal coil, and the puritan empire he created crumbled without his leadership. Charles II was welcomed back into England, and the monarchy was reinstated with widespread public acclaim. Much of what so many people had died fighting over was rendered largely moot with incredible ease.

King Charles II ordered Cromwell's corpse to be exhumed, hanged, and beheaded. Cromwell's head was impaled on a pike and raised on the roof of Westminster Hall where it stayed for a century until it blew down in a storm. A soldier recovered the skull and sold it for the price of a drink.

Cromwell's conquest of their island continued to haunt the Irish even long after his death, as the British rule over the Ireland was anything but beneficial to its people. By the 1840s Ireland's Catholics were squeezed onto tiny plots of land owned by mostly Protestant landlords who often lived in England. The only way these scraps of land could provide enough food for the people to survive was through the growing of potatoes, which are both caloric and nutritious.

In 1846 a disease called potato blight spread like wildfire throughout Ireland, and the populace faced starvation. What started out as a natural disaster quickly turned into a man-made catastrophe as the British response to the great famine was, at best, woefully inadequate. The British government did almost nothing to alleviate the starvation in Ireland. Soup kitchens were set up and then quickly discontinued as they were seen as a needless burden on British taxpayers. Grain grown in Ireland was exported to foreign markets for the profit of the landowners while the famine killed the Irish in staggering numbers.

Why were the British so indifferent to the plight of their neighbors? There were two primary reasons. First, there was a belief that free market forces would provide the solution to the problem. It was thought that any government intervention in the crisis would merely exacerbate the situation, so a laissez-faire policy of non-intervention was adopted. Second, the Catholics of Ireland were seen by the British as being people of an "alien faith" (as Prime Minister Benjamin Disraeli called them) and were thought to be dirty, lazy, and even semi-human. Furthermore, there was a widespread belief amongst the British that the famine was a divine punishment against the Irish.

This was certainly the feeling of Sir Charles Trevelyn, a British civil servant who was largely in charge of the government's famine relief program. Trevelyn was thoughtful enough to write a book about his mismanagement of the Great Famine so that future generations could see the prejudice and hate that guided his thinking during the crisis. In it, he describes the famine as "a direct stroke of an all-wise and all-merciful Providence" that would expose the "root of social evil." He said, "The judgment of God sent the calamity to teach the Irish a lesson." He called the famine a "great opportunity" to remedy the social ills of Ireland.

After six years of starvation, the potato blight began to ebb, and the harvest began to increase. The free market solution to the famine also began to show itself. It turns out that dead people don't require much food, and since Ireland lost about a million people to starvation and disease there were a lot fewer mouths to feed. Additionally, some two million people gave up and left Ireland for good, further reducing the demand on the island's food supply. More surely would have left if they had been able to scrape together the funds to buy a one-way ticket out of Ireland. Appeals to the British government to help the Irish emigrate were rejected. In all, Ireland lost three million people out of the eight million that lived there at the onset of the famine. Nearly all the dead from the famine were Catholics.

Maximilien Robespierre

Robespierre is remembered as the architect of the Reign of Terror that consumed tens of thousands of lives in post-revolutionary France. He is almost never thought of as a religious leader, yet he was. Robespierre's drive to control almost every aspect of French life led him to create his own religion and to force it upon France as the official faith of the nation. That Robespierre was actually able to pull off such a feat is a testament to the enormous amount of power he held; yet it was also the single greatest catalyst for his eventual downfall.

Maximilien Robespierre was born in Arras, France in 1758. He studied law in school and established his own legal practice that struggled to survive. The revolution was a godsend for Robespierre as it allowed him to leave his failing career as a lawyer and to reinvent himself as a patriotic politician. In 1789 he was elected to represent Arras in the Third Estate. The French government at the time was still under the rule of King Louis XVI. The estates were a concession Louis made to allow the people to have a voice in the governing of their own country, but the system was set up in such a way that common people would be given no more than the illusion of representation. There were three estates, the first two of which were the clergy and the nobility. These two groups nearly always voted together and concert with the king. The third estate, the one that represented nearly everyone in France, was routinely outvoted two-to-one and therefore had no real ability to impact French policies. The inherent unfairness of this situation inevitably led to the violence that would overthrow the monarchy.

Robespierre was a paranoid man who lived in constant fear of conspiracies that he was sure were always being carried out against him. He was virtually unknown when he first arrived in Paris, but he soon earned a reputation as a relentless radical with unswerving opposition to the monarchy. As the power of the third estate rose, it broke down into factions. Robespierre joined, and eventually took control of, the Jacobin faction. The Jacobins, in turn, gradually became the ruling faction within the government. The monarchy fell in 1792, and the royal family was eventually put to death. Robespierre was central in the decision to kill the king. "Louis must die so the country may live," he proclaimed. Those who favored the removal of Louis as king but voted to spare his life were themselves branded as traitors at Robespierre's urging. Robespierre was no longer an elected official by this time, and he had personally seen to it that men could not serve back-to-back terms. It seemed as if his power was checked, but he got himself appointed to the Committee for Public Safety, which was overseeing practically everything in France. Furthermore, his prominence within the Jacobin faction ensured that his voice was the one that carried the real power within the group.

Robespierre abused his authority to no end. Always on guard against conspirators, he rounded up and executed people by the thousands. These were people he felt were royalists, aligned with competing French factions, in league with foreign governments or just plain anti-revolutionary. An act as simple as cutting down a tree could get one branded as an enemy of the state. There were even certificates of good citizenship issued. To be without one was to be at grave risk.

Religious life in France was undergoing a dramatic upheaval all the while. When the royal government fell the Catholic Church largely fell with it. With no small amount of justification, people saw the Church as having been an instrument in their repression under the king. In 1790 the government required that the clergy in France be elected. Naturally, the pope refused to recognize bishops who had been elected by the people rather than appointed by the Church. Clergy members were also required to take an oath to uphold the new constitution of France, but half of them refused to do so. As the revolution gathered steam the Church found itself on the outside looking in. For the first time in history, atheism took off and claimed widespread acceptance. Such a thing would have been unthinkable only a generation before, but this was the age of enlightenment, and the revolutionary fervor in France left no sacred cows. In 1792 the Cult of Reason was established. This was an atheistic group that worshipped not God, but the ideals of truth, liberty and reason. Unable to imagine life without the social cohesion of religion, they formed congregations and even held services. They held their most legendary service at Notre Dame, complete with a woman dressed as liberty. The Catholic Church had become so marginalized by this time that they were powerless to stop them.

But not everyone was a fan of atheism. Amongst these people was Robespierre, although he had described himself as being a "pretty bad Catholic," and he probably kept a mistress as well. Early in his political career he strongly identified with a group called the Jansenists who believed in predestination and were condemned as heretics by the Catholic Church. He made numerous appeals on behalf the Jansenists in his speeches and described their genocide at the hands of the Church in greatly exaggerated detail. As early as 1789 he started making weepy speeches praising what he called the "Supreme Being" and the immortality of the soul. He praised providence, which he said "always looks after us so much better than our own wisdom." He even declared before the Jacobin club that religion was a necessary sentiment of his heart while the members of his own faction booed him. In 1794 he had the leaders of the Cult of Reason rounded up and put to death.

But this left an obvious problem; if the Church was forbidden, and atheism was also unacceptable what were people supposed to—or not supposed to—worship? Robespierre solved this dilemma by inventing a new religion, which he called the Cult of the Supreme Being. He decided to drop his new religion bomb on France on May 7, 1794, only four days after he was elected speaker of the National Convention, an accomplishment that cemented his stranglehold on power in France. He was a bit vague on the details of what the dogma of this new religion was, but he made it the official religion of France. He declared that a festival for the new faith would be held on June 8th.

And what a show that turned out to be! There can be no doubt that no religion has ever had such a gaudy debut as the Cult of the Supreme Being. The neoclassical painter Jacques Louis David created sets for the ceremony, and a manmade mountain was thrown together on the Champ de Mars for the event. A half a million people, nearly the entire population of Paris, turned out to see the festival. The ceremony started in the Tuileries Gardens where Robespierre set fire to a structure meant to represent atheism. Then a figure representing wisdom "miraculously" emerged from the flames only slightly burned. Robespierre gave a speech after which the action turned to the newly created mountain. Robespierre descended the mountain in a style mindful of Moses carrying the Ten Commandments. He then delivered another speech and led the people of Paris in the singing of patriotic hymns.

Robespierre was consumed with euphoria throughout the whole spectacle, but few of the onlookers shared in his joy. Atheists were naturally offended by it, and Catholics found it blasphemous. But there was something else about the whole thing that was even more disturbing to a lot of people. The Festival of the Supreme Being was the first time Parisians had ever seen Robespierre acting as the head of state, and here he was parading around like he was a king or a pope. Some even thought he was presenting himself as God. Wasn't this unchecked authority what the people of France had just revolted against? The sight was so ridiculous that even his fellow Jacobites openly laughed and mocked Robespierre during the Festival within his earshot. He brushed off their comments as the work of conspirators, but his image suffered a hit from which it would never recover. Robespierre planned for similar festivals to be celebrated every ten days, but the first one was such a debacle that no other celebrations in honor of the Supreme Being ever took place. The Festival also marked the only occasion in which Robespierre ever appeared in public as the leader of France.

But he still held onto power, and he wielded it ruthlessly. The summer of 1794 was the heart of the Reign of Terror. Robespierre sent thousands of people to the guillotine and severely censored all media coverage of the events. No one dared to publicly oppose him, but he had his delusions of conspiracies that ensured that he would never run out of opponents to murder. Outside of Paris, however, his power was not as strong as it was in the city. The city of Lyon, in particular, seemed happy to do without Robespierre's edicts and his Supreme Being. This proved to be a big mistake as Robespierre sent the military to Lyon to enforce his authority. Once the city was secured, the executions began. So many people were condemned to death that the guillotine could not keep up with the demand. Firing squads were set up but they still could not dispatch people to meet the Supreme Being fast enough, so cannons were loaded with grapeshot and fired into masses of the condemned in order to speed up the killing. Robespierre declared, "Lyon is no more" and renamed what was left of the city "Ville-Affrachie." In all of this, it never seems to have crossed his mind that he was killing innocent people.

The members of the National Assembly took note of the developments with horror. They must have figured it was only a matter of time before they were put to death themselves. With their backs against the wall, they hurriedly plotted against Robespierre.

On July 27 Robespierre was arrested. Knowing that he would be guillotined the next day, he decided to dodge the fate to which he had doomed so many others by committing suicide first. He shot himself in the head, but somehow managed to miss his cranium despite firing at point-blank range. Instead he shot himself in the jaw and merely insured that his last hours would be miserable ones. The next day his newly disfigured head was cut off.

In 1799 Napoleon Bonaparte seized control of France and outlawed the Cult of the Supreme Being. He went on to crown himself emperor at a ceremony attended by Pope Pius VII.

One of the men arrested in Robespierre's Reign of Terror was the American revolutionary figure, Thomas Paine. Paine was in France to support the revolution, but his opinions, including his dislike for organized religion, ultimately annoyed Robespierre and landed him in jail. Paine was to have been guillotined, but he escaped death by the luckiest of accidents. When the guard went around the jail marking the cells of the condemned with chalk letters he failed to notice that the door to Pain's cell was wide open. When the door was later shut, the mark was hidden inside the cell, so no one brought Paine out to be killed. Robespierre's arrest came only days later.

Joseph Smith

Joseph Smith Jr. was the son of an obsessive treasure hunter who rejected conventional religion and who claimed to have had numerous miraculous visions. The junior Smith was an apple who would not fall far from the tree.

Joseph Smith Sr. was convinced there was gold in them thar hills, and he was determined to be the one who found it. His treasure hunting (or "money digging" as he called it) included unorthodox methods such as the casting of spells, the reciting of incantations, and the use of paranormal instruments such as divining rods and "seer stones," which were rather like inelegant crystal balls in that they were ordinary rocks rather than crystals. Times were tough for the Smiths. Coming up with a pile of gold would have been the early nineteenth century equivalence of hitting the lottery, but like nearly all modern lottery players, Joe Sr. was never to strike it rich.

All this took place against the backdrop of an area of New York State that was so alive with revivalist, fire-and-brimstone preachers that it was referred to as the "burned-over" area. As such, Joseph Sr.'s rejection of prevailing religious beliefs, and his proclamation of his visions made him stand out. Even a neighbor who liked him was sure Smith engaged in witchcraft.

All of this seems to have made quite an impression on Joseph Smith Jr. who pretty much followed in his dad's footsteps, but with a lot more success. For Joe Jr. was destined to become the founder of the largest religion ever created in the United States.

When Joseph Jr. was fourteen-years old, he claimed God the Father and Jesus Christ visited him in the woods near Palmyra, New York. He said they told him none of the world's religions were true. A few years later he would say a gleaming white angel named Moroni appeared to him in his bedroom with further instructions from above. And what were Moroni's instructions to young Joseph? If you guessed "treasure hunt," you're a winner!

More specifically, Smith said the angel told him to search for golden plates containing the word of God and silver seer stones called Urim and Thummim that would allow Smith to translate the plates. After a time, Smith claimed to find the golden plates and the seer stones. The plates, which Smith claimed he could show to no one, were written in a language he said was called "Reformed Egyptian."

You would think that finding golden plates containing the heretofore-unknown word of God was pretty much the ultimate strike and would have sated Smith's hunger for further treasure hunts, but you would be wrong. Smith unsuccessfully continued the treasure hunting he had first engaged in as a child. He got people to bankroll a treasure hunt in which he used seer stones to try and find gold. He was slapped with criminal charges and called a con man for this stunt. His case went to trial, but the verdict is unknown.

During this time period, Smith won the affection of a young lady named Emma Hale, and the pair hoped to marry. You can imagine how she informed her father of her choice of lover. "Well daddy, he's a prophet of the Lord who rejects our religion, he found golden plates that no one can see, and don't pay any attention to that silly old trial." Or something like that. At any rate, Smith was obliged to meet Isaac Hale before he ran off with his daughter. Mr. Hale wanted to see the golden plates, but of course Smith told him he was forbidden to let him see them. Instead he brought his prospective father-in-law a box, which he said contained the plates, but he wouldn't let him look inside. Shockingly, Hale was unimpressed by this and by Smith in general. One wonders how his opinion would have changed had he gotten the chance to get a load of the whole polygamy thing Smith would unveil in the future. Emma married Smith despite her dad's disapproval.

Around this time Smith decided he'd better get going on translating the word of God that had been in his possession for quite some time by then. The translation process is a bit hard to explain. Smith supposedly had the golden plates out in front of him while he looked through the seer stones. Smith kept the stones in a hat that he held against his face so no light could get in. The text of the Book of Mormon magically appeared to him one character at a time, and as it did Smith recited the words—literally talking out of his hat—to his various assistants who wrote them down diligently. Smith made sure that none of his assistants, including his wife, ever laid eyes on the plates or the stones. When all was finished he returned the plates and stones to the angel Moroni, so if you were hoping to personally inspect the plates you can forget about it.

The resulting product was the Book of Mormon, which was first published in 1830. It was sort of an addendum to the Bible that described, amongst other things, the history of the Americas, and the organization of what would become the Church of Jesus Christ of Latter-day Saints (LDS) whose practitioners are commonly referred to as "Saints."

To those outside the faith, The Book of Mormon is a profoundly boring and repetitive document. The phrase "it came to pass" appears in the book more than two thousand times. Mark Twain was moved to call it "chloroform in print." Well, no one said the word of God had to be exciting. Furthermore, the book is written in language that includes lots of words such as "ye" and "thee" which were not in common use in nineteenth century America, but rather sound like the language of the King James Bible, with which Smith would have been well acquainted. One might conclude that he was trying to make the language in his book sound the same. Or if you choose to believe, it was written that way on the plates in Reformed Egyptian thousands of years earlier. Furthermore, to unbelievers, the Book of Mormon seems to be filled with anachronisms such as steel in the time of Abraham and animals such as oxen and cattle in pre-Columbian America. What's more, the history of the Americas Smith lays out in the Book of Mormon is at odds with everything that is understood of Native Americans by modern sociologists, archaeologists, linguists and geneticists.

In the Book of Mormon's version of events, Hebrew prophets traveled to the Americas around 600 B.C.E. and established two races, the Nephites and the Lamanites. The Nephites were a peace-loving people who walked with God and were "white, exceeding fair and delightful." The Lamanites on the other hand were made of less noble stuff. While once a white race, God made the Lamanites' skin darken as they grew less virtuous "that they might not be enticing to my people." The two groups had a big battle, in which the Lamanites wiped out the Nephites and became the Native-American race that was eventually encountered by Europeans.

This was not the only example of Smith's divinely inspired racial understanding. His later book *The Pearl of Great Price* claimed that blacks were descended from Cain as well as Noah's disrespectful son, Ham. Blacks were therefore claimed to bear the mark of Cain, and as a result, they were not permitted full admittance into the LDS Church. This policy was not dropped until 1978.

Smith was nonetheless able to accumulate an ever-growing number of followers. He accumulated trouble almost as fast, however. Smith was sued several times in the 1830s and was once charged with fraud. He also created a bank that failed spectacularly.

Smith established communities for his followers first in Ohio and then in Missouri. Both times the neighbors of the Mormons grew more intolerant of them as time went by. Smith was tarred and feathered in Ohio, and after a terrible spate of violence in Missouri, he took his band to Illinois where they founded the community of Nauvoo. So numerous were the Mormons by this time that Nauvoo may have been the second largest city in the state.

In Nauvoo, Smith organized an army for himself called the Nauvoo Legion. It was an outfit that the State of Illinois itself would have been hard pressed to match. Smith took the role of Lieutenant General over his unit and held showy parades featuring his soldiers in case anyone had failed to notice their existence. But trouble followed Smith to Illinois. He was arrested on charges of complicity in a murder in Missouri, and after he pulled a legal trick to get temporarily out of jail he went into hiding for three months. The charges were later dropped for lack of evidence. Smith was also charged with a series of other crimes including treason, but in every instance the cases
against him unraveled on technicalities, and he never faced trial for any of the alleged offenses.

In Illinois, the Mormons and their unfamiliar faith once again stirred up suspicions in the surrounding communities. The situation was exacerbated as bits and pieces of Smith's unorthodox theology reached the ears of unbelievers. The Mormons believe that God had once been mortal and that he is but one in a succession of Gods. Furthermore, they believe that men could rise to become Gods themselves. This was outlandish heresy to most Christians. Furthermore, they were suspicious of Smith and all the power he had accumulated. He was a prophet, general, and the Mayor of Nauvoo. What had become of the separation of church and state? To top it off, in 1844 Smith launched a quixotic campaign for President of the United States, which made him seem mad with a lust for power to those outside the community. If all that weren't enough, it was in Nauvoo that Smith was to drop his ultimate theology bomb, polygamy.

When Smith first became a polygamist is unknown. He may have had a second wife as early as 1831. He claimed, however, that the divine revelation that faithful men were to have what he called "plural wives" came to him in 1843. But Smith kept the revelation secret from his followers, well most of them anyway. The LDS big shots were let in on the divine command and started taking on multiple wives.

No one can be sure how many wives Smith himself had, but it was a bunch. High-end estimates put the number over eighty. We do know that several of his wives were already married to other men when he married them, and he took one wife who was only fourteen years old. Emma Smith seems to have been quite upset by the polygamy revelation, but she stood by her man nonetheless.

Polygamy was too big a secret to keep quiet for long, and after rumors of it inevitably started to leak out, it shook the LDS. A number of people who were unable to come to terms with it left the religion while others learned to accept it. The effect outside of the Mormon community was predictably sharp. To many of them, polygamy validated every suspicion that had ever been nurtured against the Mormons.

Mormons who were appalled by the new wrinkle in their faith founded a newspaper called *The Nauvoo Expositor*, which published its first—and last—edition on June 7, 1844. It was an expose on immoral behavior, especially polygamy, in the Mormon leadership. The paper was particularly tough on Smith who was labeled a "scoundrel" in its pages. Smith reacted by ordering the paper's printing press smashed to pieces. In so doing, he sowed the seeds of his own destruction. There was a huge outpouring of anger against Smith after this incident, but that just moved him to declare martial law in Nauvoo. Smith was charged with rioting for ordering the destruction of the press, and the charge was somehow inflated into another treason charge as well. Smith went into hiding once again while the specter of a miniature civil war loomed over Nauvoo.

Smith was accused of cowardice and desertion of his flock after running away. He realized he would lose everything he had built if he did not return. The Governor of Illinois arrived on the scene and gave Smith assurances of his safety, so he went back into the fray to face the music. Smith and three of his closest associates were put in jail in a neighboring town. Then the governor foolishly left, essentially leaving Smith at the mercy of the crowd gathered around the jailhouse. It took little time for the self-righteous mob to smash their way into the jail where they savagely gunned down Smith and his brother. No one was ever convicted of the murders.

Smith left no indication as to who should succeed him as leader of the LDS, so a power struggle ensued upon his demise. By the time Brigham Young emerged victorious, it was clear that the Mormon days in Nauvoo were over. He packed up the remaining Mormons and headed west for parts unknown. Along the way he felt the time was right to officially reveal the holy truth about God's love for polygamy, even though that cat had been out of the bag for a long time by then.

> In 1835 Smith purchased some Egyptian mummies and claimed to translate the hieroglyphics on the accompanying papyri even though they presumably were written in unreformed Egyptian. And guess what? The writing turned out to be about Abraham! *The Book of Abraham* emanated from this translation and became part of *The Pearl of Great Price*.
>
> At the time, the late Jean-François Champollion had only somewhat recently deciphered Egyptian hieroglyphics, and no one was on hand who could authoritatively challenge Smith's translation. The papyri were lost sometime after Smith's murder, but in 1966 fragments of the papyri were rediscovered. Modern translation of the text does not support Smith's translation.

What the Hell???

The Mountain Meadows Massacre

And it came to pass that after the killing of Joseph Smith, there was no one appointed to take his place as head of the LDS. Brigham Young won the ensuing power struggle, and he led the Mormons out of Illinois into the West where they would be far removed from those whose religious philosophies were incompatible with their own. When he reached the Great Salt Lake, Young declared that this would be the new Zion: a chosen land for the flock who had followed him west and for those who were to come later.

Young became the governor of the fledgling territory of Utah and pretty much ran the place as a zealous Mormon theocracy. His unorthodox leadership style drew much criticism from the rest of the country. President Buchanan decided he had better send some troops to Utah to see what was actually going on there. When Young got word that the army was on its way, he announced the news to the people of Utah in terms that left no doubt that an invasion force was approaching. He began to talk of secession from the country. Various Mormon leaders helped to dial up the urgency of the crisis by giving speeches calling for war with the United States.

Young knew he didn't have the forces to go toe-to-toe with the U.S. Army, so he looked to the Paiute Indians—who presumably hadn't read the stuff about Lamanites in the Book of Mormon—for help. He convened a meeting with ten Paiute chiefs in which he impressed upon them that their only hope of survival was to join the Mormons in their battle with the United States.

And it came to pass that many settlers were venturing to California from the East in those days, and it made sense to cut through Utah to get there. Little did these people know that they were heading into a powder keg that was on the brink of going off. The first band to take the southern path through Utah in 1857 was the Fancher party, a band of pioneers who were emigrating from Arkansas. Though the party was loaded with women and children, and was clearly not a military unit, they encountered hostility from the Mormons right from the start. Mormons were under orders to sell the travelers none of the provisions that they desperately needed no matter what the price. One Mormon who had traded cheese to the party in exchange for a quilt was cut off from the church. Another man who gave onions to a friend of his in the party was beaten with a pole. The Arkansans responded to this cold shoulder with predictable disdain for the Mormons that only increased the tension of the situation. Rumors soon spread that the travelers were the people who had chased the Mormons out of Missouri and Illinois, though they didn't come from either of those states. It was even said that the killers of Joseph Smith were in the band.

Brigham Young was aware that the settlers were heading through Utah. He sent a letter to Elder Isaac Haight saying that they were to be left alone, but he seemed to imply that Indian attacks against the emigrants would not be unexpected and should not be interfered with.

And it came to pass that a plan was drawn up to use the Paiutes, who the Mormons now called "the battle-axe of the Lord", to attack the settlers. As the Fancher party rested in a place called Mountain Meadows, the Paiutes, and possibly some Mormons dressed as Paiutes, attacked. The party was wary of the possibility of attack from the natives, so they were able to repulse the assault and draw their wagons into a defensive circle. A standoff ensued, but the party knew they couldn't hold out for long, so they sent three men on a desperate mission to break out of the encirclement and plead to the Mormons in nearby Cedar City for help. William Aiden, who was on good terms with the Mormons, led the mission, and it was hoped he could persuade them to overlook all the animosity that had developed between the groups. Little did any of them know, however, that the Mormons were really the ones behind the ambush.

And it came to pass that when the three men encountered Mormons they were fired upon and Aiden fell dead at the scene. The other two men were able to ride away intact, but the Mormons now had witnesses who knew it was white men who had shot Aiden, so a frantic effort was made to hunt down the other men before they could get back and warn the party of what they had seen. The Mormons succeeded in catching and killing the other men.

Back at Mountain Meadows, the Fancher party was growing desperate. When they saw a white man, John D. Lee, approaching their encirclement, they must have seen him as a godsend. He offered them a way out of their predicament. He would hold off the Paiutes, but the settlers would have to abandon their cattle and their weapons. Then the Mormons would segregate the men, women and children and lead them away from Mountain Meadows in separate groups. The settlers had wounded men who needed medical attention, and they were probably low on ammunition as well. So they had no choice but to accept the stark and strange terms Lee offered them.

And it came to pass that on September 11, 1857 wagons carried children, women, and the wounded away from the battlefield at Mountain Meadows while the men marched out single-file behind them, each with a Mormon escort at their side. As the party made its solemn procession an order was shouted out; "Halt! Do your duty!" at which point the Mormons turned to the unarmed men they were accompanying from the field and shot them at point-blank range. At this point, the Paiutes came out of hiding and rejoined the fray. Mormons and Paiutes slaughtered the surviving men as well as the women. The wounded were executed in the wagon where they lay. Before the attack, the Mormons had prayed for guidance regarding what to do with the children in the party. The divine answer they received was to kill all those who were old enough to talk. It didn't take long before everyone except the smallest children had been shot, stabbed or hacked to death. In all, about fifty Mormons and an unknown number of the "battle-axe of the Lord" had killed around 130 people at Mountain Meadows. About seventeen freshly minted orphans were left alive.

The corpses were robbed of any valuables they carried, and the wagons were looted as well. The booty was divided between the natives and the Saints as per previously agreed upon terms. The corpses of the dead were left at Mountain Meadows to rot. If they got any burial at all, it was insufficient. Witness passing through the area afterward reported seeing corpses strewn about the area being scavenged by wolves until they were stripped of all their flesh.

Almost as soon as the slaughter was over, the cover up began. Brigham Young was informed of the massacre and the fact that Mormons had been involved in it, but he signed a report in which all blame for the attack was placed on the Paiutes. This would be the Mormon story for years to come. But the scene of the crime was incompatible with the concept of an attack by Native Americans. Why would the settlers have abandoned most of their wagons and segregated themselves on a battlefield? Plus there had been too many people there for silence to be maintained and the settlers' possessions had been distributed amongst people in the Mormon community. It was a secret that wasn't going to be kept forever.

Meanwhile, the Army had reached an agreement with the Mormon leadership to enter Utah without any bloodshed. So the whole "invasion" which had precipitated the massacre turned out to be a much smaller matter than had been feared.

U.S. officials eventually took a look at the massacre, and they came to the conclusion that the Mormon version of events didn't wash. Orders were posted to arrest the Mormons who had taken part in the slaughter, but they had gone into hiding with extensive help from the Mormon community who still looked upon U.S. troops as the enemy. A $5,000 reward was posted for John Lee who called it, "A considerable reward for a man that is endeavoring to obey the gospel requirements." When the Civil War broke out it put a halt to any federal investigations into the massacre for years.

Brigham Young put the word out that the incident was not to be looked into too closely. "The more you stir a manure pile, the more it stinks," he said. In 1861 he visited the site of the massacre. There he saw a wooden cross that had been erected at the site with an inscription that read *Vengeance is mine and I will repay saith the Lord*. Young remarked that it should have said, "Vengeance is mine, and I have taken a little." On his journey back to northern Utah, Young feasted at a large party hosted by John Lee.

By 1870 there was growing disapproval of the massacre in the LDS church as the idea that it was an Indian affair had been pretty well disabused by that time. John Lee and Isaac Haight, the man who had ordered the massacre, were excommunicated.

Haight was reinstated four years later, however, as more and more, the blame for the entire affair came to rest on the shoulders of Lee.

Lee was a devout Mormon who had been adopted as a son of Brigham Young in a temple ceremony in his youth. Now, however, he was made to serve the Church by taking the blame for the massacre and thus deflecting the accusations that might implicate others. He was sent into exile in a remote area where he lived by himself for years, until his eventual arrest in 1874.

And it came to pass that Lee's resulting trial turned into a conspiracy of silence. No Mormon in good standing testified against him. Only Philip Klingensmith, a man who admitted to being at the massacre and who had since had a falling out with the LDS, was willing to come forward with the truth. He tearfully testified as to what had happened, but to no avail. The jury was deadlocked as all eight of its Mormon members voted for Lee's acquittal, and the four non-Mormons all voted for conviction.

Before Lee's second trial, a deal was struck between the Mormons and the government. The Mormons agreed that their members would testify, and an all-Mormon jury would convict Lee on the condition that no other Mormon leaders would be charged in the crime. The second trial was a carnival of perjury as witness after witness testified that they only saw Lee and Klingensmith at the scene. No one had any information about anyone else being involved in either the planning or the execution of the massacre. Lee was duly convicted and sentenced to death at the end of the trial. Lee was guilty, of course, but he was following orders, as were so many others who took part in the massacre. No one else was ever charged for the crime

And it came to pass that in 1877, twenty years after the massacre, Lee was taken to Mountain Meadows to be shot on the same killing field as his victims. In his final words Lee condemned Brigham Young who he said had sacrificed him with lies. Lee's extensive writings were taken into the possession of the LDS and kept from public view. Philip Klingensmith was murdered in Nevada, probably in retaliation for testifying against other Mormons at Lee's first trial.

The role Brigham Young played in the crime has been a subject of debate ever since. While Young probably did not directly order the massacre, he certainly helped to create the conditions that made it possible. He was also complicit in the conspiracy to cover up the Mormon involvement in it after he knew the truth.

> In 1887 Sir Arthur Conan Doyle penned the novel *A Study In Scarlet*. In it, he introduced a new character named Sherlock Holmes. What might surprise a lot of readers is that about half of the book consists of a section called *The Country of the Saints* and takes place in Utah. Doyle was apparently heavily influenced by the Mountain Meadows massacre. He used the novel to vilify the LDS and Brigham Young.

Pope Pius IX

Pope Pius IX's election in 1846 was cause for celebration in the Catholic world. The hated Pope Gregory XVI was gone, and there were high hopes for a new age in the Church. Gregory had been such a reactionary opponent of modernity that he might as well have been Amish. He hated technology so much that he forbade trains from entering the Papal States, and he banned gas streetlights as well. There was no way the new pope could fail to be an improvement over that, right?

At first Pius delivered the desired goods. He imposed liberal measures that were long overdue. Amongst his reforms, he abolished the Papal States' ghettos in which Jews were forced to live, and he stopped the practice of forcing them to spend their Sabbath days listening to stern lectures about how they must convert to Catholicism. But only twelve days after the ghetto walls came down in Rome, Pius showed his conservative side when he condemned the growing popular movement clamoring for the unification of Italy. What's more, he supported Austria's move to send troops to occupy part of the Papal States to ensure that his theocratic kingdom would never join in any secular Italian state.

This move immediately cost Pius his popular support. In 1848 a great uprising in Rome demanding an Italian state and an end to papal rule erupted. Pius was forced to don a disguise and sneak away to a fortress to preserve his safety. For a while it looked like the end had come for the Papal States, but Pius succeeded in getting France and Austria to come to his aid, put down the nationalists, and restore his temporal kingdom.

After this, there would be no more Mr. nice guy from Pius. The liberal reforms he had enacted were revoked, and the ghetto was the mandatory home for Jews once more. Pius would be a rock-ribbed conservative for the rest of his life, and for those who lived in the Papal States there would be a high price to pay for this.

On the evening of June 23, 1858, a knock came on the door of the Mortaras—a Jewish family living in the city of Bologna. It was the police, and they were looking for the family's six-year-old boy, Edgardo. For the Mortaras this was a nightmare come true. In the Papal States the law stated that no Christian child could live in a Jewish household. If a child were to be baptized then he was considered a Christian, and he must be removed from his family. This was true even if the baptism took place without the consent or knowledge of the parents. Other Jewish children in he Papal States had been taken from their homes, so the Mortaras knew immediately what the police entering their home would mean. Edgardo's mother threw herself over her sleeping son and wailed that the police would have to kill her before she would give him up. An ugly scene was quickly developing until the Inquisitor in Bologna (yes, inquisitions were still going on in the later part of the nineteenth century) agreed that the police would wait one day before taking Edgardo, but he would be kept under guard the whole time to prevent any escape attempt. Momolo, the boy's father, was convinced this would give him enough time to show that a mistake had been made, and that would allow him to keep his boy. He was wrong. The next day Edgardo was taken from his father's arms in an act of injustice so transparent that the police who took him were in tears as they carried out their orders. Edgardo was whisked from Bologna to Rome where he was immediately taken to the House of Catechumens, a building paid for with special taxes levied against Jews and designated for the purpose of converting them to Catholicism. It was here that Edgardo began his indoctrination into Catholic theology.

Edgardo's parents desperately pled with the Church for the return of their son, but their cries fell on deaf ears. The boy was Catholic now in the eyes of the Church. In those days, Jews were considered Christ killers and they were routinely accused of killing Christian children so they could use their blood to make their matzah. As such, the Church would have considered it to be an act of great cruelty to return the boy to a Jewish home. It was enough that the Church tolerated the presence of the Jews in the Papal States in the first place. In fact, Jews had been completely forbidden from living in Bologna not long before Edgardo was seized. What's more, it was the Mortaras who were deemed to have brought this whole incident upon themselves by hiring a Christian worker in the first place. This was in clear violation of the laws of the Papal States that forbade Jews from employing Christians. It was this servant girl who claimed to have baptized Edgardo on a night when he had fallen ill.

The Church held all the cards, but this case would not be like the cases of other Jewish children who had been taken before. The age of enlightenment had been around long enough by this time to change society. In the United States the separation of church and state had taken hold, and the French ideals of liberty, equality, and fraternity had been carried into Italy from France. A free press was blossoming, and it was unafraid to tell the story of Edgardo. The Church was condemned for the kidnapping in France and England, and protests over the case were held across the U.S.A. The French government appealed to the pope concerning the boy, but the appeals were first ignored and then rudely rejected. Pius was not about to let some secular state tell him how to run his Church; as he himself put it, "I couldn't care less what the world thinks." What Pius seemed to forget, however, was that he was entirely reliant upon France to protect Rome from the Italian people. It is no coincidence that it was at this time the French Emperor Napoleon III decided to start maneuvering to push the Austrians out of the Papal States and to turn the land over to Sardinia. This move would end up costing the Pope two thirds of his territory.

But the Church would not take all the uproar over Edgardo lying down. There were a number of Catholic newspapers in Europe, which got out the Church's side of the story. They told the miraculous and heartwarming story of how Edgardo was overcome with joy upon his first vision of the Virgin Mary. They claimed that this occurred almost immediately after his being taken from his family. It was said that his parents meant little to him now as they lived outside of the salvation of Christ. He considered Pope Pius to be his father and the Virgin Mary his mother, and he yearned to become a missionary. Remember these words allegedly came from a boy who was all of six years old. The Catholic press also had a lot to say about the Mortaras; claiming they were cruel, Christian-haters who would rather see Edgardo killed than to see him worshiping Jesus.

On June 12, 1859, the Austrians abandoned Bologna in the wee hours of the morning. In almost no time anti-Church crowds waving the red, white, and green tri-color flag of Italy overtook the city. Bologna and a good chunk of the Papal States were annexed to Sardinia with widespread popular consent. New rights such as the freedom of religion and the equality of all citizens were put into place. Fr. Pier Gaetano Feletti, the Inquisitor of Bologna, was arrested on charges stemming from the Mortara affair. He defended himself by saying he was only acting under orders from Rome. All this came about a mere seventeen months after the kidnapping of Edgardo.

Pius was infuriated by these developments. He saw the secular world as a horror show that was offensive to God. To him it was as if people had lost all their senses. It was bad enough when atrocities occurred outside of his domain. For instance, he had been appalled when the city of Turin allowed Jews to attend universities, but now these debacles were occurring in what he still considered to be his own territory. He forbade priests from cooperating in any way with the new government in Bologna, and he ordered that communion be withheld from any secular leaders. In 1861 the first Italian parliament was elected, but the Church demanded that all Catholics boycott the vote. Pius' fury with the new order culminated in the publication of the *Syllabus of Errors* in 1864. This document, which was distributed to parishes worldwide, summed up everything Pius felt was wrong with the world. In it, he condemned modernity, liberalism, and progress. He vilified the freedom of religion and the separation of church and state. He also lashed out against Catholics who felt that the Church should not hold temporal power.

That same year, almost as if to prove to the world that the Church would do as it pleased, the Church abducted *another* Jewish boy. This time the victim was Giuseppe Coen, a nine-year-old from Rome. For France, this move was the straw that broke the camel's back. The French began a phased pullout from the territories surrounding Rome leaving Pius to hold off the Italian nationalists on his own. When France was defeated in the Franco-Prussian war the pullout was expedited, and Rome was left with only the Church forces for its defense. The Italian King Victor Emmanuel wrote to Pius asking for a surrender of the city to avoid a bloody fight, but Pius angrily rejected the offer and excommunicated Victor Emmanuel for good measure. Italian forces then overran the Pope's puny army and captured the city. Eventually the Pope was allowed to retain control over the Vatican itself, an area of only 44 hectares in size. In a way, it was now the pope who lived in a ghetto.

In 1870 Pius convened the First Vatican Council and it gave the world the dogma of Papal Infallibility. This doctrine does not say the pope is perfect, but rather it lays out a number of conditions for when the pope is speaking in an infallible fashion. Even so, with a pope in office who appeared to be nothing *but* fallible the Church could hardly have picked a worse time to unveil the concept, and predictably, many people greeted it with ridicule.

Pius was the longest serving pope in the history of the Catholic Church. By the time he finally died in 1878, he was so wildly unpopular that his funeral procession was attacked by a mob of Italian nationalists intent upon seizing his corpse and throwing it into—you know this is coming—the Tiber River. The valiant efforts of the police were just barely enough to prevent this final insult to the pope whose cruelty and stubbornness had caused him to loose everything he had fought so hard to preserve.

So whatever happened to Edgardo Mortara?

By the time the Italian forces crushed the feeble papal army, Edgardo was nineteen years old and was too old to figure into custody battles any longer. Nevertheless, the Church feared what would happen if he fell into the hands of the nationalists, so Edgardo was spirited out of Rome and sent to a monastery in Austria. By this time, he was well on his way to becoming a priest. Having been raised by the Church it was really the only life he knew and the only thing he aspired to. He did become a priest and specialized in trying to convert Jews to Catholicism. He was reunited with his mother (his father died without having seen his son since 1858) and was able to form a bit of a relationship with her, but his efforts to convert her fell flat. Edgardo lived a long life. He died in Belgium in 1940, only one month before the Nazis invaded the country and eventually rounded up and killed everyone of Jewish descent that they could find, including those who were members of the Catholic clergy.

What the Hell???

The Protocols of the Elders of Zion

The document was never meant to fall into the hands of the gentiles. It was a top-secret record of the sinister goings on during twenty-four meetings held at the First Zionist Congress held in Basel, Switzerland in 1897. Yet *The Protocols of the Elders of Zion* did somehow end up in the possession of the very people who were absolutely never meant to see it, and they published what they had found for the entire world to see.

The Protocols detailed a massive Jewish conspiracy to destroy all the world's monarchies and nations. The Jews would promote a liberal agenda including the freedom of religion and the press, compulsory education, universal suffrage, and constitutional governments with separation of powers. Such ideas would inevitably lead to socialism, then to communism, and finally the destruction of the states themselves, leaving them unable to defend themselves from Jewish conquest.

The French Revolution had been the work of this Jewish conspiracy. Its promise of liberty, equality, and fraternity was a textbook Jewish ploy. In the wake of the revolution, Church lands were confiscated, and much of the French nobility were ousted from their positions. Sure, it didn't appear that Jews were behind any of this nor did they seem to be profiting from it, but that's the sly way the Jews operate. They stay out of sight and use puppets, especially Freemasons, to do their dirty work for them.

World War I was brought about by the Jews, as are all wars. The war weakened all of the participants and allowed Bolshevism to break out in Russia. Jews also spread disease, famine, and economic turmoil to further wreak the civilizations they so despised.

Furthermore, the Jews plan to launch a reign of terror in which world leaders will be assassinated in droves so they can be replaced with those submissive to Jews. Other leaders will be so intimidated by these killings that they will acquiesce to the Jews as well. Once the Jews have subjugated the entire world, they will create a Jewish world empire led by an absolute dictator who will rule the planet ruthlessly. All the liberal reforms the Jews had promoted previously will be revoked because the Jews know better than to allow such nonsensical liberties to weaken their own empire. Non-Jews, including the fools who carried out their plots on their behalf, will be reduced to the level of slaves who dare not defy their Jewish masters. The Jews also crafted a plan to fill the subway tunnels under Europe's major cities with explosives to destroy them in case their plots fell apart. There is no explanation of how the Jews themselves, with an overwhelmingly urban population, would evade these explosions, but come on, those people are sneaky; they'll find a way to survive.

So where did his relentlessly grim—and utterly ridiculous—scenario come from?

The *Protocols* were most likely written in France at the end of the nineteenth century under the supervision of Pyotr Ivanovich Rachkovsky, who was the commander of a Russian secret police force operating outside of the motherland. No one knows who wrote the document, and no original draft of it exists. The first publication of the *Protocols* appeared in Russia in 1903, but this was an abbreviated version. The first long version of the document came out two years later, also in Russia. In 1920 the first non-Russian edition came out in Germany.

In 1921 the *Times* of London published a devastating three-part investigative piece entitled "The End of the Protocols" which exposed the document as a forgery. Not only was the work fraudulent, but it was plagiarized to boot. Most of the *Protocols* was ripped off from two sources. The first of these was *Dialogue Between Machiavelli and Monesquieu in Hell* by Maurice Joly. This work was a French satire that ridiculed the rule of the Emperor Napoleon III. It was tweaked by the forger of the *Protocols* to turn its venom from away from Napoleon III and toward the Jews. The other major source for the *Protocols* was an 1868 novel called *Biarritz* by Hermann Goedsche, which featured a spooky scene in which Jewish leaders from across Europe gather in a dark cemetery to discuss their plans for world domination. The *Protocols* was not merely inspired by these books, but it stole from them so flagrantly that many passages are nearly word-for-word identical to the source material.

The *Protocols* had been exposed as a fraud, but it scarcely mattered. To the people who were dumb enough to believe in such an outlandish conspiracy in the first place, evidence of a hoax would make no impact. Indeed, the life of the lie was just getting started.

In Detroit, the automobile magnate Henry Ford took a shine to the *Protocols* and spent a staggering $5 million to publish them in a volume called *The International Jew*. This was reprinted in Germany where Adolf Hitler so admired Ford that he kept a photograph of him. In 1927 Ford apologized for *The International Jew*, but only when he was faced with a libel lawsuit over it.

And speaking of Germany, it should come as no surprise that this is where the *Protocols* made its biggest splash. By 1933, 100,000 copies of the document were in print there. Hitler said he was instantly convinced of its truth when he read it. He used the *Protocols* to explain Germany's hyperinflation crisis and to blame the Jews for the humiliating Treaty of Versailles that Germany had been forced to sign at the end of World War I. After 1933 the Nazis ramped up the printing of the *Protocols* so even more people could enjoy them. They became required reading for boys in the Hitler Youth. It is impossible to say how much of an impact the *Protocols* had on paving the way for the Holocaust, but this could only have helped to create a German public that—at best—was indifferent to the plight of their Jewish neighbors.

After the Holocaust left most of Europe's Jews dead, the *Protocols* still wouldn't die. You would think that such a wholesale slaughter of Jews would serve as ample proof that it was not Jews who were orchestrating all the events in the world, but no (and I guess all those subway bombs turned out to be duds). The establishment of the state of Israel created a new audience willing to believe anything about Jews, and there were nations willing to take advantage of this gullibility to draw attention away from their own failings. In Egypt, President Nasser disseminated copies of it to foreign journalists. A Jordanian minister used it to explain Israel's victory in the Six Day War. Libyan dictator Muammar Gaddafi promoted the *Protocols* and called them "important and enlightening." Saudi Arabia reportedly paid for 300,000 copies to be printed. These are just a few examples of the new life the *Protocols* have taken on in the Middle East. No Arab-language refutation of the *Protocols* has ever been published.

And it's not just the Muslim world where the *Protocols* live on. They have been published in every part of the world, even in places like Japan where there are no Jews to speak of. In the United States, right-wing groups such as the John Birch Society and the Christian Defense League have republished the *Protocols*, and some Black Nationalist groups have used them to buttress anti-Jewish claims such as the notion that Jews created the AIDS virus.

The lie of the *Protocols* is now more than one hundred years old and it shows no sign of fading away.

Reading this book, one could get the impression that Christians are bad while Jews are good. While the history of anti-Semitism is staggering (and this book is far from a comprehensive study on the subject,) I think it's better to look at the persecutions of the Jews as examples of the strong dominating the weak than it is to look at Christians as born villains and Jews as their inevitable victims. After all, it's not like no Jewish leaders have ever been deplorable people. For an example one need look no further than the Israeli Rabbi Dov Lior.

Lior is the Chairman of the Yesha Rabbinical Council and Chief Rabbi of Kiryat Arba. He has used his positions to make some pretty damned hateful comments. Take for instance his stance on Jews hiring Arabs; "since this is a matter of endangering souls, it is clear that it is completely forbidden to employ them and rent houses to them in Israel. Their employment is forbidden not only at yeshivas, but at factories, hotels, and everywhere." But Lior didn't stop with that. In 1994 a Jewish settler named Baruch Goldstein went on an unprovoked rampage in which he killed twenty-nine Palestinians and wounded another 125 before he was beaten to death. Rather than recoiling at this senseless slaughter, Lior praised Goldstien and his actions saying, "a thousand non-Jewish lives are not worth a Jew's fingernail." Lior also urged Jewish women not to use sperm donors to get pregnant because "negative genetic traits that characterize non-Jews" could contaminate the Jewish gene pool. Not that everyone who isn't Jewish is bad in his mind, however, "there are some honorable people among the goyim. A few, but they exist. I think that even in Hebron there are a few who are human beings—which doesn't mean I'm saying they shouldn't all be sent to Saudi Arabia. They should all be sent to Saudi Arabia!"

It goes without saying that Lior's views are on the right-wing fringe in Israel, yet he was once elected to Supreme Rabbinical Council. Israel's Attorney General, however, barred Lior from taking the post because he had once recommended that medical experiments be conducted on captured Arab terrorists.

Fr. Charles Coughlin

In September of 1926 WJR radio in Detroit was approached by a Catholic priest about the possibility of doing Sunday broadcasts on the station with the intention of raising money for his tiny church, The Shrine of the Little Flower. No one at the time could have imagined that such an unassuming event would be the first step on an inglorious path that would shake the nation in ways that still reverberate today.

The priest was Fr. Charles Coughlin, a Canadian firebrand who had a gift for the dramatic, a massive ego, and a limitless interest in listening to himself talk. WJR agreed to put Fr. Coughlin on the air and in October he made his first broadcast. In it he proclaimed, "We avoid prejudicial subjects, all controversies and especially all bigotry." As it would turn out, nothing could have been further from the truth.

Fr. Coughlin's broadcasts were successful both in raising money for his parish and in inflating his ego. By 1930 he had settled in behind the microphone quite comfortably, and his show was picked up by the CBS radio network. He started using the show as a platform to lambaste socialism, which he felt stemmed from an international conspiracy. His audience had grown to the point where that same year he was invited to testify before congress as an expert on communism, though in truth he knew very little about it. In his testimony he predicted there would be a revolution in the United States by 1933.

The next year Coughlin planned on doing a show about what he felt was an international conspiracy of bankers, a profession he detested. CBS got wind of his plans, and wishing to avoid offending any of their potential sponsors, made him promise not to go through with the show on that subject. Coughlin honored his promise and didn't harangue bankers on that day. Instead he spent the entire show trashing CBS. The next week he did his banking conspiracy show. CBS dropped Fr. Coughlin from their network soon afterward.

But Coughlin was a hit. His attacks on bankers and the like struck a resonant chord with a listening public that was in the grasp of the Great Depression. After CBS abandoned him he quickly assembled his own informal network of radio stations to carry his broadcasts across the nation.

He used the airwaves to attack President Hoover for doing nothing about the depression. When Hoover belatedly did take action, Coughlin called him a socialist. Coughlin preached that the cure for the depression was simply to print more money. He supported Franklin Roosevelt's presidential campaign, and Roosevelt was willing to put up with the wacky priest because of the huge radio audience (maybe thirty million listeners at its peak) he could draw.

Coughlin renewed his attacks on bankers, which were so savage that he drew fire from within the Church. The *Detroit Free Press* attacked him as well. He also incurred the lasting, but still unspoken, hatred of President Roosevelt. Coughlin was able to parry all of the attacks though. He found a defender in Bishop Michael Gallagher of Detroit who shielded Coughlin from any censure from the Church. He attacked the *Free Press* as vigorously as they attacked him, and he felt that Roosevelt owed his landslide victory in 1932 to him. It still hadn't registered with him that the president had no use for him.

He demanded the U.S. switch from the gold standard to silver and fully expected Roosevelt to back him on the matter. When Roosevelt showed that he had no intention of listening to Coughlin's economic advice the priest turned on him in a way that would eventually become open warfare on the president.

Sick of Coughlin's nagging on the subject, the Roosevelt administration released the names of America's major silver holders to the public. It turned out that Coughlin's personal secretary owned two and a half million ounces of the metal. Everyone knew who the silver really belonged to, and the fallout was the first dent in Coughlin's public image. It was now obvious he had been engaging in the same kind of financial speculation that he had been railing against on his radio show.

Soon afterward, Coughlin began a tour of speaking engagements at sports stadiums in which he theatrically and vehemently denounced Roosevelt in front of tens of thousands of people at every stop. He was determined to make Roosevelt pay for turning his back on him. He lobbied against Roosevelt's programs in congress and assailed his congressional allies, including Representative John O'Connor of New York. O'Connor, however, was not intimidated by the priest as is evidenced by a telegram he sent to Coughlin after he had been berated by him on the air.

Just read your libelous radio ramblings. The truth is not in you. You are a disgrace to my church... If you will please come to Washington I shall guarantee to kick you all the way from the Capital to the White House with clerical garb and all the silver in your pockets which you got from speculating on Wall Street... Come On!

When Coughlin got the telegram he went ballistic. He went into training in preparation to fight the congressman. It was only at his bishop's firm insistence that he gave up the thought of a rumble on the Potomac.

Coughlin's hatred for Roosevelt had by now grown to the point where he had convinced himself that if Roosevelt were reelected in 1936 he would become a communist dictator of the United States. Coughlin, overflowing with confidence in his own power to shape public policy, formed The Union Party in an attempt to bring down Roosevelt. The party was nothing more than a front for Coughlin's own ambitions. He recruited North Dakota congressman William Lemke to serve as the presidential nominee for the Party. Lemke's main qualification for the presidency was that he was a milquetoast who would be perfectly pliable to the will of Fr. Coughlin who, as a priest from Canada, could not possibly make a presidential run himself. Coughlin brought in Newton Jenkins, a known Nazi sympathizer, to help run the party.

Coughlin overshadowed Lemke at every campaign stop. He promised that if Lemke got less than nine million votes he would leave the airwaves. At one campaign stop the hot-tempered Coughlin attacked a reporter from the Boston Globe named John Barry by ripping his glasses off and punching him in the face. On election night Coughlin found out just how much power he really had. Roosevelt won every state in the union except two, despite Coughlin's fiery denunciations of him. No solely Union Party congressional candidate won anywhere in the country. Lemke didn't come close to winning a single state nor did he come close to getting one million votes let alone the nine million Coughlin had guaranteed. In the South, where Catholics were scarce, Lemke got well under five *thousand* votes. Coughlin made good on his promise and left radio in the wake of Lemke's defeat—for two months.

Sadly, this would not be the low point of Coughlin's career.

In 1936 he started publication of his own newspaper, which he called *Social Justice*. The paper was, naturally, nothing more than a vehicle for Coughlin's opinions about communists, Roosevelt, bankers, and increasingly, Jews. In Coughlin's mind all these entities merged together to create one great evil. For instance, he saw bankers as Jews who funded the Soviet revolution, and he referred to Roosevelt as "Rosenfeld." In 1938 *Social Justice* printed the *Protocols of the Elders of Zion* in serialized form and argued for the validity of the document. That same year, when he was unable to find a radio station in New York City that was willing to carry his show he became convinced that Jews had conspired to keep him off the air.

Things only got worse after that. Fr. Coughlin organized an anti-communist group called the Christian Front, which organized "buy Christian only" campaigns and prohibited Jewish membership. Jews were beaten in New York City by thugs calling themselves "Fr. Coughlin's Brownshirts." The outrageous behavior of the Christian Front inspired a group of prominent American Catholics including former presidential candidate Al Smith, Bing Crosby, and movie director John Ford to form the Committee of Catholics for Human Rights in an effort to create an alternative to it. When seventeen members of the Christian Front were arrested for planning to overthrow the U.S. government, Fr. Coughlin started to distance himself from the group a bit, but he still referred to them as fine Christians.

By now the wheels had come off of whatever reason Coughlin had once had. He defended Hitler's treatment of the Jews as necessary in the fight against communism. The *Free Press* called Coughlin's show "his weekly attack on the Jews" while papers in Nazi Germany praised him. A December 1938 article in the *New York Post* demonstrated that a speech Fr. Coughlin had made was almost word-for-word the same as a speech made by Nazi propaganda minister Josef Goebbels.

Coughlin approved of Germany's annexation of Sudetenland in Czechoslovakia, and when Germany invaded Poland in 1939 Coughlin blamed the British and the Jews for the war. He campaigned against aiding Britain in the war. He singled out Jewish congressmen as the focal point of this crusade. He defended Germany's bombing of Britain, and he said the U.S. should be remodeled in the mold of Mussolini's fascist Italy.

In 1940 a new government code on broadcasting aimed largely at Fr. Coughlin pushed the priest off the air, but it did not apply to his newspaper. And what a newspaper it was. *Social Justice* cheered Nazi conquests in Europe and characterized the Nazi invasion of the Soviet Union as a Russian offensive against Germany. When Japan attacked the United States, Fr. Coughlin—uncharacteristically—had no comment, but soon afterward *Social Justice* accused Roosevelt of having conspired to bring the U.S. into the war.

As the U.S. went to war, the pages of *Social Justice* were filled with defeatist articles ridiculing the American war effort. Tokyo Rose and Axis Sally themselves could not have done much better. Theodor Seuss Geisel, who later became known as Dr. Seuss, penned a cartoon published in a competing newspaper showing Adolf Hitler reading *Social Justice* with the caption "Not bad Coughlin...but when are you going to start printing it in German?"

1942 would prove to be Fr. Coughlin's Waterloo as that year the Postmaster General asked *Social Justice* to demonstrate why its second-class mailing privileges should not be revoked. No one showed up to defend the paper at the hearing. Additionally, the Catholic Church finally decided it had had enough of the priest and ordered him to cease all publishing and broadcasting or be defrocked. As if all that were not enough, a grand jury was convened to investigate Fr. Coughlin and his associates on charges of sedition. Evidence was presented at those proceedings that connected Fr. Coughlin to axis propaganda, but this was not made public until after the war. Since Coughlin was no longer in the media, and since the government had no desire to drag a man of the cloth through a sensational trial, the whole matter was quietly dropped.

In 1966 Fr. Coughlin celebrated the fiftieth anniversary of his ordination to the priesthood. At the gathering, Cardinal Richard Cushing praised him as "a man ahead of his time." Looking out over the wasteland of demagoguery that exists on the AM radio dial and elsewhere today one can't help but think he was right.

> One tactic used to sell *Social Justice* was to have children hawking the rag on the streets start crying when people passed by. When asked what was the matter they responded, "A big Jew hit me."

Bob Jones

In the spring of 2000, the South Carolina Republican presidential primary loomed with George W. Bush and John McCain locked in a tight campaign for the nomination. Bush opted to make a campaign speech at Bob Jones University, a school most Americans had probably never heard of at the time. When the spotlight was turned on the institution, its discriminatory racial and religious policies were laid bare for the whole nation to see, and controversy exploded.

But who was Bob Jones, and where did this school come from?

Bob Jones Sr. was born in Alabama in 1883. As a child, he became adept at public speaking and took a shine to fundamentalist Christianity. He dropped out of college in 1904 to pursue a career as a traveling evangelist. He preached in an unrestrained fire-and-brimstone fashion. During one of his sermons, he pounded on an alter so hard that he broke it. Such theatrics worked for Jones, and he became a big hit on the preaching circuit.

On his travels Jones met and befriended former secretary of state and three-time failed Democratic presidential candidate, William Jennings Bryan. The two men shared a deep hatred of the theory of evolution that was becoming more and more firmly supported by scientists since Charles Darwin had first proposed it in 1859 in his book *On the Origin of Species*. For Bryan, his hatred of evolution would take him to Tennessee where he argued for the prosecution in the now infamous "Scopes Monkey Trial" in which a schoolteacher named John Scopes was put on trial for teaching evolution, which was against the law in Tennessee at the time. Bryan won the case, but it was a hollow victory on several levels. National media coverage of the trial made the creationist side into laughingstocks, and the financial judgment against Scopes was later thrown out. What's more, Bryan died five days after the trial concluded. Bryan's death robbed the creationist side of its most prominent voice.

Jones had a plan though. If the liberals and their universities were going to spread what he considered to be the lie of evolution then he would create his own school where the "truth" could be told. Thus was the impetus for the creation of Bob Jones College, which opened its doors in Florida in 1927. It was here that Jones could mold students to have, as the school's mission statement puts it, a "Christlike" character and to be "others-serving, God-loving, Christ-proclaiming and focused above."

Just as the school was getting going, Jones inserted himself into politics. He was offended that Al Smith, a Catholic, had won the Democratic nomination for the presidency in 1928, so Jones threw his support behind Herbert Hoover. It was unusual for a Southerner to support a Republican in those days, but the prospect of having a Catholic in the White House caused Jones to take this drastic action. Jones also supported a number of members of the Ku Klux Klan for public office. He befriended and received support himself from several other members of that prestigious organization.

His school struggled though. In 1933 he made the decision to relocate the college from Florida to Tennessee. Things went better there, and eventually he moved to a larger location in Greenville, South Carolina where he changed Bob Jones College into Bob Jones University. The school today often refers to itself as BJU, apparently unaware of the giggle-inducing qualities that those initials might possess.

As the civil rights movement got going in the South, Jones kept BJU off-limits to blacks. He railed against civil rights saying that segregation was the will of God, and anyone who opposed it also opposed God. When President Lyndon Johnson signed the Civil Rights act into law in 1964, BJU was able to maintain its no-blacks policy because it was a private institution.

Jones also had an ax to grind with Billy Graham. Graham was the hot new evangelist on the scene and was capturing the attention of the nation's Christians. But he was doing so with a message of inclusion and ecumenicalism that offended Jones. In 1966 Graham focused most of his preaching on the area near BJU in a direct affront to his outspoken critic. Jones in return decreed that any student who attended Graham's meetings would be expelled from school. Also in 1966 BJU conferred an honorary degree on the Reverend Ian Paisley, a vehemently anti-Catholic Northern Irish politician.

Jones died in 1968, but the Jones legacy at BJU was just getting started. The school's presidency has been much like a monarchy as the title has always been passed down from father to son. When Bob Jones Sr. died, it was Bob Jones Jr. who took control of BJU. Bob Jones III succeeded him, and his son, Stephen Jones, is now running the place.

Bob Jones Jr. was a chip off the old bloc in many respects. Take, for example his attitude toward the Catholic Church. He said of it, "it is a satanic counterfeit, an ecclesiastic tyranny over the souls of men." He went on to say, "It is the harlot of the Book of Revelation." He also said that all popes were demonically possessed.

But he also did what his dad would never have done. In 1971 he allowed blacks into BJU. Now this offer was extended only to blacks that were already married so there would be no horrors such as interracial couples at BJU, but progress was on the march. Four years later school policy changed again to allow unmarried blacks to attend, but a strict rule banning interracial dating helped to keep the gene pool pure at BJU. This policy became the grounds for a lawsuit against BJU. Though a private university, BJU was still receiving local taxpayer funding. The school's segregationist policies were incompatible with federal law, and the resulting suit went all the way to the Supreme Court of the United States. In 1983 the court ruled that BJU's refusal to allow interracial dating made it ineligible for tax-exempt status. Not only was the government teat pulled from BJU, but they also had to refund money they had already collected from taxpayers.

In 1998 BJU sent a letter to an alumnus of the school after they had been tipped off that he was gay. The letter informed him that he was banned from campus, and he would be arrested if he were to try entering school grounds. The "no gays on campus rule" still applies today.

So this was the backdrop against which George W. Bush appeared when he chose BJU for a campaign stop. Bush, it should be noted, was not the first politician to use BJU as a stump spot. Ronald Reagan, Dan Quayle, Bob Dole, and other conservative icons had all given speeches at the school previously and had never been taken to task for it, but with Bush things were different. News stories erupted across the nation about the school's racist dating policy and to a lesser extent about its staunch anti-Catholic philosophy. Bush claimed that he knew nothing of the school's racial policies or its anti-Catholic rhetoric. Bush's opponent, John McCain, tried to take advantage of the situation especially by appealing to Catholic voters, but the fact is that few Catholics or blacks vote in South Carolina's Republican primaries. What's more, a BJU faculty member started a rumor that McCain had fathered an illegitimate child. The truth is that McCain had adopted a Bangladeshi child, but he had not fathered the kid, either in or out of wedlock. But the rumor was pushed along by the Bush campaign (with the added bonus that the child was of "mixed race,") and McCain was sunk. He lost the South Carolina primary, and his campaign never recovered from the blow.

Bob Jones University was in the public eye like never before, however, and they felt obligated to explain their policies to America. The school issued statement claiming they were not racist saying, "For there to be discrimination one race would have to treated differently than the other." They went on to use the biblical story of the Tower of Babel as evidence of God's desire for segregation. "God wanted a divided world," they said. They didn't budge on the subject of Catholicism either. The school urged the Catholic to "leave the false system that has enslaved his soul."

But the school didn't stick to its guns for long. A few months after the Bush visit, BJU opted to drop its interracial dating policy. In 2008 BJU apologized for its racial policies of the past, but blamed them on the influence of the surrounding culture. Perhaps no one at BJU noticed that the surrounding culture gave up segregation first, and BJU was the racist hold out. Nor did BJU's apology concede that their Biblical interpretations supporting segregation might have been imperfect.

Today, life goes on at BJU. The school still maintains a set of rules so strict they make Brigham Young University look like the Burning Man festival. Students must dress very conservatively. For example, men cannot wear T-shirts or jeans to class. Suits and ties are required attire on Sundays. Men are prohibited from wearing jewelry, and no facial hair is allowed. For the ladies skirts or dresses must be worn in class, visible panty lines are forbidden, sleeveless garments are out, and necklines are to be "no more than four fingers below the collarbone." The dress code does not say whose fingers are to be used in this measurement. Oh, and don't even think about buying your BJU school duds at Abercrombie & Fitch. As the dress code puts it "Abercrombie & Fitch and its subsidiary Hollister have shown an unusual degree of antagonism to biblical morality. Therefore, BJU asks its students not to patronize these stores, wear their clothing or display articles containing their names or logos."

But of course, there's more to college life than dress codes. The BJU website offers a few hints at what your college experience will be like on the BJU campus. First off, there's no TV allowed on campus. While off campus, students are not permitted to visit movie theaters nor can they watch any video that has a rating harder than "G." (Tip for BJU students: porn movies are not rated by the Motion Picture Association of America, so technically you're not breaking the rules if you watch *Weapons of Ass Destruction* while off campus). Also, don't expect to get your groove on in the dorms as all rock, country, jazz, and rap music is banned. This includes contemporary Christian music. You have to go to prayer meetings every night and then it's curfew at 11:00. Keep your room clean, as it will be inspected—*Daily!* Posters of movie or music stars and fashion models are prohibited. Personal photographs displaying "immodest" contact are also out. You can't play any video games rated above "E10" on the TV you don't have, and first-person shooter games are also banned. But hey, actual firearms *are* allowed at BJU (although not in the dorms). Personally, I would need a good four fingers of scotch after one day of this routine.

But you're not there to have fun; you're there to get an education. And what an education you will receive at BJU! Do you want to major in Bible? Bible Counseling? Or is Christian Ministries more your thing? In any case, BJU has got you covered from a ministerial standpoint. In fact, no matter what your major you will be getting religion at Bob Jones. Even if you major in automotive service you be taking plenty of Bible study. You can major in music although you presumably won't be playing any rock, rap, country or jazz in the program. You can even major in cinema although you can't actually attend cinemas while at BJU.

But let's not forget Bob Jones' original vision for the school. The teaching of science the way God intended it, specifically non-scientific, biblical literalism. You'll be glad to know Bob Jones' dream is still very much alive at his namesake today. As BJU themselves put it, "While offering scientific and philosophical refutation of the theory of evolution, our program teaches each course within a biblical creationist framework." But might that biblical framework be a bit constraining to science? Again from BJU,

"The Christian teacher of science must be thoroughly grounded in the Word of God. Moreover, he must have firmly implanted in his mind a biblical framework of truth which serves as the touchstone for his decision making. True science will fit that framework; anything that fails to fit the biblical framework must be rejected as erroneous. The present discussion demonstrates the need for a distinctively Christian philosophy of science teaching and surveys the differences between Christian and secular science education."

In other words, at BJU "true" scientists consult the Bible to arrive at conclusions first, and then they work backward looking for whatever they can find to try and prop up these pre-ordained conclusions. It's the polar opposite of how actual science works.

So what is a degree from BJU worth? Well, up until 2005 it was worth about nothing. Since then it's become slightly better than nothing. The issue here is accreditation. Bob Jones didn't want his school to be accredited so he made no effort to get it (though it's far from certain he could have gotten it anyway). The tradition continued down through the years. The problem is that a degree from an unaccredited institution is little more than a piece of paper. Many employers won't count such degrees, and graduate schools are even more dismissive of them. Finally, in 2005 the school won accreditation from the Transnational Association of Christian Colleges and Schools (TRACS).

But TRACS is a story in and of itself. This outfit was created in 1971 with the objective of giving accreditation to schools that teach an inerrant Bible and creationism. If this sounds like a lousy system to you, then you are not alone. TRACS had to get approval from the government before it could hand out accreditation, but for years the government refused to go along with the gag. TRACS tried for certification repeatedly, but got shot down every time. The tide turned for them, however, in 1991. The Department of Education still advised against their request, but Secretary of Education Lamar Alexander went ahead and approved it anyway. Alexander went on to run twice unsuccessfully for the Republican Presidential nomination and today represents Tennessee in the U.S. Senate.

TRACS also gave accreditation to Jerry Falwell's Liberty University at one time, but Liberty withdrew from the agreement in 2008.

If BJU students are only allowed to watch G-rated videos when off campus, all of the following smutty PG or harder films would be off-limits to them.

The Chronicles of Narnia
Ice Age
The SpongeBob SquarePants Movie
Stuart Little
E.T. The Extraterrestrial
Bridge to Terabithia
Miracle on 34th Street
Up
The Preacher's Wife
Nanny McPhee
Alvin and the Chipmunks
The Goonies
The Incredibles
Lassie
Cloudy with a Chance of Meatballs
The Prince of Egypt
The Passion of the Christ

What the Hell???

Snake Handlers

In a 1992 episode of *The Simpsons* Homer attempts to sway the hapless bartender Moe to a new religion he has recently concocted. Moe lifts his heavily bandaged arms and professes his faith, "I was born a snake handler, and I'll die a snake handler." But come on, snake handling? That has to be an urban legend, right?

Wrong. Snake handling is no tall tale.

The practice got started around the year 1908 in Tennessee when a preacher named George Hensley had box of snakes dumped in front of him during a sermon. He picked up the creatures and held them aloft before his congregation without interrupting his sermon. His rationale for this stunt came from the Gospel of Mark, which says,

> *And these signs shall follow them that believe; In my name shall they cast out devils; they shall speak with new tongues; They shall take up serpents; and if they drink any deadly thing, it shall not hurt them; They shall lay hands on the sick, and they shall recover.*

The practice caught on as Hensley traveled around rural Tennessee and thrilled the rubes in the pews with his holy snake show. Coincidentally, another preacher named James Miller (who apparently had no knowledge of Hensley) independently started doing his own snake-juggling sermons in Alabama and Georgia starting around 1912, proving that great minds do indeed think alike. This is not to say the practice was catching on in a big way, in fact it never has, but it was able to stay alive.

Which is more than can be said for some of the snake handlers (or "serpent handlers" as they prefer to be called) themselves. The Gospel of Mark doesn't say the snakes won't bite, and sometimes they do. And it isn't like these people are fiddling around with garter snakes. They use potentially lethal snakes such as copperheads, water moccasins and rattlers. A number of serpent handlers have been dispatched to the great snake pit in the sky by the scaly beasts. In a 1993 article in *National Geographic*, religious psychologist Ralph Hood said, "There are over one hundred documented deaths from serpent bites. In every tradition, people are bitten and maimed by them. If you go into any serpent-handling church, you'll see people with atrophied hands, and missing fingers. All the serpent-handling families have suffered such things."

You may have noticed that passage from Mark also mentioned the drinking of deadly things. It therefore may not surprise you to learn that a few serpent handlers may have died of strychnine poisoning. They may be drinking other harmful substances as well, but it is unknown if any snake handlers have ever been brave enough to attempt to quaff down a bottle of SunnyD. And it's not like Mark is the only part of the Bible that these people have read. A passage in Luke reading, "Behold, I give unto you the power to tread on serpents and scorpions, and over the power of the enemy: and nothing by any means shall hurt you" has also had a big influence on the faithful. This quote is both more vague and more reassuring since it seems to say you won't get hurt no matter what ill-advised activities you engage in. This has led to other snake-handler traditions such as playing with fire and the insertion of fingers into live electrical outlets.

While all of this doubtlessly makes going to church on Sunday a lot less boring, it hasn't done much to win new sheep to the flock. It also probably doesn't help that snake handling has been outlawed in most southern states in the U.S., so parishioners have to practice their faith somewhat on the sly. So it stands to reason that The Church of God with Signs Following (which is the main snake-handling denomination) hasn't had much luck bringing in converts. Most of the Church's members are from traditional snake-handling families that pass the tradition on through the generations. Nevertheless, the practice has broken out of the Deep South in which it had traditionally been confined. New snake handling churches have now opened in British Columbia and Alberta, Canada.

195

Pope Pius XII

In 1939 Germany invaded Poland and thereby launched World War II in Europe. The war and its corresponding Holocaust would be the greatest calamity to ever befall the human race. Faced with the coldly efficient evil of the Nazis, the Catholic Church desperately needed a bold, resolute leader who had the moral courage to stand up to Adolf Hitler and let it be known in no uncertain terms that his murderous schemes were intolerable to anyone who claimed to follow Jesus. Instead they got Pope Pius XII, who was none of these things.

His predecessor, Pope Pius XI—while certainly not without his own faults—had at least been a critic of both racism in general and the Nazis in particular. He had vacated Rome in protest when Hitler visited, and he chewed out a Viennese bishop who had publicly celebrated Hitler's takeover of Austria. The days of Church diffidence toward the Nazis ended with his death just before the outbreak of the war, however, as Pius XII had no desire to confront them.

There were three main reasons for this. First, Pius fancied himself an expert diplomat, and he felt that he could bring about peace in Europe through his own deft handling of the war crisis. This delusional view of his own abilities precluded him from taking any open stance against Nazi Germany. Pius's total failure to ever bring about anything resembling peace didn't dissuade him from thinking he could pull it off. Second, and more importantly, Pius saw Germany as the wall of defense the Church needed for protection from the godless commies in the Soviet Union. The Church had long taken a hardline stance against communism, including fervent support of the fascist Francisco Franco in the Spanish Civil War, and Pius was not going to be the one to let that tradition die. Indeed, Pius' fixation on communism would guide his actions for the rest of his life. Third, Pius was deeply concerned that the Vatican would be bombed. When one bomb was errantly dropped on the Vatican, Pius publicly ripped the United States for the act (though it later turned out that it wasn't an American bomb). This is the same man who did not condemn Germany's bombing blitz of Britain in 1941 and 1942.

Pius has also been accused of anti-Semitism. This charge is not well supported, but it would be hard to deny that the plight of the Jews was not the primary concern of the pontiff's. The plight of Germans, on the other hand, was another matter. Pius spoke fluent German and considered himself an expert on German culture and history. In short, the German people had a friend in the Vatican that the Jewish people did not.

Not that non-Jews were especially lucky to have Pius looking out for them either. When Germany initially occupied Poland it was regular Poles rather than Jews who were the first to feel the wrath of the Nazis. Pius was more worried about the Soviet threat than the welfare of Poles, so he held his tongue as the Germans went about their vicious business. By 1945 twenty percent of the Catholic clergy in Poland had been killed by the Nazis—most of them early in the war. Yet the Pope did not condemn Germany for the crimes. Many Poles began to wonder if the pope had abandoned them. During this period, Pius' greatest concern was not German atrocities, but rather the non-aggression pact Stalin had signed with Hitler, as he feared this would strengthen the Soviet position in Europe.

The non-aggression pact turned out to be nothing but a Nazi stunt, however, and Hitler invaded the Soviet Union in 1941 with the intention of wiping out communism. It was shortly thereafter that the Church received multiple reports of a systematic, widespread Nazi campaign to murder Europe's Jews. Pius chose to let the matter slide. He did not speak out against genocide or anti-Semitism. He did not instruct Catholics that they must not participate in such atrocities nor stand idly by while others committed them. He did not urge Catholics to protect or hide Jews. He did not warn Church leaders in Western nations such as France that the Nazis had embarked on this campaign in the East. He did not call for Catholics in places like the Americas to rise up in outrage against these atrocities. He did not excommunicate Hitler, Heinrich Himmler or other prominent Nazis who were lapsed Catholics, nor did he excommunicate Italy's nominally Catholic leader Benito Mussolini, Croatia's Ante Pavelic or other fascist, Catholic thugs.

When the Germans decided to round up the Jews of Rome for relocation to Auschwitz in 1943, the pliant pope did not protest. In fact, he asked the Germans to station *more* police in Rome to protect the city against communist agitators. After the Allies captured Rome, he still refrained from speaking out against Germany even though Nazi troops could no longer reach him.

What the Pope did do was to deliver a short, vague, almost cryptic message in a 1942 Christmas address that criticized unspecified atrocities without mentioning the Jews. He also, on occasion, used his papal offices to intervene in cases that did save the lives of some Jews. Pius' apologists make a great deal out of these limited gestures. Less celebrated is the fact that Pius ordered that warm and public congratulations be made to Hitler on his fiftieth birthday.

Pius opposed the allied nations' goal of the unconditional surrender of Germany, but the Allies had grown talented at ignoring him, and they fought until Germany ran up the white flag. With the Nazis totally defeated and the horrors of the Holocaust laid bare, the stage was set for Pius to finally condemn the Third Reich. Yet he still didn't do it.

Instead, the Vatican pressed for clemency for accused Nazi war criminals. Some Nazi fugitives from justice were assisted with papers, transportation, and pocket money provided by the Vatican. The Church also used its influence to pressure South American nations into helping to hide the accused. Among those the Church helped to escape justice was Adolf Eichmann, one of the foremost architects of the Holocaust.

In one especially perverse episode, a phony seminary was established by the Vatican that turned out to be nothing more than a front designed to hide former SS officers (who posed as seminarians) and their girlfriends and mistresses. This "seminary" even included state-of-the-art radio facilities. It was shut down by American troops when the U.S. caught wind of the scheme. No evidence connects Pius with this debacle, but a highly placed official working right under the nose of the pontiff did create the ersatz seminary.

And then there was the matter of Croatia. The Church looked at Croatia as an important front in the post-war fight against communism. Croatia was Catholic, and the Church was determined to keep it that way. The problem was that the Catholic outfit that had run Croatia during the war was the

Ustasha, a Nazi-allied group who had murdered hundreds of thousands of Serbs and sent countless Jews off to die in Hitler's concentration camps. No matter. A scheme was launched by the Vatican to return the Ustashs to power. Funds the Ustasha had stolen from the Serbs and Jews they had murdered during the war were to provide the cash for the scheme. The plot failed, however, and communist Yugoslavia took over Croatia. Once again Pius was in position to deny he knew of this scandal, but even if one were to accept that he was ignorant of the plot (which is somewhat doubtful) one would still have to conclude that Pius was asleep at the switch while a culture sympathetic to war criminals was allowed to flourish in the Vatican.

Pius refused to condemn anti-Semitism until the day he died in 1958.

Let me be clear: Pius XII never killed anyone. The Holocaust was not his idea, he did not support it, and the Nazis did not ask for his approval of their plans. Nevertheless, the pope could have taken decisive action, set himself as an example of moral courage and demanded the same of the faithful everywhere, but it was not to be. Despite all of this, Pope Pius XII is meandering toward being canonized as a saint. The increasing uproar over his actions and inactions during and after World War II is slowing the process, however.

Then there is the story of Pope John XXIII who was Bishop Angelo Roncalli during the war. Bishop Roncalli can rightfully be seen as the antithesis of Pope Pius XII, both in his actions during the war and in his pontificate. As an apostolic delegate to Turkey and Greece during the war, Roncalli recognized the crisis facing the Jews of Eastern Europe. He became deeply involved with assisting the Jewish underground and in so doing put his own personal safety at risk. His efforts helped to save many lives. He was transferred to France later in the war where he persuaded three bishops who had collaborated with the Nazis to resign.

As Pope, John initiated sweeping reforms in the Church including those of the Second Vatican Council. Vatican II, as it is commonly known, included a wholesale change in the way the Church dealt with Jewish relations and explicitly condemned anti-Semitism. John even once called a halt to a mass while it was in progress in order to have anti-Semitic material removed from the service. He then ordered a review of Church liturgy to have all such offensive material removed. Pope Benedict XVI, however, reinserted a Good Friday prayer for the conversion of the Jews decades later.

One can only speculate how differently events would have unfolded if John, rather than Pius, had been pope during the war.

In 2010 Pope Benedict XVI traveled to Scotland and unveiled a new take on the history of World War II. In his revised version of history, the war was a battle against secularism and atheism.

"Even in our own lifetimes we can recall how Britain and her leaders stood against a Nazi tyranny that wished to eradicate God from society and denied our common humanity to many, especially the Jews, who were thought unfit to live.

As we reflect on the sobering lessons of atheist extremism of the 20th century, let us never forget how the exclusion of God, religion and virtue from public life leads ultimately to a truncated vision of man and of society and thus a reductive vision of a person and his destiny."

This is an amazingly poor piece of history. First off, Hitler was nominally Catholic, and since the Church refused to excommunicate him, he remained that way until his death. He was not an atheist, in fact he repeatedly stressed that Germany was a Christian nation. German soldiers had the words *Gott mit uns* (God is with us) stamped onto their belt buckles, and the cross was emblazoned on the sides of the planes that bombed Britain relentlessly. Nearly everyone who took part in the Holocaust was Christian. Furthermore, if the Nazis were atheists why didn't Pius XII take them to task for it?

The British Humanist Association issued a response to Benedict's remarks.

"The notion that it was the atheism of Nazis that led to their extremist and hateful views or that it somehow fuels intolerance in Britain today is a terrible libel against those who do not believe in God.

The notion that it is non-religious people in the UK today who want to force their views on others, coming from a man whose organisation exerts itself internationally to impose its narrow and exclusive form of morality and undermine the human rights of women, children, gay people, and many others, is surreal."

What the Hell???

The Magdalene Laundries

In 1993 the Sisters of Our Lady of Charity, having lost their shirts (or habits) in the stock market, were forced to sell a chunk of their Dublin convent property to the Irish government to make ends meet. When Irish officials took stock of the land they had purchased from the Church, they were stunned to find the unmarked graves of 133 women on the property. As the bodies were exhumed from the graves, an additional twenty-two corpses were found unceremoniously buried in a mass grave. The sisters then had the corpses cremated with little fanfare, but the discoveries had already caused a sensation in Ireland.

The women in this pitiful cemetery were girls who had been sent to various convents to mend their wicked ways in what were called the Magdalene Laundries. Obviously, many of them never left.

The Magdalene Laundries started in the mid-nineteenth century as refuges for prostitutes. They quickly expanded in scope to encompass "bad girls" of every type. Anyone who was considered sexually active before marriage or was thought to be in danger of becoming sexually active could be sent to the laundries. Being a victim of rape or incest counted as sexual activity and could land a girl in the laundries. Unwed mothers were stripped of their children and then sent to work there. The Church put their kids into orphanages and eventually put them up for adoption to Catholic families who often lived overseas. Even being good looking could be cause enough for a girl to be sent to the laundries. All decisions about who should go to the laundries were made by the Church, which held considerably more power than the Irish government for a long time. The accused girls had no opportunity to defend themselves from the accusations against them and no way to appeal the decisions. Those sent to the laundries were given no indication as to when they might be released. The girls were essentially given life sentences.

It seems like everyone in America who went to a Catholic grade school has horror stories about the nuns that ran the school, but believe me, old Sister Doris who terrorized the lunch room with her wooden spoon would have cowered before the Magdalene nuns like a puppy in a thunderstorm.

Upon arrival at the laundries, the forlorn girls (who came to be known as "Maggies" or "Penitents") were stripped of their names and given new ones by the nuns. This was the first step in robbing the girls of their identities and their dignity. The process continued as the Maggies were outfitted with drab, shapeless gowns that hid their figures and made them all look alike. They also had to wear strips of cloth tightly tied around their chests to flatten their breasts. Since many of them were lactating mothers who had just been robbed of their babies, this could be an excruciating process. The dresses were apparently not enough to shame the girls, so they also had their hair unceremoniously chopped off. The nuns told the Maggies they were sinners whose families had abandoned them out of shame, and they beat them with impunity.

The Maggies were forced to do grueling work washing and ironing clothes in ten-hour shifts, six days a week. They had to attend mass every day as well. There were no washing machines in the laundries, so the ladies had to scrub everything by hand. The Maggies were not paid for all this work. In other words, they were slaves. They were not permitted to talk to one another. Even when doing chores such as sewing, adults were seated between the girls to make sure no communication took place between them. The Maggies had no contact with their families. They had no contact with anyone but the clergy who exploited them.

They were even forced to participate in bizarre, sexually-oriented ordeals by the nuns who lined them up naked for purposes such as comparing the girls bodies. One survivor of the laundries named Phyllis Valentine remembered such humiliation in the documentary film *Sex In a Cold Climate*, "They used to touch you a lot. They used to line us up every Saturday night, and they used to make us strip naked for them... They'd be laughing at us, they'd be criticizing us. And if you were heavy, fat or whatever, they'd shout abuse to us. We had no privacy with them at all...They enjoyed us stripped naked." This captive population of women was also easy pickings for any sexually predatory priests who might happen to visit the convents. When Maggies were raped by such men they had nowhere to turn for help. Who would ever take the word of a fallen woman over that of a priest?

The laundries were located behind high, windowless walls crowned with barbed wire or broken glass set in cement to prevent any escape attempts. When Maggies did manage to slip out of their prisons, the convent's bells would be rung to alert the whole town that there was a fugitive on the loose. The girls were never given leave or time off. The only way they could see outside the convents was to look up at the sky.

People who lived around the convents never saw the Maggies, but they still had inklings as to what was going on behind the high walls. There was an awful lot of laundry being done, and it obviously wasn't the nuns who were doing it. Chilling sayings such as "Bad girls do the best sheets" evolved in Irish culture, and naughty children were warned to shape up lest they be sent to the laundries.

Often times, the only way out of the laundries (other than death) was for a male family member to claim the girl and take the prisoner away. This was easier said than done, however. First off, the Church was not forthcoming as to the whereabouts of the girls. A search for them would be made much more difficult by the fact that the Maggies were forced to live under assumed names. What's more, the total domination of Irish society by the Church strongly discouraged the removal of the girls from their penitent work in the first place. There was an enormous amount of shame attached to fallen women, and to acknowledge that one's daughter was such a sinner in the eyes of the Church was almost unthinkable. Those who were rescued from the laundries were often collected by relatives from outside of Ireland.

Most of the Maggies were not rescued though. Some of them went on to become nuns themselves. This may sound perverse, but it was the only life they knew apart from slaving away on laundry. Many of the Maggies continued to do laundry until they died. It is likely that a number of them committed suicide.

Which brings us back to the unmarked graves discovered in 1993. In violation of the law, the nuns made no reports to the authorities when the Maggies died, so not only do we not have their names, we don't know their causes of death either. The discoveries touched off an outpouring of interest in Ireland from people wondering if the dead could be their long-lost sisters, daughters or mothers. The spotlight was turned not on just one convent, but on all the laundries throughout Ireland. It was now the Church's turn to be ashamed. After a CBS news story concerning the laundries aired in the United States, the Conference of Religious of Ireland issued a written statement saying the whole laundry episode was regrettable, but asked that people remember the context in which these events took place. They did not specify what context could possibly explain—let alone justify—this cruelty. Mary Norris, one of the relatively few survivors of the laundries who has been willing to speak out about her experiences, put it this way, "They now say they're sorry—what they mean is they're sorry they were found out."

The age of the laundries did come to an end, but it wasn't until much later than you would guess. The last Magdalene Laundry didn't close down until 1996. It is estimated that 30,000 girls and women were forced to work in the facilities at one time or another, but it's hard to say as there were no records kept, and the Church has been tight-lipped about the whole affair since it broke.

In 2002 a film called *The Magdalene Sisters* that dramatized life in the laundries was released. Although the film portrays the Maggies' lives under sadistic nuns as being utterly dismal, Norris said, "The reality of those places was a thousand times worse" than what the movie portrayed.

Without a doubt, the most famous Maggie was the singer Sinéad O'Connor who was sent to a laundry in the 1980s when she was fifteen years old and spent eighteen months there. By the '80s the laundries had mellowed out a lot from their brutal low point of the mid-twentieth century, but they were still horrible places. She was forced to wash priests' clothes in cold water with bars of soap over a sink—without pay of course.

Part III

The Marketplace of Salvation

L. Ron Hubbard

"If you oppose Scientology we promptly look up—and will find and expose—your crimes. If you leave us alone we will leave you alone. It's very simple. Even a fool can grasp that.
–L. Ron Hubbard

"The purpose of the (lawsuit) is to harass and discourage rather than win."
–L. Ron Hubbard

"If attacked on some vulnerable point by anyone or anything or any organization, always find or manufacture enough threat against them to cause them to sue for peace.... Don't ever defend. Always attack."
–L. Ron Hubbard

"We do not want Scientology to be reported in the press, anywhere else than on the religious pages of newspapers.... Therefore, we should be very alert to sue for slander at the slightest chance so as to discourage the public presses from mentioning Scientology."
–L. Ron Hubbard

"And don't underrate our ability to carry it out.... Those who try to make life difficult for us are at once at risk."
–L. Ron Hubbard

Not to worry guys. My review of L. Ron Hubbard and his Church of Scientology will be 100% positive. I include Hubbard in this book only to highlight the stark contrast between the losers in the other chapters and this truly great man.

L. Ron Hubbard was born in Tilden, Nebraska in 1911. Even as a boy, Hubbard distinguished himself. In 1924 he became the youngest Eagle Scout in the United States. The Boy Scouts of America's records of that era conveniently did not include the scouts' ages, however, so Hubbard was denied the proper accolades he deserved for this accomplishment. This type of mistreatment would become a theme in Hubbard's life.

He went on to George Washington University where the school, unable to comprehend his expansive intellect and insight, placed him on academic probation for deficiency in scholarship. Hubbard left the University without a degree.

207

Undeterred by the simpletons who would hold him back, Hubbard entered the U.S. Navy in World War II. Hubbard was given command of a small vessel and distinguished himself in battle by finding and sinking two Japanese submarines. Smaller minds again intervened, however. The Navy's investigation of the incident (which eventually occupied five ships and two blimps) concluded that there had never been any enemy subs in the area. The Mexican government eventually joined in the Hubbard-bashing by filing a formal complaint with the United States that accused him of using a Mexican island for target practice. Hubbard was relieved of command after this incident. One wonders how much sooner the war could have been brought to an end if Hubbard hadn't been stopped from terrorizing the Japanese submarine fleet in the eastern Pacific.

What's more, Hubbard had been badly injured during the war. His war wounds left him blind and crippled with injuries to his eyes, feet, and hip. In fact, Hubbard had nearly died from his battle wounds. The Navy awarded him the Purple Heart for being wounded in action twice. This is where his story turns truly remarkable. Hubbard was able to heal all of his injuries using nothing more than the power of his own mind! This was the origin of the fantastic revelations with which he would later shock the world. Oh sure, skeptics once again reared their ugly heads. An article in the February 14, 2011 issue of *The New Yorker* claimed to have obtained Hubbard's full military records and found no evidence of Hubbard having been wounded in battle at all. The article also implied that Hubbard's Purple Heart and other naval medals were bogus. That's your elitist, East Coast media for you.

Notwithstanding the Navy's clumsy handling of their brilliant junior officer, the United States defeated Japan. After the war, Hubbard continued his work for the Navy by going undercover to rid the nation of practitioners of black magic. Selflessly disregarding any risk to himself, Hubbard infiltrated a black magic group led by a rocket scientist (no kidding) named John Parsons that practiced something called "sex magic." Amongst other things, the Parsons group had a ceremony that involved a naked, pregnant woman jumping through fire in the backyard of their group home, and unsurprisingly, they did a lot of drugs. Hubbard's clandestine work for Navel Intelligence was instrumental in leading to the successful break up this nefarious group, but naysayers once again tried to rob Hubbard of his proper credit. They claim he was actually on very good terms with Parsons, and he was supportive of the group's efforts to change the world. The Navy conveniently "lost" its records of its anti-black magic program. But at least one positive would come out of the situation for Hubbard; he met his second wife Sarah at the group home. She had been Parson's lover, but traded up to Hubbard when given the chance.

Hubbard eventually left the Navy and returned to his true passion, writing science fiction. The man was a whiz behind the typewriter where he spun spellbinding yarns at a dizzying rate. Many of his books have become bestsellers. *Battlefield Earth*, perhaps his best-known work of fiction, was made into a film by Scientologist John Travolta, which has been enjoyed by millions of people despite the caustic reviews of critics who hoped to suppress the picture. Some killjoys such as *The Los Angeles Times* (in a series of articles that began on June 24, 1990) and *Time* magazine (in a story called *The Thriving Cult of Greed and Power* in its May 6, 1991 issue) have claimed that the sales figures for Hubbard's books were hugely inflated by Scientologists who bought the books in massive quantities in an effort to make them look more popular than they really were. The Church of Scientology slapped *Time* with a $400 million lawsuit over the incredible charges leveled at the Church in that story. Unfortunately, *Time* was able to get the courts to dismiss the suit.

In 1950 Hubbard made the breakthrough that would change his life—and the world—forever. He wrote an article in a magazine called *Astounding Science Fiction* in which he claimed that he had discovered the cause of humanity's problems. This article would eventually grow into the book *Dianetics: The Modern Science of Mental Health* that launched Hubbard to international fame. The science fiction writer Harlan Ellison, who was doubtlessly jealous of Hubbard's superior storytelling skills, tried to throw cold water on the article by claiming he was present at the moment the idea was invented. He said Hubbard was complaining about the low pay he made as a writer when "(author) Lester del Rey then said half-jokingly, 'What you really ought to do is create a religion because it will be tax-free,' and at that point everyone in the room started chiming in with ideas for this new religion. So the idea was a gestalt that Ron caught on to and assimilated the details. He then wrote it up as *'Dianetics: A New Science of the Mind'* and sold it to John W. Campbell, Jr., who published it in *Astounding Science Fiction* in 1950."

Dianetics explained how people can achieve anything they want if they can only free their minds of the litter that holds them back in a process known as becoming "clear." The book took off despite the objections of psychiatrists who dismissed the whole thing as nonsense. Psychiatrists had good reason to be worried about the book because in it Hubbard was beginning to expose their entire profession as a despicable fraud that was stealing money from good people, while keeping them enslaved to their repressive natures at the same time. He once said that if psychiatrists "had the power to torture and kill everyone they would do so." When the Scientologist actor Tom Cruise famously scolded Matt Lauer on the *Today Show*, saying, "You don't know the history of psychiatry. I do," this is what he was referring to.

Dianetics was not Hubbard's only breakthrough. He was the first person to realize that thoughts have mass. This discovery was so far ahead of its time that mainstream scientists today still haven't acknowledged it. This discovery allowed Hubbard to invent the E-meter, a device which has two metal tubes attached to a box with some gauges on it. In the hands of an experienced operator, the E-meter can measure a person's mental condition. Hubbard was such an ace at using the machine that he could use it to detect the pain tomatoes feel while being sliced. Naturally, the government got in the way of his progress when the FDA warned that the E-meter has no curative power and is ineffective in diagnosing or treating disease.

In 1953, Hubbard used the principles laid out in *Dianetics* to form the Church of Scientology, and the Church took off. This was despite the constant barrage of insults Hubbard was forced to endure from people hoping to stymie him, including his own wives. Hubbard's first wife Margaret had said Hubbard was "not normal" and "sadistic," so it looked like a move up when he met his second wife, Sarah. Alas, Sarah also turned out to be a loser. She said Hubbard tortured her and was possibly a paranoid schizophrenic. She later came to her senses and retracted her charges. After Hubbard patriotically informed the FBI that his estranged wife Sarah might be a communist, they foolishly dismissed him as a "mental case."

A lesser man would have wilted under such withering assault, but not Hubbard. He endured these slings and arrows with grace and in 1967 removed himself from all this vitriol by taking to the high seas. Hubbard—still an expert seaman from his Navy days—bought a boat called the *Apollo*, created a group of crack Scientologists called the Sea Organization (or Sea Org for short) to man it, and set sail for the Mediterranean. The members of the Sea Org are so dedicated to Scientology that they sign one billion year contracts when they join this elite force. Alas, the persecution that plagued Hubbard in the U.S. followed him to Europe. Several nations wound up banning Hubbard's Sea Org from docking in their ports. In a truly bizarre episode, Hubbard's ship was attacked in Portugal by a violent mob that was convinced the Scientologists were actually CIA agents.

Ex-Scientologist Bent Corydon in his outrageous book *L. Ron Hubbard: Messiah or Madman* accused Hubbard of numerous misdeeds at this time. His book portrays Hubbard as an out-of-control hothead who would throw people (who were sometimes blindfolded) off his ship from as high as twenty-five feet as a form of punishment. He also accused Hubbard of punishing people by shutting them away in a dangerous chain room in the vessel. Corydon claimed this was done to people as young as the age of four. He also accused Hubbard of taking amphetamines, barbiturates, hallucinogens, cocaine, peyote, mescaline, uppers and downers called "pinks and grays," phenobarbital, and opium in addition to the heavy use of alcohol and tobacco. These charges must be false, however, because drug abuse is forbidden in Scientology.

I suppose some of you might be wondering exactly what Scientologists believe anyway. Contrary to what the mainstream press might have you believe, it's not some weirdo cult with outlandish beliefs. They believe in the almost limitless possibilities of the human mind once it has been set free of the negative influences that hold it back. These possibilities include the ability to move objects, heal injuries, and eradicate illness all with only the power of thought.

So how did the human mind become so ensnared in negativism in the first place? A good question, but one with an answer so shocking that the Church of Scientology carefully prepares its members for it before springing the horrible truth upon them. In fact, this truth is so disturbing that it has been claimed that people are at risk of dying from pneumonia if they are exposed to it without first becoming clear and advancing through the lower ranks of Scientology with a lengthy program of what I'm assured are reasonably-priced counseling sessions called "auditing." In fact, Hubbard called this information the "Wall of Fire" and said of it, "The material in this section is so vicious, that it is carefully arranged to kill anyone if he discovers the exact truth of it… I am sure that I was the first one that ever did live through any attempt to attain that material."

I am about to reveal the truth to you here gentle reader. I have bolded the section so the unprepared can safely skip it. You've been warned, so if you read it anyway and then die of pneumonia don't come looking for me.

Seventy-five million years ago an evil space alien named Xenu ruled a galactic confederation of seventy-six planets that had become hopelessly overpopulated with hundreds of billions of inhabitants on each planet. Xenu solved the population problem by bringing billions of alien beings to Earth (then called "Teegeeack") on spaceships that looked just like DC-8 airplanes. Xenu laid his prisoners out around Earth's, or Teegeeack's, volcanoes and dropped hydrogen bombs on them. As the victims died, their thetans (which are rather like souls) flew away from their corpses, and Xenu captured them. He implanted the thetans with horrible things such as sexual perversions and traditional religious beliefs. When people are born on earth today these thetans attach themselves to the newborns and immediately begin to suppress them. Only through Scientology can people hope to shake off the thetans and liberate the true power of their minds. Xenu was eventually overthrown and imprisoned beneath a mountain, where he remains today.

Crazy? Obviously not. Yet the poorly animated TV show *South Park* thought so. They made a goofy-looking cartoon mocking these beliefs in an episode called *Trapped In The Closet*, which included a caption saying, "THIS IS WHAT SCIENTOLOGISTS ACTUALLY BELIEVE." Would the *South Park* creators have made fun of anyone else's sacred beliefs like this? I don't think so. This underscores the unique persecution that Scientologists are continually forced to endure.

As if that weren't enough, some people have pointed to a number of seemingly anti-homosexual comments in Hubbard's writing and have suggested that he took a dim view of such people. Nothing could be further from the truth. The fact is that a bigot sabotaged Hubbard's work and inserted the gay-bashing parts. The Church edited out some of the offending passages in a timely fashion (decades later).

As the unquestionably heterosexual Hubbard grew older, he gradually withdrew from public life. On January 24, 1986

Hubbard passed away, or at least that's what was reported in the mainstream media. In reality, Hubbard had advanced to such a high level of understanding that he was able to shed the shell of his body and ascend into the heavens to chart a path to immortality for humanity to follow.

David Miscavige succeeded Hubbard as leader of the Church of Scientology. While obviously not at the same level of greatness as Hubbard, Miscavige is still an amazing force for good in the world. Yet just like his predecessor, he has become a whipping boy for those with lesser minds. He has been publicly accused of being a violent, abusive, hot tempered, and cruel dictator who lives like a prince off of the backs of Scientology's members. Alas, visionary men are seldom appreciated in their own time.

> If you think that Scientology was the only faith to originate in the mind of a science fiction writer, you can guess again. In 1994 a man named Steve Galindo founded the Church of Ed Wood. This faith is based upon the works of the legendary filmmaker Edward D. Wood Jr. who created such hounds as *Glen or Glenda*, *Bride of the Monster*, and of course *Plan 9 from Outer Space*, which became widely regarded as the worst movie of all time—or at least it was until *Battlefield Earth* came out. The Church of Ed Wood regards Wood as their savior and celebrates his birthday as "Woodmas Day." I know what you're thinking; this is some sort of a joke. But the group's website puts it best, "To answer your first question—yes, we're TOTALLY serious!" They also claim to have baptized more than 3,000 people into the faith.

Jim Jones

As a child growing up in the small town of Lynn, Indiana, Jim Jones displayed an early flair for religious drama. Though he was the son of non-religious parents, Jones often attended fundamentalist Christian services and soon took to preaching himself. He set up a pretend church at which he presided over a congregation of other neighborhood children. He also conducted funerals for their pets when they passed on to the great litter box in the sky. Few people doubted that Jones would go on to run his own church someday, but no one could have foreseen how tragically it would turn out.

What might be surprising about Jones is how unremarkably his career began. In 1952, a Methodist church in Indianapolis agreed to let him preach in their church, although Jones was not a Methodist himself. He put on rather buoyant services, but he wasn't building much of a following. Since the money coming in was paltry, he had to take an outside job to make ends meet. So Jones went into business for himself as a door-to-door salesman. The product he was selling? Live monkeys.

Jones knocked on doors and schlepped his pets throughout Indianapolis while a monkey climbed around on his shoulders. Apparently, there was some pent-up demand in the Hoosier state for diaper-wearing, dung-flinging simians, as Jones was actually able to sell a number of the beasts. Alas, the monkey business was never the howling success Jones had hoped it would be. The problem was on the supply end. He had his monkeys shipped to Indiana via mail from the tropics at all times of the year. The trip proved to be too much for many of the delicate creatures, and Jones was often left opening box after box of dead monkeys that he still had to pay for.

What's more, Jones' preaching gig ran into problems of its own. He preached a message of racial inclusion and started attracting African-Americans to his sermons. This freaked out the parish that was letting him use their church, so they pulled the welcome mat out from under him. It might have been the end of the road for the man of God-cum-monkey salesman, but Jones was not a quitter.

215

He started his own ministry called the Community Unity Church. Without the Methodists around to keep an eye on him anymore, he was free to do things his way, which was flashy and unorthodox. He started practicing faith healings in his services. He informed the faithful that they had cancer and would make them choke out the tumors right in front of the congregation. He also demonstrated his psychic powers by knowing things he seemingly could not have known about the people in his church. As word got out about the miracles he could perform his following grew larger. He even took his show on the road, traveling around the Midwest performing his wonders and expanding his ministry. He wasn't about to let money problems get in his way again either. Those in his flock who failed to contribute enough coin to the Church received home visits from officials who were often verbally abusive to the cheapskate parishioners. Jones continued his outreach to the African-American community as well. This may have inspired some backlash against him in the white community as there were several threatening incidents directed against him. Jones most likely embellished the animosity by making up stories about harassing phone calls he allegedly received; he may have staged many of the other threats as well. The stories of harassment may have been largely false, but they helped to burnish his reputation as a racial reformer.

Jones' preaching continued to become more outlandish. In 1961 he predicted that Indianapolis would be consumed in a nuclear holocaust on June 15, 1967. Jones moved to Brazil after *Esquire* magazine ran an article about the safest places in the world in the event of nuclear war. He moved back to Indiana only after getting word that his followers were drifting away from his Church. He didn't remain in Indiana long, however. In 1965 he packed up and moved to Ukiah, California, which was near another of the safe areas mentioned in the *Esquire* piece. This time he asked his believers to follow him when he left. As his predicted apocalypse was only two years away, many people felt they had no choice but to go west with Jones.

When he got to Ukiah he had little trouble getting his Church set up again. He seemed like a pretty decent guy to the locals and his Peoples Temple (as he now called his Church) was sanctioned by the mainline Protestant faith, The Christian Church (Disciples of Christ). Jim Jones was ordained as a minister by the Disciples. It didn't take long, however, before the Peoples Temple became an armed camp that shooed away any outsiders who happened to come by to visit.

Jones had good reason to keep anyone other than his devoted followers from seeing his services, as they were truly a theater of the bizarre. Jones would perform miraculous healings before his wildly cheering congregation. He would often predict the imminent death of a parishioner only to see that person keel over minutes later. Jones would then resurrect the person from the dead. He also held punishment sessions for anyone in the Temple who had violated any of the faith's innumerable rules. The accused were brought up before the congregation and made to bend over so Jones could beat them. In the early years Jones lashed his wayward sheep with a belt, but as time went by he graduated to progressively more damaging tools such as a wooden paddle and then a rubber hose. While the beatings were being administered the congregation screamed "Harder! Harder!" until Jones would decide the victim had had enough. Then the poor sap would have to shout "Thank you Father!" (Jones was now always referred to as "Father") or he would face further punishment. Other people were stripped naked before the crowd and forced to jump into an unheated swimming pool. Still others were beaten senseless in lopsided boxing matches that Jones arranged.

While all of this must have been great fun, the main part of the services at Peoples Temple were Jones' sermons. And what sermons they were. He would rant and rave for hours on end spewing out bewildering, offensive nonsense that the worshippers were supposed to lap up like manna from heaven. During his various sermons he claimed to have a ten-inch penis, he said he was the world's greatest lover, and that he had to masturbate thirty times a day. He once urinated in a can on stage, and he pulled out a live rattlesnake during another service. The services at Peoples Temple started in the afternoon and did not break up until the wee hours of the morning. During that time no one was allowed to use the bathroom, and no one could leave except for handicapped people who invariably raced out the front doors of the temple after Jones had miraculously healed them. Anyone who drifted off to sleep during one of the marathon sermons would be severely punished.

And what exactly was being worshiped at these services? It was Jones himself. He claimed to be the reincarnation of Jesus, Gandhi, and Mohammed. He routinely lashed out against the Bible and spat and stomped on it during his sermons. He preached the virtues of communism constantly as if it was salvation itself. Whatever theological connection he had once had with standard Christianity was gone by the 1970's.

Putting up with Jones' excruciating services wasn't even close to all that he demanded of his followers. They were expected to dig deep into their pockets to give to the Temple as well. At first Jones demanded that all Church members tithe, or give ten percent of their income to the People's Temple. He later raised that to twenty-five percent, but that still wasn't enough. He pressured people into giving everything they had to the Peoples Temple. Their cars, houses, and jewelry all made nice gifts for Father. People were instructed to sign over their social security and pay checks to Jones. Even wearing a watch was frowned upon at the Church, as people were discouraged from having personal possessions. If a member needed something such as a car they would have to get Church permission before buying one and then it could only be a used vehicle.

Those who opted to go all out on the Peoples Temple experience could move to the temple compound and partake in the thrill of communal living. Men and women were segregated into separate buildings, and sex was forbidden amongst them, even if they were married. Their children were taken from them to be raised by the Temple. The suckers who bought into this lifestyle could look forward to days working in Peoples Temple farms and attending an endless procession of pointless meetings.

The ban on sex didn't apply to Jones himself, of course. As the world's uncontested sexual champion he needed to maintain a harem of women to keep himself going. Jones derided homosexuality, but that didn't stop him from having sex (or "anal baptism" as he called it) with his male followers. Everyone Jones forced himself upon was then obliged to give public testimony that Jones was the greatest lover in the world. In 1973 Jones was arrested for lewd behavior after he exposed his erect penis to an undercover cop at a movie theater known to be a center of gay activity. The arresting officer's report of the incident failed to mention that Jones was the world's most incredible lover.

Jones stoked paranoia amongst his faithful with fanciful tales of how society was conspiring against them. He buttressed his case with a bunch of faked attacks on his Church. He had someone fire a gun outside the temple during services, and then he claimed the staged event was a real attack on him. One time he claimed to have been shot in the temple parking lot. There was a lot of what looked like blood on his shirt, but no one ever saw the wound. Jones claimed he had miraculously healed himself after the bullet hit him.

You may now be asking yourself why people didn't abandon this religion in droves. The answer is multi-faceted. First off, if you already gave Jones your house, car, and all your money, you had no home to go back to and no way of supporting yourself. Furthermore, if you lived in his commune you would be living apart from your spouse and children. Leaving Peoples Temple meant abandoning them forever. Fear was another factor. There were horror stories about what happened to people who left Peoples Temple and some defectors did indeed die under suspicious circumstances. Temple members were also required to sign blank pieces of paper so that Jones could type any confession he wished on the page in the event of a defection. But all of this still wasn't enough to explain the hold Jones held over his people. By all accounts the tall and charismatic Jones was a very persuasive man. When he spoke, people believed him. They had seen the miracles he could perform with their own eyes, and they lived in a community where every moment was dedicated to reinforcing the notion that Jones was God.

By the mid 1970's the Peoples Temple may have had the largest Protestant congregation of any house of worship in California. More than 10,000 people (and a chimp named Mr. Muggs) belonged to the Temple. The Temple quietly changed from a non-profit corporation to a California Corporation so Jones could more easily keep the financial windfall he was reaping. The nuclear war he had prophesied had never materialized, and he denied he ever had made such a prediction. The Temple moved to the suddenly safe city of San Francisco and immersed itself in politics. Jones ordered his people into the streets to get George Moscone elected mayor. When Moscone won (possibly with the help of electoral fraud committed by Peoples Temple) he rewarded Jones by making him a member of the San Francisco Housing Authority. This was to be the high-water mark for Jim Jones.

Jones brought an entourage of admirers along with him when he attended the Housing Authority meetings; this fan club cheered wildly every time he said anything. Such shenanigans going on in a major city invariably drew the attention of journalists who started poking around into Peoples Temple. But the story of the Peoples Temple was a hard one to break, as almost everyone involved was too afraid to talk about it. In 1972 the *San Francisco Examiner* did a damaging series on the Temple, but threats of lawsuits from Jones caused the paper to drop the series after only half the planned articles were published, and those that been printed had been censored to remove the more inflammatory information in them. Jones would not be so lucky in 1977 when the magazine *New West* published a scathing expose of Peoples Temple. After that article broke, investigations into allegations of Temple involvement in murder, arson, tax evasion, kidnapping, and more were initiated by various government agencies. *New West* braced itself for an onslaught of legal challenges and public protests from the Peoples Temple, but they heard almost nothing from them. Jim Jones had fled the country.

Jones had run off to Jonestown, which was the Temple's mission in the South American nation of Guyana. He took about a thousand of his most dedicated followers with him. This was the "Promised Land" Jones told them. Here, they would live free of government interference. They would also escape the upcoming race war and concentration camps for blacks that Jones was now predicting would soon sweep across the U.S.

Jonestown was a primitive, communal-living settlement hewn out of the Amazonian rain forest. Peoples Temple portrayed it as heaven on Earth, but it sounds more like it was hell. The people were made to work all the time without pay. They toiled away clearing the jungle in tropical heat and humidity eleven hours a day and got only meager rations on which to live. All the while, Jones would preach to them over loudspeakers that were set up throughout the site. Jones was consuming vast quantities of drugs by this point of his life, so his diatribes made even less sense than before. He warned his followers that the CIA was out to get them. He even said the agency was responsible for the rains that plagued the settlement. He warned that soldiers were liable to parachute into Jonestown at any time to kill everyone's babies. He held drills in the middle of the night in which everyone armed themselves with whatever they could to fight off the CIA baby killers that were everywhere around them, but nowhere to be seen. They also practiced committing suicide as the ultimate form of non-compliance. Anyone caught trying to escape from this Shangri-La was cast into irons.

Relatives of those in Jonestown succeeded in getting Democratic congressman Leo Ryan to go to Jonestown so he could see the conditions of the commune and hopefully get people out of there. In November of 1978, Ryan was able to force Jones to allow him to visit Jonestown. He went with a small number of relatives of Peoples Temple members and an NBC news crew.

Jones and his people knew how to deal with important visitors. Whenever they arrived Jones refrained from making his endless sermons, the laboring stopped, and everything was made to look fun and normal. This was the sight the Ryan delegation was treated to in Jonestown. There was music, dancing, and a feast was laid out for them. On the second day of the visit, however, some cracks formed in Jonestown's façade of happiness. First one person and then another told Ryan they wished to leave. Ryan promised he would take with him anyone declaring an intention to go. The number of defectors was relatively small, only fifteen people wished to go, but they represented a crisis for Jones. He figured that once the people got out they would talk to the press and tell them about the horrid conditions in Jonestown. It would be another devastating blow to the Peoples Temple. Then one of Jones' people pulled a knife on Ryan and held it to his neck saying, "Congressman Ryan, you are a motherfucker." The assailant was wrestled away from Ryan, but the die had now been cast. There was no way this incident would not cause a tsunami of negative attention to crash into Jonestown. Jones ordered one of his closest followers, Larry Layton, to pretend to defect, so he left with Ryan and the others. When the Ryan party got to the airstrip, a team of men sent by Jones pulled up behind them in a tractor-drawn trailer. They pulled out weapons and opened fire on Ryan and everyone who was with him. Ryan and two NBC employees fell immediately.

Layton pulled out a gun he had brought with him and started shooting the defectors who had already boarded an airplane. Ryan was then shot in the face with a shotgun at point-blank range to ensure that he was dead. He became the only congressman in American history to have been killed in the line of duty. His assistant, Jackie Speier, was shot five times and survived by pretending to be dead. She and the rest of the survivors—who were nursing various gunshot wounds of their own—would have to wait twenty-two hours for help to come.

Back at Jonestown, Jones knew his days as a living God were over. He ordered two tubs of punch to be whipped up and spiked with cyanide. He then ordered everyone to drink it. Only one woman objected to his command, and she was shouted down by the faithful. Children were the first to be poisoned. The punch was drawn into syringes and squirted into the mouths of babies. Cyanide poisoning is an extremely painful way to die. When the kids started screaming, Jones reassured them that "It's only hard at first." More and more people started drinking the poison. So many people were lined up that a third tub of punch had to be brought out. Armed guards encircled the camp to shoot anyone who tried to escape their fate. Eventually the guards drank the poison, and finally Jones himself died from a single, self-inflicted gunshot wound to the head.

More than 900 people died at Jonestown. At the time, it was the largest loss of civilian American lives (excluding natural disasters) in history; a record that would stand until another religiously motivated slaughter took place on September 11, 2001.

Perhaps the most enduring part of the Jim Jones tragedy is the notion of people willingly lining up to drink poisoned Kool-Aid. "Drinking the Kool-Aid" has now become a standard insult for anyone who wishes to allege that someone is blindly following another person. It is so common that many people who have never even heard of Jim Jones use the term without knowing what it alludes to.

Not to ruin things for everyone, but the Jonestown folks may well have used a Guyanan knock-off product called "Flavor Aid" rather than Kool-Aid to make their cyanide cocktails. They had both products in Jonestown, but we don't know which of them was used for the mass suicide and murder.

What the Hell???

Faith Healers

There is no question that Jim Jones' miraculous ability to heal people was crucial to the recruitment and retention of members, and there are plenty of other preachers who seem to be able to heal the faithful. So how do they do it? Here's a look at some of the most famous faith healers of the last century.

Jim Jones

The Jim Jones parade of miracles was little more than an amateur magic show performed by a team of assistants he created. The "tumors" he removed from people were actually putrefied chicken guts and cow brains. A little sleight of hand on the part of his assistants would make the "tumors" appear to come out of the victims' mouths or anuses. The assistants would also put small dabs of tapioca pudding on tissues that Jones used to wipe the eyes of his victims. He then claimed he had removed their cataracts and used the dirty tissues for evidence. How did he make wheelchair bound people walk? Jones' assistants donned disguises and pretended to be crippled so Jones could miraculously "cure" them. After being cured, the assistants would flee the Temple so no one could get a good look at them. Additionally, Some congregants of the Temple were drugged, so they passed out stiff during services. Jones knew beforehand that the person was going to be slipped a mickey, so he would then predict the person's death and simply wait for the drugs to kick in. When they did, the victim would appear to be lifeless. "Nurses" (actually the assistants again) would try to revive the victim for a while, as Jones would wait until about the time the drug was to wear off and then say his magic words over the person. Not only did this "resurrection" look impressive, but the victim himself would also think Jones had actually saved his life. Jones' assistants also sneaked into the homes of prospective members and made notes of everything they could find about their lives. They would pass this information on to Jones in advance of his meeting with the marks. Jones then pretended to know all these things about the people by means of clairvoyance.

The most outrageous, cruel, and dangerous trick Jones played was another ploy to make the crippled walk. His assistant would spot an elderly person walking around town. The assistant would follow the victim until she was near a staircase and then creep up behind the person and push her down the stairs. As the person was lying dazed at the bottom of the steps the assistant would race around from another direction and say she was a nurse from the Peoples Temple and that she saw some thugs push her down the stairs. The "nurse" would "help" the person by loading her into a car to drive her to the "hospital," which was actually the Temple. She would tell the victim her glasses were broken so the victim would not be able to clearly see the fake equipment and x-rays she got at the fake hospital. The victim would be told she had a broken leg and would be put into a cast. Then after her glasses had been "fixed," she would be told of the marvelous healer, Jim Jones. She would be brought to see Jones who proclaimed her broken bones healed and when her cast was removed she could walk! Again, this was not only an effective show for the sheep in the flock, but the victim was likely to be converted to the Temple as well.

Peter Popoff

In the 1980's Peter Popoff was riding high. He traveled the country healing the sick and raking in millions of dollars per year from the faithful. He could miraculously call out the names of people in his audiences and deduce what was wrong with them without being told. He knew numerous details of their lives such as their relatives' names and their street addresses. He put his hand on the sick and cast out devils. People were so overwhelmed with the miraculous forces he released that they often fell over backward. After the Popoff touch was applied, the people were cured. If they had cancer it disappeared. If they used a wheelchair or a walker they could walk again without them.

So how did he do it? The main ingredients of his success were prayer cards that worshipers filled out upon entering his presentations and a wireless communication set. Popoff's wife would read information from the prayer cards to Popoff while he was on stage. He then repeated the information as if it was coming to him from God. People claiming their cancer was gone were merely taking Popoff's word for it when he told them it was gone. Popoff's people provided wheelchairs to worshipers who had walked into the presentation, so when they got out of them later it was only surprising to those who didn't know the healed persons were not actually wheelchair bound. And people who use walkers can still walk, especially if someone such as Popoff is lending them a helping hand to hold them up.

James Randi, a magician and skeptic who has dedicated much of his life to exposing frauds who claim to have paranormal powers, attended one of Popoff's healing performances with a radio scanner and recorded Mrs. Popoff's transmission to her husband. Randi went on *The Tonight Show* and played a videotape of Popoff's supposed healing with the clandestine transmission he had picked up layered onto the soundtrack. Popoff's trickery was laid bare, and his sheep bolted from his flock. In 1987 Popoff declared bankruptcy.

Having been chastened, Popoff decided to clean up his act and got an honest job. Yeah, right. No, Popoff went back into the God business (he calls himself a "prophet" now) and today is as successful as he ever was. His new shtick is something called "Miracle Spring Water." This water will not only cure any illness you may have, but it will also make you rich. He gives the water away for free on his televised infomercials. Of course, anyone foolish enough to order the water will be bombarded with dozens of mailed requests for money from Popoff's ministry. In 2005 his ministry received over $23 million in donations in the U.S. alone, and that's just a fraction of the take as Popoff runs the Miracle Water ads around the world.

John of God

Step aside all you garden variety faith healers, for John of God is putting you to shame. While the average faith healer may cure hundreds or even thousands of people over the years, John of God is claimed to have cured *tens of millions* of people.

John of God is a former farmer in Brazil whose real name is João Teixeira. He claims to be the reincarnation of a variety of healers throughout history ranging from the biblical King Solomon to the mythical German, Dr. Fritz. These people (including the ones who never even existed) passed on their healing powers to John of God, and he has been generous enough to share his gift with the rest of us. In the 1960's he started healing people and his reputation exploded around the world. Today people travel to Brazil from every part of the globe to feel the healing touch of John of God.

And what a touch that is! John of God's main healing tools are scissors that are invariably shoved up patients' noses, and scalpels that are used to make slashes across their bodies and to scrape the surfaces of their eyeballs. Since John of God single-handedly treats more people than the Mayo clinic, you can bet your session with him will be short. If you're female, you can also be fairly sure you're going to get felt up by John's blessed hands during your examination. Hey, the Lord works in mysterious ways. And just like Jim Jones and Peter Popoff, John of God does not charge money for his wondrous cures. He does prescribe special herbal medicines to his patients, however, for the cost of a few dollars, which really isn't much unless you multiply that by the thousands of people he treats each week.

So how does he do it? Once again we turn to James Randi for insight in this matter. He has explained how the forceps-up-the-nose stunt is actually an old carnival trick that has been performed for years with a nail in the place of the scissors that John of God uses. A little knowledge of how the sinuses are laid out allows the carnie to drive the nail into a person's nose at a seemingly impossible angle. Unlike John of God, however, carnival folk don't claim that this stunt will cure cancer. The old eyeball scrape ploy may well be a matter of coming close to the eye without touching it. Even if the blade did lightly touch the eyeball, it shouldn't cause trouble unless it were to hit the cornea or the lens of the eye, and those are not hard to avoid. In both tricks a local anesthetic may be surreptitiously applied. As for the random cuts on the body, well there's not much of a trick there. A few superficial cuts are not likely to kill anybody, although they are even less likely to cure any chronic disease. Many times John ditches the gross theatrics and does non-invasive miraculous healing. This will require the patient to follow some sort of regimen (invariably involving his herbs) for a lengthy period of time.

Despite the seemingly shady tactics John uses to create his miracles, he has had no trouble finding supporters in the media. In the U.S. alone, Oprah Winfrey, Dr. Mahmet Oz, and ABC's *Primetime Live* news magazine have helped to whip up credulous interest in John of God.

Padre Pio

Padre Pio was an Italian Catholic priest who is most famous for displaying the stigmata of Christ on his hands. For those who don't know, the stigmata are replications of the wounds Jesus incurred during his crucifixion. These wounds are supposed to magically appear on the hands and feet of particularly holy men (and less often, women). There have been hundreds of people ranging from St. Francis of Assisi to Jim Jones who have claimed to have had the stigmata, but Padre Pio is the most famous for being a stigmatic by a good measure.

He first started showing the stigmata in 1911 and continued to display the wounds on his hands until his death in 1968. And don't think Pio's powers were limited to merely displaying the stigmata. He is credited with miraculously healing the deaf and the blind as well. He also was supposed to be clairvoyant, and he could go for super-human lengths of time without food or sleep. The blood in his wounds even miraculously smelled like perfume. Last but not least, he had the ability to bilocate; meaning he could appear in two places simultaneously. He is said to have once appeared in Milwaukee while being in Italy at the same time.

But not everyone was enamored of Padre Pio. Pio's miracles were initially met with skepticism in the Church and he was kept on a very short leash. In the 1920s he was even forbidden from saying mass in public. The founder of Rome's Catholic university hospital referred to him as, "an ignorant and self-mutilating psychopath who exploited people's credulity."

In 1919 Pio purchased a bottle of acid from a local pharmacist, ostensibly for the purpose of sterilizing syringes. He pleaded with the pharmacist to keep the transaction a secret from his brothers at the monastery though there would be no reason to keep the sterilization of needles a secret. This raises the prospect that Pio was using the acid to cause his wounds, or more probably, to irritate his self-inflicted wounds to keep them open. In fact, people around this time did notice that his wounds smelled like acid. It was then that the miracle of perfumed blood occurred as Pio's hands took on the smell of *eau-de-toilette*. Now the skeptical might be inclined to think that this miracle was more likely the handiwork of Coco Chanel than of God, but the tide in the Church was turning in Pio's favor.

Pope Pius XII took a shine to Padre Pio and actively encouraged the faithful to see the miracle monk. So while millions of people were dying in the Holocaust and in World War II, people in Mussolini's Italy flocked to see how God intervened in the world by making Padre Pio's sore hands smell like High Karate. But alas, when John XXIII became pope things went south for Pio.

John had caught Pio's dog and pony show years before he became pope and was—to put it mildly—unimpressed. He referred to Pio's mystical faith as being "almost medieval" and suspected trickery was involved. When he became pope he assigned a monsignor the task of spying on Pio to see what he was up to. His spy made clandestine recordings of Pio and discovered that his wounds were not serious enough to prevent him from associating with numerous women in relationships the pope described as "intimate and incorrect." In 1960 John wrote on the subject of Pio's alleged miracles that he felt "privileged to be free of the contamination which for forty years has clung to hundreds of thousands of souls who have been stupefied and disturbed to an unbelievable degree." He also wrote that Pio "has shown himself to be a straw idol."

But John's pontificate was a short one, and when he was gone the Church's skepticism of Pio went with him. Pope Paul VI returned to the policy of promoting Pio as though he was some sort of holy rock star and even gave him permission to ignore his vow of poverty. Pope John Paul II continued the adoration of Pio after his death, and in 2002 Pio was canonized as St. Pio of Pietrelcina.

James Randi continues to be a force for debunking paranormal and supernatural beliefs today. The James Randi Educational Foundation offers a one million dollar prize for anyone who can demonstrate paranormal abilities under controlled conditions. No one has ever come close to claiming the money.

David Koresh

When Vernon Wayne Howell was born in Houston in 1959, there was little reason to be optimistic about his future. His mother was single, and she was only fifteen years old. Little Vernon was a bad student (possibly due to dyslexia) and dropped out of high school. But he did have a knack for two things, playing the guitar and memorizing large chunks of the Bible. He moved to California to try and become a musician, but met with failure. He also joined his mother's faith, the Church of the Seventh Day Adventists, but got kicked out for being a bad influence on young people. Undeterred, Howell turned to the Branch Davidians in 1981 and found a home there.

So who were the Branch Davidians? Their story starts with the aforementioned Church of the Seventh Day Adventists, a religion with strong apocalyptic elements and a fixation on the Book of Revelation. This faith considers the Roman Catholic Church to be the Antichrist and the United States of America to be a lamb-like beast that will assist the Antichrist at the end of days. In other words, this is not your ordinary Protestant outfit. In the 1920s a Bulgarian immigrant by the name of Victor Houteff broke away from the Adventists when they failed to embrace his interpretation of scripture. He started a new faith called the herd's Rod and in 1935 set up shop in Waco, Texas where he looked forward to the restoration of the Kingdom of David. After he died, his wife Florence took over and predicted that the apocalypse would occur on April 22, 1959. When this failed to pan out, the Shepherd's Rod went down the tubes. The Branch Davidians eventually arose from the ashes of the Shepherd's Rod. They took their name from a line in the Book of Jeremiah, "I will raise unto David a righteous branch." The Davidians obviously saw themselves as that righteous branch. Benjamin Roden (who believed he was the successor to King David) led the Davidians. When he died, his widow Lois Roden took over as prophetess.

Vernon Howell was a nobody when he arrived in Waco, but he soon slept his way to the top when he entered into an affair with Lois, who was a scant fifty-four years older than he was. When she died, a power struggle broke out in the Church between Howell and Rogan's son, George. George Rogan won control of the Davidians and forced Howell out at gunpoint. Only momentarily deterred, Howell and his followers set up their own church elsewhere in Texas. This situation didn't last long though as Howell and seven of his congregants staged a raid on the Davidian complex dressed in camouflage and armed to the teeth. In the ensuing melee, George Roden was shot in the chest and in both hands (hey, the stigmata of Christ!). Howell and his boys were put on trial for attempted murder of course, but they claimed they had merely intended to shoot at trees, and things had gotten out of hand. Only in Texas could anyone buy such an implausible excuse for a game of bullet hockey (although Roden's bizarre behavior including exhuming a corpse for religious purposes probably didn't help.) Howell and his boys were fortunate enough to find enough foolish jurors to escape conviction for their amateur commando raid.

After the shooting, things went from bad to worse for George Roden as he was implicated in an unrelated murder, but was found to be too mentally incompetent to stand trial for it and was incarcerated in a mental institution instead.

With Roden out of the way, Howell took control of the Davidians. He changed his name to David Koresh, naming himself after King David and the Persian ruler Cyrus the Great (called "Koorosh" in the Farsi language). By calling himself "David" he was establishing himself as a messianic figure to the Davidians, and he fancied himself to be a modern Cyrus because the original Cyrus had destroyed the Babylonian Empire, which Koresh considered to be a symbol of the apostate Church. In Koresh's mind, the "apostates" were everyone outside of the Branch Davidians. Koresh proclaimed to the Davidians that he was Christ and an angel, and he claimed he could reveal the secrets of the seven thunders (or seals) of the Book of Revelation.

At first many of the Davidians thought Koresh was crazy, but he gradually won them over with his encyclopedic knowledge of the scriptures and his charismatic ways. He recruited new members with great success in the U.K., Australia, and elsewhere. Members of the Seventh Day Adventist faith were especially fertile ground for Koresh to till. Though his message was his own, it had enough in common with the old parent faith that it didn't sound too terribly strange to people who had been brought up in that tradition.

With Koresh calling the shots, there were some changes in the Branch Davidian culture. First off, Koresh got married. Actually he got married over and over again. He married women right and left; and by "women," I mean girls as young as eleven since any Davidian girl who hit puberty was considered to be ready for marriage with Koresh. He impregnated girls as young as twelve. In addition to his harem of wives in Texas, he also established a dormitory in California where eighteen more of his wives lived. His California neighbors rained on his parade, however, when they notified the cops that one of his brides was a twelve-year-old.

Being a kid in the world of Koresh couldn't have been a lot of fun even if you weren't married to him as he imposed severe punishment for what he considered to be misbehavior. It was not unusual for Koresh to beat children with wooden spoons or to withhold food from them for trivial offenses such as crying.

Koresh also had an interest in armaments. His gun-collecting hobby drew the attention of federal officials after they were tipped off that the Davidians were illegally modifying guns into fully automatic weapons. The government monitored deliveries of four tons of ammunition to Davidians' compound near Waco. And as if that weren't enough, a package sent to the Davidians via UPS broke open before it could be delivered and hand grenades poured out of it. Koresh transformed the Davidian compound itself from a loose assembly of buildings into a single, highly defensible structure the size of a city block complete with underground bunkers and a subterranean network of tunnels.

In March of 1993 the Bureau of Alcohol, Tobacco and Firearms obtained arrest and search warrants to scour the Davidian compound for contraband weapons and explosives. Knowing that the Davidians might resist the warrants, the ATF approached the Davidian compound with more than 100 agents. The Davidians would have none of it, however, and gunfire erupted before a single agent could enter the building. By the time the shooting stopped, twenty agents had been shot—four of them fatally. A number of the Davidian faithful had also been shot and killed, but they had repulsed the ATF and hunkered down for a standoff. The number of law officers swelled as the ATF was reinforced by a large contingent from the FBI. The lawmen laid siege to the Davidians, but they were ready for it as Koresh's apocalyptic theology had been thoroughly beaten into their heads over the years, and a survivalist mentality was entrenched in the community. The Davidians not only had enough weapons and ammunition to invade a small country, but they had generators, fuel, and food stores that could last for months, if not years.

FBI hostage negotiators tried to work with Koresh to end the standoff, but they were in a hopeless position. Koresh clung to his belief that the U.S. was the beast of Revelation that would help to usher in the end of days, so the thought of reaching an agreement with the government was unthinkable to him and his followers. Yet he did agree to surrender on the condition that he be allowed to address the country. Several Christian radio stations agreed to allow Koresh to deliver what turned out to be a rambling speech that lasted nearly an hour, but after his sermon Koresh reneged on his promise to surrender, and the standoff dragged on.

After fifty-one days the feds decided they had had enough of the stalemate and decided to break the Davidian resistance. On April 19, 1993 the FBI approached the compound with armored vehicles that they used to punch gaping holes into the walls of the structure. They then flung non-incendiary teargas canisters into the holes. The government forces knew the Davidians had gasmasks that could withstand a teargas bombardment for forty-eight hours, so they planned to gas them over and over again during the coming days until they would be forced to surrender.

But Koresh decided it was Armageddon time. He ordered his men to pour fuel all over the compound and then to set it afire. The FBI had sneaked microphones into the building that recorded his followers reacting with shock to his orders, but they did it anyway. Once the fires were set they spread rapidly. Davidians who tried to run away from the flames were shot down by Koresh's men who tried to make sure there would be no survivors. Many of those who didn't die in the smoke, flames, and gunfire were killed when the burning building collapsed upon them. The law enforcement officials surrounding the compound had no firefighting equipment with them and could only watch as the devastation unfolded before their eyes.

Not all of the Davidians in the compound died in the fire. Eight of those who escaped were later convicted of crimes ranging from violations of weapons laws to voluntary manslaughter for their parts in the affair. The way the law enforcement agencies handled the raid and siege also came under scrutiny. There is little doubt that the ATF and the FBI could have handled things better, but numerous rightwing groups went beyond criticizing the feds for bad planning and execution of the raid and accused them of wholesale murder. They rejected the notion that the Davidians had immolated themselves and instead accused the government of slaughtering innocent people in cold blood who only wished to exercise their right to bear arms. They accused the government in general, and Attorney General Janet Reno in particular, of deliberately setting the fire that consumed the compound.

In 1994 conservative radio icon and convicted Watergate burglar, G. Gordon Liddy further fanned the flames when he admonished his listeners to kill ATF agents, "Now if the (ATF) comes to disarm you and they are bearing arms, resist them with arms. Go for a head shot; they're going to be wearing bulletproof vests. They've got a big target there, ATF. Don't shoot at that, because they've got a vest on underneath that. Head shots, head shots…kill the sons of bitches!" When objections were raised over his remarks he pulled out the classic it-was-taken-out-of-context excuse. Then, in a letter dated April 13, 1995 Executive Vice-President of the National Rifle Association, Wayne LaPierre called law enforcement agents "jackbooted government thugs" who threaten to "take away our constitutional rights, break in our doors, destroy our property, and even kill us." Six days later, a man named Timothy McVeigh commemorated the second anniversary of the Waco fire by driving a truck filled with homemade explosives to the Alfred P. Murrah Federal Building in Oklahoma City and detonating it. His terrorist bombing left 168 people dead—about twice the number that had died at Waco. Amongst his victims were nineteen small children who attended a daycare center in the building.

235

The accusations against the government became so overwhelming in the aftermath of the siege and fire that it almost seemed like Koresh himself became a forgotten figure in the whole ordeal, but his remaining followers were still devoted to him. They came to believe that Koresh would return as the messiah 1,335 days after his death. And he wasn't going to be shy about it either. He would come back riding upon a white horse, slaughtering the wicked right and left. The magical 1,335th day arrived on Friday, December 13, 1996. A look at the news from that day shows that Janet Reno was about to be nominated for a second term as Attorney General, but the mainstream media makes no mention of an equestrian smiting of the damned. Even today, there are those whose faith in Koresh remains unbent and who still await his eventual resurrection.

If you think that gun-crazy, Christian fringe groups died out with David Koresh you can guess again. Case-in-point: the Hutaree.

The Hutaree are a paramilitary group based in southern Michigan. They consider themselves to be Christian warriors and believe the arrival of the Antichrist is right around the corner. They are heavily into combat training and have even posted videos of themselves on the Internet going through maneuvers while decked out in camouflage and brandishing military-style rifles. They hate the U.S. government (of course) and advocate creating something called the "Christian Colonial Republic" to replace the United States.

Now a bunch of guys playing army in the woods may seem pretty laughable, but the Hutaree are genuinely dangerous group. In March of 2009 numerous law enforcement agencies swept in on the Hutaree and arrested nine of their members. Unbeknownst to the Hutaree, an undercover agent had infiltrated their organization and discovered their plans for a terrorist attack. The group was allegedly plotting to place a phony 911 emergency call and then to ambush and kill the responding police officer. As awful is this was, it was only a prelude to the real attack as the Hutaree were plotting to use the slain officer as bait to kill more cops. They knew that the funeral of the fallen officer would draw in hundreds of law enforcement officials. They intended to charge into the funeral procession firing guns and propelled explosives to take down as many of the grieving cops as they could.

In 2012, however, the defendants were acquitted of the most serious charges.

Jerry Falwell

Born in 1933 to parents who were religiously indifferent, Jerry Falwell would not have seemed a likely candidate to become arguably the most significant religious leader in the United States of his generation. There was little in his youth to indicate this either as he was a rowdy, brawling kid who paid scant attention to religious matters. That all changed one day in 1952 when a fire-and-brimstone preacher touched the teenaged troublemaker in a way that would change his life.

After Falwell's on-the-spot conversion to the Baptist faith that day, he dropped out of the college he was attending and enrolled at the Baptist Bible College in Missouri to set about on his path to serve the Lord. He was ordained a minister in 1956 and soon thereafter started a tiny Church in his hometown of Lynchburg, Virginia. The young pastor gave lively sermons, and his church quickly grew. It would eventually become one of the largest churches in the entire country.

There was a general notion in those days that the affairs of state were not to be bandied about in Sunday sermons, and Falwell initially went along with that convention. He once said, "preachers are not called to be politicians, but soul winners." As things turned out, he would live to regret having said those words. His gradual conversion from a standard preacher to a political firebrand seems to have begun in 1954 when the U.S. Supreme Court made its landmark *Brown v. Board of Education* ruling, which mandated that racial segregation in American schools must end. Falwell was incensed by the decision. In 1958 he preached to his flock, "If Chief Justice Warren and his associates had known God's word, I am quite confident that the 1954 decision would never have been made... The facilities should be separate. When God has drawn a line of distinction, we should not attempt to cross that line." Pretty rich stuff, but Falwell wasn't finished. "The true Negro does not want integration.... He realizes his potential is far better among his own race... (Integration) will destroy our race eventually. In one northern city a pastor friend of mine tells me that a couple of opposite race live next door to his church as man and wife." The horrors! And by way, what is a "false" Negro?

Needless to say, the 1960's were not too much to Falwell's taste either. The civil rights movement was unbearable to him; in fact he called it the "civil wrongs" movement. He still railed against civil rights as he had in the '50s, but unlike then, when he was limited to damning the Supreme Court only before his Sunday church audience, he now had a new medium at his disposal. He had been one of the earliest preachers to see the potential of T.V., both to spread his message of love and as a cash-raising tool. He used his television show, *The Old Time Gospel Hour*, to blast the civil rights movement. He invited prominent segregationists onto the program to extol their views, and he castigated the civil rights movement's leaders. He said, "I do question the sincerity and nonviolent intentions of some civil rights leaders such as Dr. Martin Luther King, Jr... and others, who are known to have left-wing associations."

In 1973 the *Roe v. Wade* decision, which legalized abortion across the U.S., was the last straw for Falwell. He saw the government as the enemy of Christendom, and he set out to do everything he could to obliterate the line between church and state. In 1976 he began a tour of the country he called "I Love America" which was designed to promote socially conservative candidates for public office. In 1978 he threw himself into beauty pageant contestant-turned rabid anti-homosexual activist Anita Bryant's campaign against gay rights in Florida. He ominously warned America that "acknowledged homosexuals" were allowed to teach in public schools. It should be mentioned, however, that Falwell didn't want public schools to exist at all as is evidenced in his comment, "I hope I live to see the day when, as in the early days of our country, we won't have any public schools. The churches will have taken them over again and Christians will be running them. What a happy day that will be!"

All of this culminated in Falwell's creation of the Moral Majority in 1979. The new organization was unambiguous in its mission. It would push to elect politicians who were deemed to have the moral values that Falwell considered critical to good Christians including staunch opposition to homosexuality and unbridled support for military expenditures. The 1980 presidential election was the first big proving ground for the Moral Majority. The group worked hard in support of Ronald Reagan, and he viewed them as such a critical part of his following that he felt compelled to explain himself to Falwell when he picked George

Bush (whom the group wasn't nuts about) to be his running mate. The election resulted in a big win for Reagan over Jimmy Carter and Falwell was quick to take credit for it. A lot of people on both sides of the aisle agreed with that assessment, though how much of a role Falwell really played in Reagan's victory is debatable. The next year Reagan was again compelled to explain himself to Falwell when he picked Sandra Day O'Connor to fill a vacancy on the Supreme Court. The man who had been so incensed by previous Supreme Court rulings had now risen to the point where the president had to get his blessing for his nominees. Not everyone was enamored with Falwell's growing power, however. The slogan "The Moral Majority is neither" became commonplace, and it wasn't just liberals who were concerned about the preacher. The 1960's conservative standard bearer, Barry Goldwater was so disturbed by the O'Connor episode that he said, "I think every good Christian ought to kick Falwell right in the ass."

In 1985 Falwell made a visit to South Africa, which was then still ensconced in the apartheid era. On his visit, Falwell did nothing to make people forget about his segregationist past. He slammed those who were trying to pressure the country into dropping its crushing racial discrimination by encouraging American divestment from South Africa. In this, he was consistent with President Reagan's highly controversial policy of engaging with South Africa despite apartheid, but Falwell went farther than Reagan. He urged his followers to purchase South African Krugerrands to try and counteract the effects of the divestment campaigns. He also trashed the Noble Peace Prize-winning Archbishop Desmond Tutu, calling him a "phony." As he had during the civil rights era in the American South, he claimed that it was he who knew what South Africa's blacks really wanted. In 1989 George Bush became president, and he reversed the Reagan policy of engagement with South Africa. South Africa dropped its apartheid policy soon afterward.

That same year the Moral Majority was disbanded. Falwell claimed this was due to its having completed its mission, but in truth the organization was beset with money problems. Financial problems were also plaguing Liberty University, a school Falwell had founded to promote his brand of Christian values. The reverend turned to an unlikely source for relief, Sun Young Moon (see later chapter about him). The leader of the

"Moonies" organization bailed out the college to the tune of $3.5 million. Falwell happily took the money.

To make matters worse for Falwell, in 1993 a Democrat moved into the White House. Falwell wasn't about to take this development lying down, so the next year he started making appeals to his followers to send money to "help me produce a national television documentary which will expose shocking new facts about Bill Clinton." Falwell then secretly paid $200,000 to a group called Citizens For Honest Government (CFHG), which used the money to produce a program called *The Clinton Chronicles*. This faux-documentary was a catalogue of wild accusations against President Bill Clinton. Among the charges in the video was the allegation that Clinton had provided protection for a cocaine smuggling ring while he was Governor of Arkansas. The charge spread like wildfire on conservative radio shows and then found its way into the conventional media. The hullabaloo led to an investigation conducted by the House Banking committee, which cost taxpayers millions of dollars and found no evidence of Clinton being involved in coke smuggling. The video also made the claim that Clinton was a murderer. It even went so far as to warn the President that if any of the people involved in the creation of the video were to turn up dead, everyone would know they had been killed by the president. One of the people Clinton was supposed to have murdered was former White House Counsel, Vincent Foster. Two Arkansas state troopers appeared in the video to support the murder charges, but they later admitted they had been paid to make those statements. The CFHG also paid numerous other individuals to make similar claims about the president in mainstream publications around the country.

Falwell was not only bankrolling the smear campaign, he was its head cheerleader as well. He promoted the video heavily on *The Old Time Gospel Hour* and even ran a special program touting it. In his infomercial, he interviewed an investigative reporter who was so afraid of being killed by Clinton that he had to be interviewed in shadow. The reporter told the chilling tale of how a number of Clinton's enemies had died in plane crashes with the clear implication that Clinton was orchestrating the disasters. Falwell promised to pray for the reporter's safety.

The identity of the "reporter" in the shadows was eventually discovered to be Patrick Matrisciona who, in a shocking coincidence, was also the president of the CFHG. In an interview with *Salon* Matrisciona later admitted, "Obviously, I'm not a reporter, and I doubt our lives were actually ever in danger. That was Jerry's idea to do that... He thought it would be dramatic."

It was also rather dramatic when in 1999 Falwell irrevocably turned himself into a laughingstock when he assailed the children's television show *Teletubbies* for secretly promoting a homosexual agenda to toddlers. He claimed that a character on the show named Tinky Winky was gay because he had a triangular antenna on his head, he carried a purse, and he was colored purple, which was pretty gay in Falwell's world.

But what Falwell will probably be best remembered for are his comments made following the terrorist attacks carried out against the United States on September 11, 2001. With the nation still in shock over the deaths of thousands of people killed in the senseless slaughter, Falwell chose to exploit the attacks as an opportunity to push his hatred of Americans with different ideas than his own. Appearing with Pat Robertson (see later chapter on him) on *The 700 Club,* Falwell blamed the attacks on homosexuals, pagans, feminists, The American Civil Liberties Union, The People for the American Way, abortionists, and secularists. "I point the finger in their face and say you helped this happen," he concluded while Robertson readily agreed. After his comments drew outrage across the country, Falwell backed down in a most unconvincing way. The next day he said, "I would never blame any human being except the terrorists, and if I left that impression with gays or lesbians or anyone else, I apologize." So that whole pointing of the finger in their faces stuff was not Falwell blaming anyone, it was just you misinterpreting his words. Years later, however, Falwell reiterated his belief that the Lord had withdrawn his protection of America on the day of that attack because of people's actions that he didn't approve of.

In 2007 age and obesity caught up with Falwell as he keeled over dead in his office at Liberty University. His funeral figured to be a grand sendoff for the man who had swept Reagan into office and turned America's Christian conservatives into the base of the

Republican Party. The funny thing was, however, that the people who supposedly owed so much to Falwell didn't show up for his funeral. Reagan administration officials stayed away, as did every one of the aspirants for the 2008 Republican presidential nomination. Senators and representatives couldn't be bothered to make the short trip from Washington D.C. to Virginia. President George W. Bush blew off the funeral as well, as did every significant member of his staff. But he did send Tim Goeglein, a deputy director of public liaison specializing in relations with religious conservatives, to represent the administration. The most noteworthy group that did turn up for the funeral was the worshipers of the Westboro Baptist Church, which will be covered more in the forthcoming chapter about Fred Phelps.

The bizarre saga that was the life of Jerry Falwell never ceases to lose its ability to shock. Take this charming little tale about his dad taken from his book *Strength for the Journey: An Autobiography*

There were times that Dad's pranks bordered on cruelty. One of his oil-company workers, a one-legged man he nicknamed "Crip" Smith, complained about everything. Dad and Crip's co-workers got tired of the old man's bellyaching and decided to take revenge. One morning Crip called in sick and Dad volunteered to send by lunch to his grateful but suspicious employee. Dad and his chums caught Crip's old black tomcat, killed it, skinned it, and cooked it in the kitchen of one of Dad's little restaurants. They called it squirrel meat and delivered it to Crip on a linen-covered tray. When Crip returned to work the next morning, Dad and his co-conspirators asked him how he liked his meal. They knew he would complain even about a free home-cooked lunch, and when Crip called it "the toughest squirrel meat" he had ever eaten, they were glad to tell him why.

I'm glad this prank only bordered on cruelty and didn't go all the way to actual cruelty.

The Tinky Winky Fiasco was by no means the first time conservative Christians had seen the specter of homosexual indoctrination in pre-school entertainment. The people who bring you *Sesame Street* have been fending off complaints from such people for decades. It seems the faithful are convinced the Bert and Ernie characters are a gay couple, and rumors of their impending wedding arise regularly. In 1994 the Reverend Joseph Chambers of North Carolina tried to get Bert and Ernie banned from television with the use of an obscure anti-gay law. He failed.

Bhagwan Shree Rajneesh (a.k.a. Osho)

Chandra Mahan Jain was a rather unspectacular philosophy professor in India until he decided he was particularly enlightened and therefore qualified to be a spiritual guru. He changed his name to Bhagwan Shree Rajneesh and began preaching an unusual brand of religion. His teachings were scattershot, hard to describe, and often contradictory. He hated socialism and Mahatma Gandhi. He said that "God is the greatest fiction created by cunning priests," but the name he chose for himself means "divine one," and his followers were adamant that they were a legitimate religion. He claimed he was telepathic and said he was the "beginning of the new man." He advocated free love and claimed to have sex with hundreds of women—all of them his followers. He rejected the traditional Hindu belief in reincarnation, but nevertheless told women they could obtain benefits in their future lives by having sex with him. He also believed in smuggling and tax evasion. When the Indian authorities closed in on him he relocated to the United States.

Arriving in Oregon in 1981, Rajneesh modestly announced, "I am the messiah America has been waiting for!" About 2,000 of his followers quickly joined him in Oregon. To house everyone, the group bought a run-down, 64,000-acre plot of land called Big Muddy Ranch, which his followers (called Sannyasins) rechristened "Rancho Rajneesh." There they set about to build a utopian society based on Rajneesh's teachings. They gave all their money to Rajneesh and often severed ties with their families when they joined him. They dressed in red clothing and wore necklaces holding Rajneesh's picture. Free love was practiced at the ranch, but Rajneesh had prophesied that two thirds of the world's population was going to die from AIDS, so in order to halt the spread of the disease he banned kissing amongst his followers and required that people having sex wear both condoms and rubber gloves. Every room in Rancho Rajneesh was bugged to ensure that no one was getting out of line. Though Rajneesh despised socialism, he set up a communal living system in which his followers were made to toil in the ranch's fields for long hours, seven days a week. They were not paid for their work and were not usually permitted to have cars.

Rajneesh on the other hand did have cars, Rolls-Royces to be specific. His meditation led him to the conclusion that he should be the world record holder for owning the most Rolls-Royces, so he collected them obsessively. He eventually accumulated a staggering ninety-three of the vehicles. Not that he wasn't willing to share them with his followers, mind you. Every day the Sannyasins would have to take a break from their toiling in the fields and line up along a dirt road while the divine one would whisk past them in one of his British luxury automobiles. If you caught a glimpse of the new messiah as he rolled past, then that would be the highlight of your day. Rajneesh also demanded other outrageous extravagances such as lavish jewelry and watches for himself. And he had a taste for substance abuse. He took large amounts of Valium and inhaled nitrous oxide (better know as laughing gas) like it was going out of style.

With so much of Rajneesh's attention devoted to keeping himself pampered and inebriated, he had to delegate some of his authority at the ranch. He chose a woman named Ma Anand Sheela to be his chief of staff and to generally run the commune. Sheela was an unfortunate selection because she was a hot tempered, vulgar tyrant who had little respect for humanity.

Her first order of duty was to build and expand living areas at the ranch. There were land use laws that stymied her efforts to get this done, however. To get around them, she tried to incorporate a new city where the ranch was located. The new town was to be called "Rajneeshpuram," but she ran into opposition when she tried to create it. An environmental group called 1000 Friends of Oregon opposed the plan. When Sheela's attempts to bribe them into submission failed, she went to war with them. Eventually her fight expanded to include just about everyone in the state. She publicly insulted her enemies and had Rajneesh's followers harass them. But none of this was getting her anywhere. The Sannyasins then moved a bunch of people into the nearby town of Antelope, which had a population of less than one hundred. With so few people in town, the Sannyasins quickly outvoted the locals and took over the local government.

But the legal fights went on without interruption. Rajneesh pressured Sheela to secure a safe base for his followers who now numbered some 7,000 in Rajneeshpuram. Sheela's cruelty and vindictiveness weren't accomplishing anything, so in 1984 she escalated her war on the people of Oregon by poisoning them. She sent Sannyasins to infect a political rally and the Wasco County courthouse with salmonella. Apparently just for fun they also tried to hit other targets such as a grocery store and a nursing home. The attacks apparently failed, however, as there were no news reports of anyone being sickened by salmonella. Undaunted, Sheela ordered that a more virulent strain of salmonella be found for future attacks. She then successfully had two Wasco County commissioners poisoned as they inspected the commune, and they became violently ill.

Rajneesh came up with the idea of taking control of the Wasco County board of commissioners, and Sheela was given the task of making it happen. A Sannyasin was selected to run for the board without disclosing her affiliation to Rajneesh. Sheela wasn't going to leave the outcome of the election to chance, however, so she came up with a two-pronged approach to ensure that her clandestine candidate would win.

First, she tried to suppress the vote by poisoning as many people as she could. The Sannyasins poisoned salad bars at ten restaurants with salmonella. This time their operation was a success. More than 750 people went to emergency rooms with salmonella poisoning. The sick included very small children who are especially at danger from such an illness. This was the largest biological terrorist attack in American history. However, authorities didn't put together that it was an attack until a year later as they assumed that poor hygiene practices had occurred simultaneously at ten different places, so no immediate attempt was made to find the poisoners.

The second part of Sheela's cunning plan was to stuff ballot boxes with votes for her candidate. To accomplish this, she sent buses across the United States to pick up and bring back as many homeless people as could be carried. The transients were offered free food and beer if they agreed to travel to Oregon. About 2,000 people took advantage of the offer. As soon as they arrived in Rajneeshpuram, they were forced to fill out voter registration forms. Problems with the plan arose right away, however. The people they had bussed in weren't exactly mentally stable in many cases, and fights broke out frequently. The Sannyasins tried to remedy this by slipping sedatives into the beer kegs they had provided for their new voters. Then it became apparent that this army of the unwashed would not be allowed to vote in the election anyway. No longer having any need for their homeless horde, the Sannyasins packed them back onto the buses and dumped them into the neighboring communities under the cover of darkness. The next morning the people of eastern Oregon awoke to find their little communities swarming with street people from across the nation. The state of Oregon was eventually forced to bus everyone back to where they came from at a cost of $100,000.

Despite Sheela's insidious attempts at manipulating the electoral process, the Sannyasins were still going nowhere with their legal battles. Sheela pulled out new tricks in an effort to disrupt the legal system. She considered flying a plane loaded with explosives into the Wasco County Courthouse, but dropped the idea. She and an accomplice sneaked into the office of the Wasco County planner and set fire to it in hopes the files he needed for his proceedings against them would be destroyed, but the fire was put out before it did much damage to the office. And of course, there were always people who needed to be poisoned. At a hearing looking into the Sannyasin practice of wiretapping, one of the witnesses was poisoned with a substance that caused her jaw to freeze up during her testimony. The Sannyasins lost the case anyway and were slapped with million-dollar judgment. They also tried to poison a woman suing the group for a $1.7 million loan they had not repaid. But this attack failed, and they lost that case as well.

Rajneesh kept in close contact with Sheela. She frequently tape-recorded their conversations as proof of her special place in the community. During one of their chats he told her that if ten thousand people had to die to save a single enlightened master, then so be it. An execution list was then drawn up. It included numerous people who were investigating the Sannyasins, but unknown to Rajneesh, it also included some of his closest confidants. Sheela wanted to solidify her grip on power within the group and she took advantage of the occasion to get rid of her rivals. Her assassins managed to bungle every one of the execution attempts, however. Only one person, Rajneesh's personal doctor who went by the name of Swami Devoraj, came close to death. He was injected with a syringe full of adrenaline and barely survived the assault. But he did survive, and the attempt on his life shook the group to its foundations. Sheela's support within the commune crumbled, so she and twenty of her accomplices fled to Germany. Rajneesh, probably reeling from her betrayal, called a press conference in which he condemned her.

The blame for the attacks fell on Sheela, but Rajneesh wasn't off the hook either. He had lied to get into the country, and his immigration status was in doubt. There were a lot of other issues facing him as well, so he decided to make a run for the Caribbean, but he only made it as far as North Carolina before the feds caught up with him. When he was arrested he was carrying jewels, a handgun, and a large amount of cash. He was convicted of felony immigration offenses, given a ten-year suspended sentence, fined $400,000, and deported. Twenty-one countries refused to accept him before he finally ended up in India again. He never apologized to any of the victims of his religion.

Back in India, things didn't go much better for Rajneesh. He distanced himself from his disgrace in America by changing his name to Osho. He remained hopelessly addicted to drugs and even had nitrous oxide spigots installed next to his bed. He was so out of it that he would sometimes urinate in the halls of his home. He carried an intense grudge against the United States, which he felt had treated him unfairly. He said Americans were "sub-human" and a collection of his lectures from the late '80s was published under the title *Jesus Crucified Again, This Time by Ronald Reagan's America*. He died in 1990 at the age of fifty-eight.

Sheela was extradited from Germany to the U.S., and she spent two and a half years in prison for her various crimes. Today she lives in Switzerland.

All the drug abuse, bizarre behavior, greed, terrorism, and attempted murder haven't done much to dampen the enthusiasm for Osho's special brand of enlightenment. He is hailed today as one of the fathers of the New Age movement. Many of the 650 books he allegedly wrote remain popular, and there is a complex called a "Multiversity" in India that is dedicated to promoting his teachings. The Osho website lists a huge number of Osho meditation centers around the world including about forty in the United States, so sub-humans can still bask in the glow of Rajneesh's wisdom.

Rajneesh/Osho wasn't the only Indian religious import into the United States. The Hare Krishna faith migrated into the U.S. in the middle of the twentieth century and is still practiced here today. One of its leaders was Swami Bhaktipada who earned his own place in infamy.

Born Keith Ham in 1937, Bhaktipada joined the Krishna movement and became a swami in 1967. He set up a magnificent palace called New Vrindaban on a 4,000-acre site in West Virginia. He adorned the palace with gold leaf decorations, crystal chandeliers, marble floors, and much more. New Vrindaban grew into the largest Hare Krishna congregation in the United States.

But not all was well at New Vrindaban. One of its members, a man named Charles St. Denis, was murdered in 1983 after he allegedly raped the wife of another member. Even worse, another member named Steve Bryant made accusations that staff members—including Bhaktipada himself—had molested children at the community's school. Bryant was murdered shortly thereafter. The feds took a close look at Bhaktipada and charged him with mail fraud and racketeering for encouraging the two murders. Bhaktipada pled guilty to the most serious of the charges and spent several years in prison. He was excommunicated from the Hare Krishna faith as well. He died in 2011 in India.

Sun Myung Moon

When I was a teenager, I had a job working behind a counter at a rather slow-paced store. One day, a forlorn-looking, young Asian woman entered the store and half-heartedly tried to sell me some cheap paper fans. She told me in a very soft voice with unsure English that they were to benefit the Unification Church. I shook my head at her offer, and she dejectedly slid out the door.

So what is this Unification Church, for which this girl was willing to march all over town, facing endless rejection, in a quest to raise pennies? It all revolves around Sun Myung Moon, who was born in 1920 in Japanese-occupied Korea. Raised a Presbyterian, Moon claimed he was visited by Jesus in 1936. Moon said that Jesus had admitted to him that he had failed in his mission on Earth by getting himself killed before he could start the "True Family." It would now take a new messiah to finish the task of creating the perfect family and also to unite all the world's religions into one. Thankfully for humanity, Moon was up to the job.

But history would get in Moon's way before he could fulfill his duties as the messiah. Soviet troops conquered the part of Korea Moon lived in during World War II. By 1950 he had gotten on enough of the communist authorities' nerves to be shipped off to a labor camp. He languished there for years before he was freed by U.N. troops during the Korean War. He then made his way to South Korea where he started his first Church, which he named The Holy Spirit Association for the Unification of World Christianity. This ungainly title was later pared down to The Unification Church, though virtually everyone outside of the Church refers to its practitioners as "Moonies." The Moonies, in turn, refer to Moon as "Father" since he is supposed to be the patriarch of the perfect family.

In 1960 Moon dumped his wife and married one of his followers. Later that year he arraigned the first blind wedding amongst the faithful. This practice of blind marriages between strangers—which sometimes involve thousands of couples in mass weddings—has become to many people the defining feature of the Moonies. The marriages are supposed to be part of the mission to create pure bloodlines of the faithful, and they serve the additional purpose of eliminating the possibility of premarital sex amongst the couples as people who have never met seldom have a sexual history together. The practice also did wonders to demonstrate Moon's total power over the lives of his followers, who were usually separated from their families and friends and who often gave everything they owned to his Church.

Moon had said that Pyongyang, North Korea, was to be the New Jerusalem in what he said would be the "New Messianic Era," but he gradually started looking away from Korea and toward America. In 1973 he moved the headquarters of the Church to New York City. Moon's relationship with the United States was to be an odd one. He referred to the U.S. as the "kingdom of Satan," yet at the same time he saw the country as the world's only hope in the battle against communism, and he threw himself into supporting conservative American political leaders. In 1973 he took out full-page ads in newspapers such as *The New York Times* and *The Washington Post* declaring that Richard Nixon (then embroiled in the Watergate scandal) had been chosen by God to be president. In the coming months he organized street rallies in America, Europe, and Asia in support of Nixon. Nixon repaid the favor by inviting Moon to the White House where he gave him a big hug.

But why buy ads in newspapers when, for a few bucks more, you can start your own paper that broadcasts your message every day? In 1982 Moon founded *The Washington Times*, a daily love letter to America's political right. The paper and its sister publication, *Insight* Magazine, have "broken" numerous false stories that were picked up by other right-wing media outlets and became mantras of conservative thought in America. A couple of examples of this were the false tales that Iraq's non-existent weapons of mass-destruction were sent to Syria for safe keeping after Iraq was invaded by the United Sates in 2003, and that President Barak Obama was educated in a hardline Islamic madras. Moon went a step further when he purchased the United Press International news service in order to make his feelings felt all over the world, but his takeover of UPI effectively destroyed the organization, and today it is nothing more than an afterthought in the news industry. *Insight* has gone out of publication while the *Washington Times* is hanging on, despite the massive financial hemorrhaging it has incurred since its inception due to Moon's willingness to cover its losses. The Moon media empire also includes newspapers in South America and Asia. Furthermore, he bought a cable T.V. network called The Nostalgia Channel (now called ALN) and suffered years of losses on it before selling it to an evangelist.

Moon's news empire might not be winning many Pulitzer Prizes, but that doesn't mean it doesn't have its fans. President George Bush gushed over the *Washington Times* saying, "Normally, when I think of the Washington beltway press corps, I think of, well, I'm not going to say it. Wouldn't be prudent. But when I think of the *Washington Times* I think of a publication that has brought much needed balance to the way the way Washington is covered these days." Perhaps it was the *Times* story that claimed that Bush's 1988 opponent, Michael Dukakis, was insane that won him over.

In the wake of the Iran-Contra scandal in the 1980's, Moon founded The American Freedom Coalition to drum up popular support for Oliver North, who was one of the scandal's core conspirators. The group spent millions of dollars on its mission and distributed thirty million pieces of campaign literature on behalf of conservative candidates in the 1988 campaign season before it quietly went away.

The same year that Moon founded the *Times* he was convicted of tax evasion and was eventually sentenced to eighteen months in prison. These charges had been brewing since 1978, when a congressional investigation found that the Moonies had been systematically violating U.S. tax laws and were also attempting to infiltrate the American Congress on behalf of South Korean intelligence.

The early '80s would turn out to be a busy time for Moon. In addition to founding the *Washington Times* and being busted by the law, he threw himself into the world of film and released the legendary box office bomb *Inchon,* which was based on the Korean War and was financed by Moon. The Church tried to keep Moon's connection with the film secret, but word got out, and protesters showed up at screenings of the movie. Unfortunately for Moon, protesters were about the only people who showed up at theaters as the movie earned less than $2 million in its North American release. This was not quite enough to cover the $42 million budget for the flick. The picture would likely have been a commercial failure even without its poisonous connection to the Moonies, however, as it was trashed by critics from coast to coast. Surprisingly, even the *Washington Times* gave it a bad review. The movie was triumphant at the Golden Raspberry Awards, however, as it "won" the awards for worst picture, director, actor, and screenplay of 1981.

After his release from prison for the tax evasion rap, Moon laid low and let the *Washington Times* do the talking for him. In the 1990's he soured on the United States and spent a great deal of his time living in South America. He denigrated the U.S.A. in sermons he made at the time. He said, "God hates the American Atmosphere." He called the U.S. a hell on Earth created by Satan. He compared American women to prostitutes and trashed America's tolerance of homosexuals, who he referred to as "dung-eating dogs." But not all hope was lost because at least there are Asians in America. "In the Last Days, it is natural that Western women will long for Oriental men, and Western men will long for Oriental women" Moon said. "Orientals are here to save your nation of America."

But sadly for Americans, he wasn't quite done with the country. As long as there was business to conduct, Moon would be there to do it. He quietly took a seafood company called True Foods and built it into a giant in the sushi industry. The company is so dominant in fact, that it supplies most of America's sushi restaurants. He also made a killing by collecting tax dollars from the U.S. government through a vast number of front companies he started. These firms supposedly provide services ranging from abstinence-only sex education to homeland security. He even got government funding for a company he owned that was allegedly building a device for communication with the dead. Moon's extensive political connections left him well placed to get such largesse sent his way. He also held huge commercial interests in his native Korea; yet most of Moon's revenues were thought to come from his business interests in Japan. And Moon probably needed the money, as the *Washington Times* wasn't the only money pit he had going. It's thought that most of Moon's business ventures in the United States were cash burners, and he persisted with them in an effort to earn credibility for himself and his faith.

In 1998 Moon's daughter-in-law, Nansook Hong, published a book called *In The Shadow of the Moons: My Life in the Reverend Sun Myung Moon's Family*. The book was a tell-all concerning her disastrous marriage to Moon's eldest son, Hyo Jin Moon. She was married to the younger Moon in one of his dad's infamous mass weddings and soon found him to be an abusive, unfaithful, drug addict. Hyo Jin Moon died of heart failure in 2008 at the age of forty-five. The book also describes Sun Myung Moon's extensive dealings in money laundering, his rampant sexual relationships (which were said to be part of some type of a "purification" ritual,) and the distant relationships he had with his many children. Hong appeared on the news magazine *60 Minutes* to lay out these charges against the True Father and was joined on the broadcast by one of Moon's estranged daughters, Un Jin Moon, who backed up her story. Remember, Sun Myung Moon's divine mission as the messiah was to create the perfect family.

After the turn of the century, Moon ramped up his efforts toward unifying all the world's faiths. Part of this effort was to get rid of the Christian cross. He implored churches to tear down their crosses, and astonishingly, a few of them in the American South complied with his request. On Easter Sunday, 2003 Moon held a burial ceremony for a cross in Jerusalem.

In 2004 Moon and his wife were coroneted in an elaborate ceremony in the Dirksen Senate Office Building in Washington D.C. Several congressmen were on hand as Moon and his wife were crowned king and queen of god-knows-what. Most of the congressmen present later said they had been duped into attending the event. That may be, but two of them actually participated in the bizarre event by presenting the Moons with a crown and robes as part of the ceremony.

Moon's son, Preston, took control of the *Washington Times* in 2006 and decided to try and right the paper's financial ship by laying off scads of staff members and cutting coverage of things like sports that were outside the paper's right-wing mission. He hoped to sell the paper to finally stop its drain on his family's fortune. When he finally did sell it in 2010, however, the buyer turned out to be none other than his dear old dad, who paid the princely sum of one dollar for the esteemed publication. It was expected that the elder Moon would turn the money spigots back on again at the paper.

In 2012 Moon died. The issue of what will become of his empire after his death remains. The Church side of the family business seems to have been dead in the water for some time. By many accounts, the number of the faithful has been dwindling for a long while, and it's rather hard to imagine the Church picking up steam after the loss of their messiah. The business side of Moon's holdings is more interesting. He controlled a vast fortune, but much of it revolved around his personal charisma and political contacts. Whether his children can hold together his financial empire after his death is an open question. Moon, for his part, has promised to lead the Church from beyond the grave.

Speaking of things from beyond the grave, in 2003 Moon revealed that he had communicated with all of America's deceased presidents. Wow! Can you imagine what it would be like to talk today with George Washington, Thomas Jefferson, Abraham Lincoln, and all the rest? What would they say? Well, as it turns out the only thing any of them are interested in is how great Sun Myung Moon is. Moon, in his infinite modesty, made their alleged comments available for the world to enjoy.

George Washington: "I realize that the American people are blessed by the mere fact that the Messiah is present on American soil. Yet, they appear unable to realize this deeply. I am deeply distressed over this."

Thomas Jefferson: "People of America, rise again. Return to the nation's founding spirit. Follow the teachings of Rev. Sun Myung Moon, the Messiah to all people, who has appeared in Korea."

Abraham Lincoln: "I am making a request to the people of America because I love you with an earnest heart. Rev. Sun Myung Moon has appeared as the Messiah and the True Parent of humankind."

Teddy Roosevelt: "When I listened to lectures on Rev. Moon's Divine Principle and Unification Thought here in the spirit world, I was so moved that I feel an ever-growing urge to be resurrected on earth every day."

It's not just dead presidents who swoon over Moon. The Bush family had an affinity for the man that defies belief. Oddly, none of this ever damaged the Bushes' standing with the Christian conservative voters in their electoral base. Here are a few examples of Bush–Moon ties…

President George Bush: In addition to the glowing comments about the *Washington Times* mentioned earlier that Bush made to a reception honoring Moon and his fish wrapper, Bush took in over $2 million in contributions from Moon and has traveled extensively on his behalf.

Neil Bush: Neil is the son of George Bush and the brother of President George W. Bush. He has sucked up $1 million in contributions from Moon for an education company he runs. Neil Bush has also traveled extensively with Moonie officials and with Moon himself.

President George W. Bush: Dubya accepted a $250,000 contribution from Moon to help pay for his second inaugural gala. He also endorsed a Moonie leader to head a U.N. food program.

After the Bushes die they will no doubt have many more wonderful things to say about Moon from the great beyond.

What the Hell???

Make a Joyful Noise Unto the Lord!

Religion has always been closely affiliated with music. Here are some of the more notable stories of holy (and unholy) hit makers.

The Singing Nun

In 1963 the U.S. pop charts were topped by the unlikely spectacle of a Belgian nun named Janine (or Jeanine, or Jeanne) Deckers strumming her guitar while singing in French. Her song "Dominique" was a tribute to St. Dominic who we met earlier in this book in the saga of the Cathars. The tune was lame enough to make Justin Bieber look like a death metal act, but this was the early '60s when the listening public's tolerance for twee was higher than it was during say, the Guns N' Roses era. It was able to stay at number one for four straight weeks in America and was a smash hit in the rest of the world as well.

Deckers was billed as the "Singing Nun" in America and as "Soeur Sourire" pretty much everywhere else. The "nun" part was a slight misnomer, as Deckers had not taken her vows when "Dominique" came out, and as it turned out, she never would. She grew disillusioned with the Church and dropped out of her convent in 1967. That same year she released a song called *La Pilule d'Or* (The Golden Pill), which was a tribute to birth control. Needless to say, this was one of the issues where she and the Church did not see eye to eye.

Sadly for Deckers, her pill song flopped, and she was doomed to go down in music history as a one-hit wonder. After her musical career went into the toilet, Deckers opened a school for autistic children in Belgium. She revived her singing career in 1982 by releasing a fresh version of "Dominique" set to a monotonous techno-disco beat in an attempt to update the song for the '80s. She even made a video for it. While this song could be considered a laughable piece of kitsch, the story behind it was anything but funny.

The Belgian government had slapped Deckers with a gigantic bill for back taxes they said she owed from her rock star days. Deckers argued that she shouldn't owe any taxes because she had given all the money she had made to her convent, but she had no proof she had done so. The matter left her destitute and her hackneyed comeback was a desperate attempt to keep the wolf from the door. When that failed, she and her longtime companion Anne Pécher, committed suicide by ingesting large amounts of alcohol and barbiturates.

In 2003 a forty-seven song, two-disk Soeur Sourire "Best of" album was posthumously released. I think it's fair to say that the breadth of this record is stunning for a musician that only had a single hit.

While the Catholic Church now condemns artificial birth control, Deckers was not the only prominent Catholic to ever support it. The thirteenth-century pope John XXI was not only cool with birth control; he actually tried to *invent* it. John was the only physician ever elected pope and in his pre-pontiff days he wrote a book called *Thesaurus Pauperum* that laid out workable contraceptive solutions. When John became pope he ordered the construction of a study/laboratory at the papal apartments so he could conduct his medical work without interruption. Unfortunately for John, the building was poorly put together, and it collapsed while he was in it. He died of his injuries a few days later.

It would almost be unfair to talk about the Singing Nun without mentioning the world's other famous singing nuns.

Maria Von Trapp is surely the most famous of these. The classic film *The Sound of Music* was the true* adaptation of the story of Von Trapp and her family's flight from the Third Reich. Like Deckers, however, Von Trapp never truly was a singing nun because she never took her vows.

Sister Janet Mead on the other hand, is an Australian nun who did take her vows. She was intent on making the Catholic mass more interesting by inserting contemporary music into it. In 1974 she released a "rock" version of "The Lord's Prayer" that was an inexplicably huge hit. This led to a boom in contemporary music being played in church services. So if you find yourself stuck listening to some guitar-strumming, folk music washout during church someday, you now know who you have to blame for it.

* *The Sound of Music* is historically accurate except that in real life Captain Von Trapp was a warm, loving father who encouraged his kids to take up music while Maria was given to fits of rage. She did not need to teach music to the children, as they were already quite good at it when she arrived to work as a governess to one of the kids. There were ten Von Trapp children rather than the seven portrayed in the movie and the movie kids are the wrong genders, ages, and all their names are false. Furthermore, the Von Trapps did not flee from Austria to Switzerland on foot through the mountains with the Nazis in hot pursuit. They simply boarded a train bound for Italy while openly telling people they were going to continue on to America. No one tried to stop them. And this did not happen immediately after the Von Trapps' wedding, as was the case in the movie, but rather eleven years later. Okay, pretty much the whole movie was bunk

The Peters Brothers

In 1966 John Lennon set off a firestorm when he said, "Christianity will go. It will vanish and shrink. I needn't argue with that; I'm right and I will be proved right. We're more popular than Jesus now; I don't know which will go first—rock 'n' roll or Christianity. Jesus was all right, but his disciples were thick and ordinary. It's them twisting it that ruins it for me." For few months no one took any notice of his comment, but after a magazine picked up the quote "We're more popular than Jesus" and printed it out of context, a series of Beatles record burnings took place in the American South. Lennon later clarified his remarks saying, "If I had said television is more popular than Jesus, I might have got away with it, but I just happened to be talking to a friend and I used the words "Beatles" as a remote thing, not as what I think—as Beatles, as those other Beatles like other people see us. I just said 'they' are having more influence on kids and things than anything else, including Jesus." The whole controversy gradually died down.

But the precedent had been set for rock and roll record burnings. In the 1970s Dan and Steve Peters started organizing seminars in which they vilified rock music and held record burnings. By the early '80s they claimed that millions of dollars worth of records had been burned at their seminars.

The artists that the Peters despised ran the gamut of music history. Everyone from the Rolling Stones, to John Denver, to Conway Twitty, to Prince (whom they thought was a group) has been trashed by the Peters boys. Earning the wrath of these evangelists didn't take much. Anyone who lives an immoral life by, say using drugs or supporting gay rights is an evil influence on America's kids—or so they claim. They also claim to hear the influence of the devil in song lyrics and see it in the cover art of various bands.

Other preachers were also trashing rock music, but the Peters lads separated themselves from the others with their assertion that there are secret, subliminal, backward messages imbedded into rock music that are part of the musicians' hidden agendas to corrupt Christian youth. So they spent countless hours spinning records backward listening for the voice of the devil coming out of the noise. They produced two famous examples of this. One was from Led Zeppelin's "Stairway to Heaven," which they claim says "my sweet Satan" when the words "and there's still time" are played in reverse. They also complained that the song says you can buy a stairway to heaven, which they say is blasphemy. The lyrics to that song are largely nonsensical (a bustle in your hedgerow?) but even a casual listening would quickly reveal that the song mocks the notion that you can buy your way into heaven, yet the Peters somehow couldn't figure that out.

The other infamous example of backward masking they "uncovered" is from the Queen song "Another One Bites the Dust." When the titular line is played backward it is supposed to say, "Decide to smoke marijuana." The Peters say this can be heard "clearly," but to me it sounds more like an asthmatic snake is gasping out the words "Inside the snow nary wanna." At any rate, why would the guys in Queen give a rat's butt as to whether their listeners smoked pot or not? And how would this "clear" when played backward recording advance that supposed agenda?

The Peters cavalcade toured the world denouncing popular music and roasting records and tapes afterward. They appeared on the ABC News program *Nightline* and were confronted by host Ted Koppel who compared their record burnings to the book burnings of the Third Reich. The Peters lamely defended themselves by saying they didn't personally burn any music.

The Peters brothers published book after book on the evils of rock music. Well, not all rock music, as they heartily endorse Christian rock (though other religious figures such as Jimmy Swaggart and Jack Chick have argued that no rock music can ever be considered Christian). Yet the world mostly stopped paying attention to the Peters boys years ago. I suspect the key ingredient in their decline was the rise of the compact disk because it's impossible to play CDs backward by spinning them in the wrong direction with your finger.

> In 1986 a pair of evangelists named Jim Brown and Greg Hudson took the backward message idea to the pinnacle of silliness. They claimed the familiar "A Horse is a Horse" theme song from the *Mr. Ed* television show included the lines "the source is Satan" and "someone heard this song for Satan" when played in reverse. They made this claim during a seminar they held for teenagers about the dangers of popular music lyrics.

Satan-Worshiping Heavy Metal Bands

In the 1980's heavy metal bands wore colorful tights, had frizzy hair and worshipped Satan. There could perhaps be no clearer example of this than the band Mötley Crüe, who filled their album artwork and videos with satanic imagery such as the inverted pentagram, and constantly flashed satanic hand gestures to their fans. So these guys were pretty heavily into Satanism, right? Well, no.

The whole devil-worshiping thing is similar to the umlauts in the band's name. They might look badass, but are in fact meaningless ornamentation. The Crüe (and countless other such acts) knew that there was little that could freak out parents—and therefore appeal to kids—more than Satanism, so they went with it. Judging by the number of records they sold, I think it's fair to say the ploy worked.

It's not as if the whole pretending to be in league with Satan idea originated in the '80s either. Way back in the 1920s, the legendary bluesman, Robert Johnson, concocted a story about selling his soul to the devil at a deserted intersection in Mississippi in exchange for his mastery over the guitar. The myth has become one of the most enduring aspects of Johnson's legacy. The Crüe didn't go as far as to claim the devil gave them mastery over their instruments, however, for reasons that are obvious to anyone who has ever listened to one of their records.

So what did Anton LaVey, the founder of the Church of Satan and author of *The Satanic Bible*, think of these "satanic" hair-metal bands? Not much. LaVey thought all these groups were poseurs who didn't really worship Satan like he did—or at least like he pretended to, as LaVey himself waffled as to whether he really believed in the literal existence of the devil. So what music did LaVey think was satanic? He felt that old songs that used to be popular, but were rarely listened to anymore possessed special occult power. He cited the 1920s novelty hit "Yes! We Have No Bananas" as an example of a song with strong satanic power. So if you want a soundtrack for getting closer to the dark lord you might want to forget about Black Sabbath and dust off the old Carmen Miranda records instead.

But were any metal artists actually worshiping Satan? A case has been made for a Norwegian headbanger named Varg Vikernes who in 1994 was convicted of the murder of fellow musician, Øystein Aarseth, of the band Mayhem. Vikernes was also convicted of involvement in the arson of four Christian churches in Norway, including one church that was an irreplaceable 900-year-old landmark. In the wake of his conviction, it was widely reported that he was a Satanist, but in truth that claim is hard to back up. Vikernes certainly isn't part of the Church of Satan. He describes himself as a pagan and he is a neo-Nazi as well. His motive for destroying the churches was revenge against Christianity for its offenses against pagans in past centuries. Despite the serious nature of the crimes for which he was convicted, Vikernes spent only sixteen years in prison. Four years after his release, he was arrested in France on suspicion that he was planning a massacre there.

Also from Norway comes the band Gorgoroth, which is an actual Satan-worshiping band. Or at least the band's lead guitar player and only consistent member, Roger Tiegs, (who goes by the stage name of "Infernus") is a Satanist. Gorgoroth gained some notoriety for playing a gig in Poland that included severed sheep heads, buckets of sheep's blood, and naked models on crosses.

But let's face it, you've never heard of Gorgoroth. And you might wonder if anyone genuinely famous has actually taken Satanism seriously. To find someone who did, look not to metal musicians, but rather to the blonde bombshell actress Jayne Mansfield. She was a committed follower of Anton LaVey and credited Satanism for saving her son's life after a lion had mauled him. She was even ordained a priestess in the Church of Satan. When she was killed in a car accident in 1967 LaVey claimed he had magically foreseen her death, but naturally he didn't tell any one about his premonition until after she died.

The Insane Clown Posse

The Insane Clown Posse (ICP) is another band young people might get into solely for the sake of upsetting their parents. Purveyors of the underappreciated genre of music known as "horrorcore," ICP songs feature profoundly misogynistic and ultra-violent rap lyrics set against a backdrop of banal beats. ICP is composed of two fellows who go by the pseudonyms of "Violent J" and "Shaggy 2 Dope." Messrs. J and Dope wear clown makeup during all the band's highly theatrical performances.

News reports showing members of the band's devoted fan base (who call themselves "Juggalos") being arrested for homicides have helped to whip up ICP's murderous, bad boy image. At least one of the killers was considerate enough to be arrested while wearing a t-shirt with the ICP logo on it. For those of you who are too old and square to know this stuff, the logo consists of a maniacal-looking person wielding a butcher knife. In other words, this band is as far from wholesome Christianity as you can get.

Or so it seemed. After about twenty years of parading around as hell-bent hedonists, ICP had a little surprise in store for its fans; the band was actually Christian and had been secretly proselytizing for God the whole time. They summed up their religious position in the song "Thy Unveiling," which includes the lyrics…

Fuck it, we got to tell.
All secrets will now be told
No more hidden messages
…Truth is we follow GOD!!!
We've always been behind him
The carnival is GOD
And may all Juggalos find him
We're not sorry if we tricked you.

And their brand of Christianity is of the fundamentalist persuasion that includes a rejection of science as is seen in the song "Miracles."

Hot lava, snow, rain and fog,
Long neck giraffes, and pet cats and dogs
Fuckin' rainbows after it rains
There's enough miracles here to blow your brains…
Fuckin' magnets, how do they work?
And I don't wanna talk to a scientist
Y'all motherfuckers lying and getting me pissed.

267

It's reassuring to know that their embrace of Christianity didn't diminish ICP's adoration of the F-bomb.

In 2010, The British publication *The Guardian* published an interview with the boys concerning their newly proclaimed evangelicalism. On the subject of people mocking the band for thinking that giraffes are miracles, the band had this to say,

Violent J: "A giraffe is a fucking miracle. It has a dinosaur-like neck. It's yellow. Yeah, technically an elephant is not a miracle. Technically. They've been here for hundreds of years..."

Shaggy 2 Dope: "Thousands"

Violent J: "Have you ever stood next to an elephant, my friend? A fucking elephant is a miracle. If people can't see a fucking miracle in a fucking elephant, then life must suck for them, because an elephant is a fucking miracle. So is a giraffe."

The Christian thing didn't pan out too well for ICP in some ways, however. A lot of Juggalos thought the switch was a betrayal of what they thought the band stood for. The phrase "Fucking magnets, how do they work?" has been so widely mocked on the Internet that it has become a cliché used to ridicule any example of anti-scientific stupidity. Furthermore, the boys were afraid that the *Guardian* article made them look like morons (although to be fair, they had a major head start in that area long before the interview hit newsstands). The band tried to back away from the idea that they were really hardcore Christians by claiming they never even go to church. I don't doubt this, but the witnessing they did in their songs, and their defense of it in subsequent interviews isn't something they can now just walk away from because it makes them look foolish.

Jerry Lee Lewis

Jerry Lee Lewis was one messed up piano player. He was brought up in an intensely religious family (the infamous preacher Jimmy Swaggart was his cousin) and lived in constant fear of the fires of hell. As a teenager, he and Jimmy would sneak off to a black nightclub to listen to the music there that was thought to be the devil's music in the white part of town. Lewis loved the music, but feared it would lead him to moral ruin.

After dropping out of high school, Lewis went to a Bible college, but dropped out of that as well. This didn't stop him from taking up preaching, however, though he didn't stick with that for long either. What he could stick with was music. He played a rollicking, tempestuous style of rock and roll on the piano, and when he presented himself to the legendary Sam Phillips at Sun Records he was quickly snapped up and launched into stardom.

The problem was that Lewis still thought that the style of music he was playing was ungodly at best. When Phillips brought the song "Great Balls of Fire" to him Lewis balked at it because he apparently thought the word "fire" in the title was a reference to the devil. He and Phillips got into a big debate over the song that was recorded for posterity when a studio technician inadvertently turned on the recording equipment while the discussion was in progress. The argument is a startling revelation of a performer who was convinced he had damned himself to hell because his music honored not God, but Satan. At one point in the recording he states, "Man, I got the devil in me. If I didn't I'd be a Christian." In the end Lewis obviously agreed to do the song, but not because Phillips had succeeded in convincing him that the song wasn't satanic, but rather because Lewis had convinced himself that his chances of salvation were already hopeless, so he had nothing more to lose.

The song was a smash hit of course, but Lewis would sabotage his own success when he married his thirteen-year-old cousin who was so naive that she still believed in Santa Claus. As if that weren't bad enough, he hadn't bothered to divorce his first two wives before entering into the union with this the third Mrs. Lewis. When the news of his odd marriage reached the public his career was ruined. His strange sexual behavior had destroyed him in the same way his cousin Jimmy's would decades later.

Jimmy Swaggart

Jimmy Lee Swaggart was born in 1935 in Ferriday, Louisiana. His cousin, Jerry Lee Lewis, was born in the same house as Jimmy a few months later. The two boys (and a third cousin, future country music star Mickey Gilley) were raised together for the most part and were as close as brothers. When Jimmy was a mere eight years old, he claimed that he heard the voice of God talking to him. When he was nine, he started speaking in tongues. This was a boy who was clearly destined for the pulpit.

But getting there wasn't as straight a path for Jimmy as one might have expected considering that he had heard the voice of God and all. He and Jerry Lee both dropped out of high school and took to lives of petty crime. It was in these days that Jimmy married his wife Frances when she was only fourteen or fifteen years old.

It was Jerry Lee who got religion before Jimmy, but Swaggart followed suit soon after, and—unlike his cousin—his rediscovered love for Christianity took hold of him permanently. He became a reverend in the Pentecostal Assemblies of God Church and started preaching in backwater areas and very slowly worked his way up. While Jerry Lee was becoming an internationally famous rock-and-roll star, Jimmy was just barely scraping by back in Louisiana. He had to dig ditches to make enough money to make ends meet. Jimmy despised his cousin's music and the rock genre in general. When the Beatles broke out Swaggart remarked, "You boys and girls that have Beatle records at home, this is the most rotten, dirty, damnable, filthy, putrid filth that this nation or the world has ever known. And you parents that would allow this filth to be in your home, you ought to be taken out somewhere and horsewhipped, you hear me. And I mean it, my friend." So if you ever meet Swaggart, you might not want to ask him who his favorite Beatle was.

In 1969 he got his first chance to reach out to a wider audience by appearing on the radio, and in 1973 he showed up on television for the first time on a station in Nashville, Tennessee. A couple of years later, he started to cobble together his own broadcasting empire, and then he really took off. At his peak, Swaggart claimed that his broadcasts aired in 145 countries and reached half of the world's households. He claimed to have 500 million viewers (I wish to point out, however, that none of these numbers were independently verified). His broadcasts were translated into languages ranging from Farsi to Icelandic for his worldwide audience. He claimed that God wished for him to appear on every television in the world, though he also said the media was controlled by Satan.

And what a message Swaggart had for his viewers! He used his televised pulpit to lash out against homosexuals. He bristled at the term "gays" saying they should be called "perverts," "queers," and "faggots" instead. He warned that "AIDS can be contracted by eating at a restaurant where food is prepared by homosexuals." He didn't think much of the Catholic Church either, calling it a "false cult" and a "monstrosity of heresy," though he claimed he was not anti-Catholic.

He also hated the government. He said the Supreme Court of the United States and Congress were demonic institutions and that public schools teach incest to children. He ripped them for teaching evolution: "Evolution is a bankrupt speculative philosophy, not a scientific fact. Only a spiritually bankrupt society could ever believe it. ... Only atheists could accept this satanic theory." Of sex education he said, "I saw pictures the other day of what they're wanting to show our kids. And I want to tell you, if I ever hear of one teacher that shows my boy that filth, I'm going to get in my car and go to that school and pull off my coat, and when I get through with him, his face is going to be rearranged." At one time Swaggart had seventeen shows on the air at the same time. I don't now how many times you can say gays and Catholics suck and still keep your message fresh, but Swaggart was up to the challenge.

He proclaimed all this "wisdom" in an over-the-top flamboyant style with yelling, crying, and screaming to get his hate-filled points across. And it worked like a charm. By 1986, his ministry was pulling in an estimated half million dollars per day. He had a ministerial complex in Baton Rouge that received so many mailed-in pledges that it was assigned its own ZIP code. The complex included the Jimmy Swaggart Bible College and another school for K-12 education. It also hosted the headquarters for his global missionary work and a branch that worked to assist poor children around the world. A media investigation found that little—if any—of the money donated to help the poor actually was used for that purpose, but it barely ruffled Swaggart's feathers as the money kept pouring in.

Swaggart got to be filthy rich from all this donated lucre. He lived in an opulent mansion and drove expensive cars. He even built a two-story, air-conditioned playhouse for his grandkids.

Though he lived the good life, Swaggart always seemed to want more. He cast a jealous eye at other preachers who had built large ministries, and looked for ways to bring them down. He heard rumors that Jim Bakker (see the later chapter on him) was bisexual and he used that information to try and elbow him out of his lucrative Praise the Lord television ministry. After that strategy failed, Swaggart found out about a heterosexual affair Bakker was having and Swaggart wasted no time in using it to destroy him. The reverend Marvin Gorman, who led the First Assemblies of God Church and who had the largest congregation in the state of Louisiana, also fell into his crosshairs. Here too, Swaggart learned of a sexual indiscretion that he used to attack the competition. He forced Gorman to step down from his ministry and to make a humiliating public confession of his misdeeds. Swaggart was only too happy to take over Gorman's ministry in the wake of the scandal. Gorman was furious with Swaggart and carried a fearsome grudge against him.

And revenge would be his when, years later, Gorman heard stories of Swaggart regularly cruising for hookers on a seedy street near New Orleans. He sent his son and son-in-law on a private investigation to see what they could uncover. They were able to photograph a hotel room where local prostitutes rendezvoused with their johns. Amongst the numerous men going into the room was none other than Jimmy Swaggart. Gorman's boys sabotaged the tires on Swaggart's car so he couldn't leave the hotel after one of his romantic trysts there. Gorman then confronted Swaggart while he was stranded in the parking lot. He offered Swaggart terms similar to those that he had been forced to endure years earlier. He demanded that Jimmy step down and publicly confess his sins. He told Swaggart he would give him some time to think it over, but he made it clear that he had no option.

Swaggart carried on as if nothing had happened, but there was no way Gorman was going to let this worm wriggle off the hook. When Gorman's deadline came and went without Swaggart responding to his demands, he broke the story in the news media. Swaggart tried to deny that he had been with a prostitute, but he was quickly forced to concede the fact. On February 21, 1988 he made a sobbing, stammering confession in front of a packed church audience. Part of the confession was made public in video form and his tearful words "I have sinned against you my Lord" became an icon not just for Swaggart's fall, but for televangelists in general, who were going down in scandals right and left. The speech was shown over and over again on T.V. and was widely mocked and parodied. Swaggart had once claimed that it was God's wish that he be on every television in the world; this moment was the closest he would ever come to achieving that goal.

Swaggart claimed that he had only met the prostitute on one occasion, but the lady in question, Debra Murphee, told a different story. She claimed that Swaggart was a regular customer of hers and that his routine was to pay her to masturbate while he did likewise. She claimed that Swaggart had repeatedly asked her to bring her nine-year-old daughter into their meetings so she could watch too, but she refused to do so.

His local branch of the Assemblies of God suspended Swaggart from preaching for three months, but the national organization gave him a two-year suspension. This was still far more generous than the terms he had inflicted upon Gorman, but Swaggart couldn't even bring himself to abide by this mild ruling. Swaggart had come to believe that he—and only he—could do the work that God needed to be done. He claimed that if he didn't return to preaching millions of people would go to hell.

So on Easter Sunday 1988, Swaggart strode on stage during services at his church and took to preaching again though his suspension was far from over. A young man in the congregation yelled "liar" and "hypocrite" at him, but ushers dragged him out of the building. Jimmy Swaggart was back, but his defiance of his suspension led to his being defrocked by the Assemblies of God. He decided to continue preaching in a more generic version of the Pentecostal faith without the blessing of the Assemblies of God.

But his ministry had run into hard times. Many of the stations carrying his broadcasts stopped airing him. Students of the Jimmy Swaggart Bible College dropped out *en masse* and many of those that had degrees from the school tried to get them revised to remove Swaggart's name.

Swaggart slowly started to rebuild his ministry, however, and nothing was going to stop him. That included getting busted with *another* prostitute. In 1991 Swaggart was pulled over by the California Highway Patrol for driving on the wrong side of the road. Swaggart tried to make up an excuse to explain the odd situation, but the lady in the car with Swaggart told the patrolman, "He asked me for sex. I mean, that's why he stopped me. That's what I do. I'm a prostitute." Swaggart had been caught with his pants down again, but there would be no tearful contrition this time around. Swaggart said of the incident, "The Lord told me it's flat none of your business."

Nevertheless, Swaggart continues his preaching, and his broadcasts once again supposedly reach huge numbers of people worldwide. His webpage claims he is seen in 104 countries, but that includes people watching on the Internet, so it's a rather meaningless boast. There is a biography of Swaggart on his site that makes no mention of his scandals, but there is a large "Donate" link for anyone wishing to send some cash his way.

Jimmy Swaggart was not the first Pentecostal preacher to gain national broadcasting fame. That honor belongs to a Canadian woman named Aimee Semple McPherson who gained notoriety with radio broadcasts in the 1920s in which she railed against the teaching of evolution in schools and so forth.

In May of 1926 McPherson disappeared and was thought to have drowned. Her grieving followers made every effort to find her, and two people died in the search for her, one from drowning and another from exposure. Five weeks later, McPherson walked out of a Mexican desert and claimed that she had been kidnapped, tortured, and drugged, but had escaped and walked for thirteen hours across the desert to freedom.

It later turned out that a male associate of hers had gone missing at the same time as McPherson. He admitted to having rented a hotel room in Mexico for the purpose of having an affair with a woman who he said was not McPherson. Witnesses said the woman looked like her, however, and documents taken from the hotel room were said to match McPherson's handwriting. Moreover, the police didn't believe that McPherson had walked so far through the desert because she was in remarkably good condition, especially considering that she had supposedly been tortured beforehand. Furthermore, her shoes showed little wear from the thirteen-hour walk, and she was found fully clothed despite having disappeared while wearing only a bathing suit.

McPherson turned out to be not just a pioneer in the area of electronic evangelism, but also in the area of sex scandals involving electronic evangelists.

Lest you think Jerry Lee Lewis and Mickey Gilley got all the musical talent in this family, allow me to set you straight. For you see, Jimmy Swaggart himself is a legend of gospel music. Swaggart has released scores of albums and claims to have sold more than fifteen million records although, once again, this number cannot be verified.

So what do Swaggart's songs sound like? Well, they all sound pretty much the same. Swaggart's voice has no range, and his singing voice sounds almost the same as his speaking voice. He does occasionally disrupt the monotony by breaking down and blubbering—at least on his live recordings.

One little piece of advice for Jimmy; when you have a sex scandal-ridden past such as you do, it may not be the best idea to put a song called "He Touched Me" on an album called *The Message of His Coming* like you did.

Jim and Tammy Faye Bakker

Jim Bakker loved to tell the story of his underprivileged upbringing in a slum in Muskegon Heights, Michigan where he grew up in an orange, cinder-block house. It seems that in reality Bakker came from a middle class family, and the tale of his impoverished childhood was more for effect than anything else. In other words, his life of deceit started early.

Bakker had a powerful need to be popular. When he was in high school he was known for throwing parties He was even a deejay at a school sock hop, despite his conservative Christian beliefs that prevented him from participating in the dancing. But his party boy ways were about to take a back seat to his Christianity, or so it seemed. He would later tell the inspiring story of how, in 1957, he had driven over a boy and seriously injured him. An emotionally ravaged Bakker pounded on the walls of the hospital where the boy was taken and sobbed and wailed over the horror of the accident. When the child miraculously pulled through, the overjoyed Bakker dedicated himself to the service of God as thanks for his intervention in the tragedy. The story was partly true. Bakker did run over a kid, but it happened two years before he claimed it did, and no one remembered it being a particularly life-changing event at the time. In any event, Bakker was off to do the work of the Lord. He went to Minnesota to attend the North Central Bible College and while he was there, he chanced to meet the girl of his dreams.

Tammy Faye LeValley grew up in the small and famously frozen town of International Falls, Minnesota. She too could tell of a spartan upbringing, but unlike Bakker, she didn't have to fake it; her family was genuinely mired in the lower class. Due to either her family's harsh Christian faith, their lack of funds, or both, she wore no makeup—not even lipstick—until she arrived at college. When she got there, she fell so in love with cosmetics that she caked them on as if she would never get another chance. She even wore makeup to bed. She also fell in love with Bakker, and the two quickly decided to marry. The school forbade marriage amongst the students, so they both dropped out and got hitched. The newlyweds headed for the Carolinas where they launched their own impromptu traveling ministry. At first, things didn't go well for the Bakkers. Money was so scarce that they were lucky to eat on some days. Then Tammy came up with the idea of making puppets out of bubble bath bottles, and their fortunes changed for the better. Between her puppet show and Jim's story of the "miracle" involving the pedestrian he had driven into, they had something resembling a serviceable act. It was enough to get them noticed by Pat Robertson who offered them the chance to do a show on his fledgling *700 Club* broadcasts. The Bakkers did a show aimed at children that included their puppet theatrics, and they found a receptive audience. They became stars at the station—to the growing consternation of Robertson. He strongly considered firing them because he apparently felt they were too ambitious, but God somehow told him not to do it, so he kept them on. Eventually the Bakkers got on his nerves so much he decided to can them anyway, irrespective of God's wishes. The Bakkers were forced to set out on their own, and they would never look back.

They eventually ended up in Charlotte, North Carolina where they started a show called *PTL Club* with the "PTL" standing for "Praise the Lord." The show was a smash hit, and it allowed Jim to set up a satellite network to take his PTL network nationwide. At its height, the Bakkers' programming was seen by thirteen million people a day on 171 stations. Jim Bakker's prestige grew to the point that he prayed with President Carter aboard Air Force One, and he was a prominent guest at President Reagan's inauguration and the following ball. In 1978 the couple opened Heritage USA, a resort and theme park in South Carolina based upon Christian virtues. Heritage USA had it all: a man made lake, a 200-foot water slide, and a shopping mall where one could buy Saks 5th Avenue merchandise as well as Tammy's personal line of cosmetics for the tastefully impaired. The park was such a raging success that it was said to attract six million visitors a year, trailing only Disneyworld and Disneyland as tourist attractions in the United States.

Yet the *PTL Club* remained the centerpiece of the Bakkers' public image. Their daily shows featured the two of them smiling so hard it looked like it made their faces hurt. Tammy sang gospel tunes while Jim preached and begged for money. He always needed more and more money. They could never get enough to do the Lord's work, as it seemed that PTL was always on the brink of ruin. Jim's heartfelt pleas for cash were punctuated by Tammy's emotional collapses. Tears poured from her mascara-encrusted eyes and ran across her painted face until she looked like she was melting. Cynics rolled their eyes at this spectacle, but the ploys brought in cash by the barrelful. One especially effective marketing technique was to sell memberships in Heritage USA. For a thousand dollars, you could buy such a membership, which would entitle you to stay three nights per year at the hotel located in the Bakkers' kingdom of kitsch, free of charge.

But there was much going on behind the scenes. Jim Bakker was earning more than two million dollars a year at PTL despite his constant pleas of poverty. He had a secret bank account and kept a second set of books for PTL's finances. Cash donations to PTL were often stuffed directly into suitcases for Bakker without ever being accounted for. The couple had numerous homes and a houseboat. They had two Rolls-Royces, furs, and perhaps most famously, an air-conditioned doghouse. Tammy got breast implants and liposuction on the dime of the faithful. And although the Bakkers' presented themselves as the perfect couple, they fought constantly. They drove separately to the television studio because they couldn't stand one another's company. Once there, they would bicker and battle with each other backstage until the moment the cameras started rolling at which point their heartwarming grins would consume their faces.

And there was good reason for tension in their marriage as Jim was far from an ideal husband. Austin Miles, one of the Bakkers' assistants, reported seeing Jim "frolicking in the nude" with two other men in a steam room. They took turns messaging each other until Tammy found out what was going on. She pounded on the door yelling, "I know what you're doing... Do you think you're fooling anyone? Well I want you to know right now that you're not!" But that was only the tip of the iceberg for Jim Bakker. He visited gay bars while wearing women's clothes including wigs, pantyhose, and prosthetic breasts. He hired consultants to set up Roman-style sex orgies for him, and he carried on a four-year affair with his male masseuse.

And then there was Jessica Hahn. Hahn was a secretary at PTL who caught the eye of Bakker. In 1980 another preacher named John Wesley Fletcher set up a tryst between Bakker and Hahn at a hotel where the two holy men joined Hahn in a threesome. A third man was invited to the festivities, but when he got there he found Hahn "prostrate on the floor and unable to accommodate" him, so he left. And people say romance is dead.

But it turned out that Hahn had more on her mind than group sex with men of God. She knew that Bakker was loaded, and she wanted to get a piece of the action. She blackmailed him to the tune of $265,000. Baker recruited a man named Roe Messner to make the payment to Hahn so it would not be traced back to him. Messner was a building contractor who had done much of the construction at Heritage USA, so he was able to turn around and bill PTL for the hush money he had paid to Hahn without arousing suspicion.

For seven years the fling with Hahn stayed secret, but in 1987 Jimmy Swaggart caught wind of it and was going to use it to ruin Bakker, so Bakker made a desperate move to head off the destruction of his empire. He arranged a meeting with Jerry Falwell in California and there he confessed his liaison with Hahn to him. Only in Bakker's version of the events, Hahn had been the aggressor. The harlot had raped poor Jim Bakker when she was able to get him alone. His only sin had been to get himself into the situation where he was vulnerable to her advances. He neglected to mention to Falwell all the other aspects of his wild and unconventional sex life, not to mention his financial misdeeds. He turned the control of PTL over to Falwell temporarily until he could get the whole Hahn scandal resolved. Falwell, perhaps motivated by the thought of combining Bakker's huge media reach with his own, believed Bakker's version of events and agreed to run PTL.

The scandal hit the airwaves and many outraged contributors stopped giving to PTL. Furthermore, many other people who remained loyal to the Bakkers were appalled to see Falwell running things and withheld their money to show their contempt for him. Bakker had pilfered so much money from PTL that the organization could not withstand the crisis, and its financial underpinnings began to teeter. Furthermore, the whole issue of the lifetime memberships was blowing up. Bakker had sold far more memberships with the free nights stays at Heritage USA than the hotel could possibly accommodate. Many times people showed up to claim their free vacations only to be turned away. The inn had no room, and it was all by Bakker's design. The feds became interested in how the facility had been grossly oversold, and they began a fraud investigation. While all this as going on, Bakker whiled away his days hidden away in one of his homes where he spent much of his time curled up into a fetal position, cursing the world that had failed to appreciate him.

But he eventually got over it. When he reemerged from hiding, he went on the ABC news program *Nightline* and used his appearance to galvanize opposition to Falwell. Then he and Tammy made an unannounced visit to Heritage USA where they were received like returning heroes. It was clear that the Bakkers were ready to resume control of PTL, so Falwell decided it was a good time for PTL to declare bankruptcy. The move blocked any effort on the part of the Bakkers to retake control of the outfit, and it escalated the tension that had existed between the two sides into outright vilification. Conspiracy theories involving Falwell swirled amongst the Bakker supporters while Falwell paraded out a document from Bakker in which he demanded a $300,000 annual salary for himself plus another $100,000 for Tammy even though they were no longer working at PTL. Bakker also wanted scads of other perks from PTL such as a maid and cars. In the end, PTL could not withstand the strain of all this infighting and scandal. The firm went out of business, and its assets, including the air-conditioned doghouse, were auctioned off.

But that wasn't the end of the ordeal for Bakker. He was charged with dozens of counts of fraud for his part in the PTL debacle. His trial turned out to be the three-ring circus that one would have expected it to be. Crowds gathered outside the courthouse everyday cheering for Jim while Tammy (who somehow managed not to get charged with anything) sang for them and sobbed hysterically. At one point during the trial, Jim curled up in the corner of his lawyer's office with his head under a couch, prompting the judge to order him to undergo a psychological evaluation. He was deemed fit to stand trial, and he was found guilty on all counts. He was sentenced to forty-five years in the slammer, but this was reduced on appeal to eight years, and he got out after serving only five. Other members of the PTL staff also got jail time for their participation in the scandal.

Tammy Faye Bakker ditched her husband not long after he entered prison. She married Roe Messner, the same guy who had paid the blackmail money to Jessica Hahn. Messner was married at the time the two of them started their relationship together, but Mrs. Messner stepped aside for Tammy with little resistance saying, "Any man who would want Tammy Faye is not the man for me!" Messner's construction firm went bankrupt, and he was sentenced to two years in prison for committing fraud during the bankruptcy proceedings. Tammy sure could pick 'em. She died of cancer in 2007.

Jessica Hahn was the big winner in this whole fiasco. She made a nude appearance in *Playboy* for which she was paid a cool million dollars. So she ended up making at least $1,265,000 off of the episode.

> Tammy Faye's romantic escapades may not have held a candle to her hubby's carnival-like sex life, but that's not to say she didn't have her own illicit affairs of the heart. First up was record producer Gary Paxton, who did musical production work for PTL. Paxton was no ordinary gospel musician; he had some big hits to his name. In 1960 he sang a tune called "Alley Oop" with a group called the Hollywood Argyles that he had hastily thrown together. Though the song was awful—even by the standards of novelty tunes—it rocketed to number one. Two years later, Paxton scored again when he produced and performed on the recording of the song "Monster Mash," which not only hit number one, but also became the definitive Halloween song of all time. Notwithstanding Paxton's musical pedigree, Jim fired him as soon as he found out that he had become close to Tammy, even though both Tammy and Paxton swore they had never had sex with each other, while Jim seems to have been copulating with half the population of South Carolina. Tammy took up with another man and nearly ran away with him before Jim chased him off. It wasn't until Jim was safely ensconced in prison that she successfully dumped him for the blackmail-paying, future jailbird Roe Messner, who would be the love of her life.

Pat Robertson

The story of Pat Robertson is eerily similar to that of Jerry Falwell except that Robertson has said even dumber things than Falwell, and perhaps not coincidentally, has been even more successful.

Pat Robertson was born in Virginia in 1930. He was the son of A. Willis Robertson, who served many years in the U.S. Senate and House of Representatives as a conservative Democrat. Pat Robertson went into the military during the Korean War and later told tales of his combat experience including claims that he had received multiple combat citations during the war. In reality, it seems he never saw any combat in Korea as his powerful dad kept him out of harm's way. Robertson passed the war in Japan keeping an eye on an officer's liquor supplies. He also nailed an unknown number of prostitutes while in the service.

When he returned from serving his country overseas, his heart turned to thoughts of love. He married Adelia "Dede" Elmer in 1954. She gave birth to their first son a scant ten weeks after the wedding. Robertson had entered Yale Law School just before his marriage with hopes of setting about on a career in law, but that plan got sidetracked when Robertson proved himself incapable of passing the bar exam after graduating. He eventually gave up on it and considered suicide for a time.

It was shortly after this that Robertson found God and had his born-again conversion. He enrolled in a theological seminary, and in 1961 he was ordained a Southern Baptist minister. Even before his ordination, he had purchased a tiny T.V. station in Virginia and started what he called the Christian Broadcasting Network (CBN).

Though he had bought the station for chickenfeed, he was in constant need of funds to keep the venture going. In a 1963 telethon for the station, he asked 700 contributors to pledge ten dollars a month to keep him on the air. This was the genesis of *The 700 Club*, a television program he started soon afterward that rocketed Robertson to fame and fortune and gave him a daily podium to spread his bizarre beliefs around the nation.

His sermons were as much about politics as religion, and he left no doubt where he stood on such matters. He preached an ultra right-wing agenda that he felt could only be advanced by the Republican Party. He railed against the idea of the separation of church and state, saying it was a Soviet plot to undermine America, and he said that only Christians and Jews were qualified to hold office in the United States. He regularly lashed out at the Supreme Court and said their decisions were not the law of the land, and he opined that congress is free to ignore Supreme Court decisions as they see fit. He also suggested that the U.S. Constitution should not be allowed into the hands of non-Christians. Is it any wonder this guy was never able to pass the bar?

In 1985 he claimed credit for diverting Hurricane Gloria from Virginia after the hurricane veered toward New York. Yes, the storm killed several people in the northeast U.S., but Pat's beloved Virginia had been spared. In 1986 Robertson said God had told him he would usher in the return of Jesus, and this event would take place on the Mount of Olives in Jerusalem. Robertson didn't say when this would happen, but he did promise that CBN would have live coverage of it when it did.

This may all seem like a bunch of insanity, but Robertson built a huge following with these and many other extremist positions and wild claims. By 1987, he had become such a powerful figure that he resigned his position in the Baptist Church and threw his hat in into the ring in the race for President of the United States. His fortune and television audience made him a viable candidate for the Republican nomination despite his having never held any previous public office. In fact, he took second place at the Iowa caucuses in 1988, coming in ahead of George Bush.

That would be the high water mark of Robertson's run, however, as his campaign was beset with problems. Not the least of these was the testy relationship he had with the media. He had never been forced to stand up to scrutiny in all his years of pontificating on *The 700 Club*, and he was ill prepared for it when it inevitably came during his presidential run. He thought it was entirely out of bounds for reporters to notice that his wife had been seven months pregnant when he married her even though he routinely chastised what he considered to be moral deficiencies in others. He bristled at being called a televangelist even though that is clearly what he was. When challenged on his positions on issues he demonstrated a lack of knowledge that did not inspire confidence. One example of this was his incredible claim that the Soviet Union had nuclear missiles based in Cuba.

Robertson claimed that God had told him to run for president, but apparently God's plan did not include Robertson's winning. At the New Hampshire primaries he faced an electorate far less religious than he had in Iowa, and he finished at the bottom of the pack. He did better in the Bible-Belt state of South Carolina, but he didn't get the win there that he needed. After winning no states on Super Tuesday, he was forced to end his campaign. Robertson said he would run again in 1992, and it was God's plan from him to be president, but he never did make another run for office. Nevertheless, his quest to influence American public policy was far from over.

In 1990 Robertson formed the Christian Coalition, which was essentially a replacement for Jerry Falwell's failed Moral Majority. Although the group claimed to be non-partisan they were founded in part with a $64,000 donation from the Republican Senatorial Committee. The Christian Coalition works to this day to push right-wing policies in the American political body ranging from local school boards to the White House.

Once Robertson was free of the shackles of trying to look "mainstream" for his presidential run he was really able to let his freak flag fly. His comments and writings became even more extreme and nuttier than before. In 1991 he released a book called *The New World Order*, which laid out his worldview for everyone to see. In the book he presented vast conspiracy theories involving the Illuminati, Freemasons, the Trilateral Commission, and all the other groups who are favorites amongst the sort of people who like to talk to you on the bus. It probably goes without saying, but it seems that Jews are bankrolling these conspiracies.

In 1989 Robertson panned feminism saying, "Now the male mind thinks in certain attitudes. But the key in terms of mental—it has nothing to do with physical—is chess. There's never been a woman Grand Master chess player. And if, you know, once you get one, then I'll buy some of the feminism."

There have been several female Grand Masters of chess and some of them predated Robertson's foolish comment, but it seems he still did not "buy some of the feminism" as is evidenced by a 1992 document bearing his signature which said, "The feminist agenda is not about equal rights for women. It is about a socialist, anti-family political movement that encourages women to leave their husbands, kill their children, practice witchcraft, destroy capitalism, and become lesbians."

Robertson also spoke out on the subject of the racist government of South Africa saying, "I think one man, one vote—just unrestricted democracy would not be wise." Like Jerry Falwell, Robertson supported South Africa's apartheid regime until its bitter end. He also supported the brutal regime of Mobutu Sese Seko in what was then Zaire. He praised the tyrant repeatedly, lobbied to get him a U.S. visa after the dictator was banned from visiting the country in response to his human rights violations, and he made a visit to Zaire to meet with his buddy against the expressed wishes of the George Bush administration. The contact was quite profitable for Robertson as he had diamond and logging interests in Zaire that were well looked after by the strongman.

Robertson had a lot of business interests by this time. He had been nearly penniless when he launched CBN, but he had parleyed the small loan he used to buy the station into a vast fortune. His widespread holdings included such familiar brand names as the Family Channel and the Ice Capades. His net worth rose to more than a hundred million dollars.

But this wasn't enough to prevent his poor Christian followers from being persecuted. In 1993 he made the incredible statement, "Just like what Nazi Germany did to the Jews, so liberal America is now doing to the evangelical Christians. It's no different. It is the same thing. It is happening all over again. It is the Democratic Congress, the liberal-biased news media, and the homosexuals who want to destroy all Christians. Wholesale abuse and discrimination and the worst bigotry directed toward any group in America today. More terrible than anything suffered by any minority in our history."

His *700 Club* forum continued to allow him to spew out such offensive nonsense on a daily basis. In 1995 he took credit for diverting another hurricane from Virginia, and that same year he said people who bomb abortion clinics may be hearing the word of God who had instructed the attacks. He suggested that Christian tribunals were the only way of judging such cases. The removal of such terrorists from the legal system was one of many proposals he has had which—if actually enacted—would convert the United States into a theocracy.

In 2001 when a bunch of religious zealots attacked the United States because they thought *their* God wanted it, Robertson was not about to reconsider the roll religious fanaticism plays in society. Instead, he piled it on even more in the wake of the terrorist attacks. It was on *The 700 Club* that Jerry Falwell made his infamous remarks about the September 11th attacks. Robertson was in agreement with him all the way saying, "Well, I totally concur" when Falwell had finished his diatribe against pretty much everyone in America. Robertson's own words of wisdom following the terrorist attacks were perhaps overshadowed by Falwell's insipid remarks, but they shouldn't be overlooked. "We have a court that has essentially stuck its finger in God's eye and said we're going to legislate you out of the schools. We're going to take your commandments from off the courthouse steps in various states. We're not going to let the little children read the commandments of God. We're not going to let the Bible be read, no prayer in our schools. We have insulted God at the highest levels of our government. And we say, "why does this happen?" So there you go. The September 11th attacks occurred because the courts, schools and legislatures didn't comply with Robertson's vision of what America should look like.

Not that all terrorism is bad, mind you. In 2003 Robertson spoke out in favor of a nuclear weapon being detonated in Washington D.C. to take out the State Department. In 2005 he preached that assassins should be sent to Venezuela to kill President Hugo Chavez.

Also in 2005, a federal judge ruled that a small school district in Dover, Pennsylvania could not teach "intelligent design" as science. Intelligent design was created by fundamentalist Christians to try and shoehorn creationism into the schools by disguising it as science. A group of reactionaries on the Dover school board had mandated it's inclusion in their curriculum as a scientific alternative to evolution, but the judge saw right through their ploy and ruled accordingly. To make matters worse for the evangelical crowd, the voters of Dover swept all eight of the Republican creationists off of the school board in favor of a bipartisan slate of candidates who dropped the attempt to teach creationism. An enraged Robertson threatened the town. "I'd like to say to the people of Dover: If there is a disaster in your area, don't turn to God. You just rejected him from your city." And he went on, "God is tolerant and loving, but we can't keep sticking our finger in his eye forever. If they have future problems in Dover, I recommend they call on Charles Darwin. Maybe he can help." And Robertson's warnings of "future problems" had some heft to them. Remember, this is the guy who can direct the path of hurricanes.

He didn't make Hurricane Katrina turn away from New Orleans, however. After the storm killed almost 2,000 people, Robertson said "But have we found we are unable somehow to defend ourselves against some of the attacks that are coming against us, either by terrorists or now by natural disaster? Could they be connected in some way? And he (the author of Leviticus) goes down the list of the things that God says will cause a nation to lose its possession, and to be vomited out. And the amazing thing is, a judge has now got to say, 'I will support the wholesale slaughter of innocent children' in order to get confirmed to the bench." Soon afterward, Robertson denied he had ever said Katrina was caused by God's wrath over abortion, but this rambling statement shows that he did.

After an earthquake devastated Haiti in 2010, Robertson again linked the disaster to God's wrath. "You know ... something happened a long time ago in Haiti... They got together and swore a pact to the Devil. They said, 'We will serve you if you get us free from the French.' True story. And so, the Devil said, 'OK, it's a deal.' And they kicked the French out. You know, the Haitians revolted and got themselves free. But ever since, they have been cursed by one thing after another." It goes without saying that Robertson's fantastical version of Haitian history is entirely false.

It appears that Robertson is simply immune to criticism, however. Since he owns his own network, his show can't be cancelled, and there is a never-ending supply of foolish people who will be willing to believe whatever he and others like him spew out.

> In addition to being a man of God and a prophet, Pat Robertson is also a super jock. In 2006 he hit the weights at the Florida State University football weight room and supposedly leg pressed 2,000 pounds. This alleged feat topped the leg press record by a staggering 665 pounds. The old record holder burst the capillaries in both of his eyes under the strain of the press. Robertson, by the way, was seventy-six years old at the time. You too may be able to achieve such accomplishments if you get Robertson's age-defying milkshake and pancake recipes, which are available only to registered members of his CBN website.

Pat Robertson is more than a spokesman for God; he also speaks with him, and God tells him what is going to happen in the future. The problem is that Robertson's divine predictions have been incredibly inaccurate. Here are a few examples of Robertson's failed prophecies...

1976: The Soviet Union would invade Israel in 1982, possibly ushering in the end of the world.

1980: The Soviet Union would invade the Middle East, and it would be a year of sorrow and bloodshed. God's kingdom would rise from society's ruins.

1985: There would be a worldwide economic collapse.

1991: Jay Rockefeller would be elected president in 1996.

1998: As punishment for Disney's support of gay rights, The city of Orlando, Florida would be struck by earthquakes, tornadoes and possibly a meteor.

2005: George W. Bush's Social Security reform plan would pass and the Islamic world would embrace Christianity.

2006: Republicans would have control of congress after midterm elections, the war in Iraq would end successfully that year, and something as bad as a tsunami would strike the Pacific Northwest of the U.S.

2007: There would be a major terrorist attack in the U.S., which could affect millions of people.

2008: Israel would bomb Iran between November of 2008 and January of 2009, thereby touching off World War III.

2009: Gold would hit $1,900 an ounce, and oil would cost $300 a barrel before the year's end.

2012: Mitt Romney would defeat Barak Obama and serve two terms as president.

For what it's worth, the book of Deuteronomy says failed predictions are a sign of a false prophet and such people should be put to death. I'm *not* calling for Robertson's assassination; I'm just sayin'.

Louis Farrakhan

Years ago, I was at a mostly deserted mall with an acquaintance of mine. We stopped and sat on a bench for a spell while a black man in a suit and a bowtie stood directly across from us. The man watched us, but made no move to approach us. Whenever an African-American person entered the area he would rush over to deliver his religious pitch to them. After being brushed off, he would return to pacing about across from us, but he never said a word to us.

The faith the man was unsuccessfully trying to spread was the Nation of Islam (NOI). The reason he wouldn't talk to us was the color of our skin as white people are literally considered to be the devil in this faith. Now in truth, I am of mixed race and the person I was with was from a Middle Eastern country whose government has been effusively praised by NOI leader Louis Farrakhan, but that didn't matter. What mattered was that we looked white.

You might expect Nation of Islam to be an Islamic group that migrated to the U.S. from somewhere in the Middle East, but nothing could be further from the truth. A man named Wallace Fard Muhammed founded Nation of Islam in Detroit sometime in the 1930's. Fard is a rather mysterious character. The place and date of his birth are unknown. What is known is that he moved to Detroit at some point and began to preach. He called his faith "Islam," but his message is radically different from the Islam of the Eastern Hemisphere. Fard taught that blacks—and only blacks—were divine. He said they were smarter and stronger than whites whom he called "devils." He claimed that original men were black, but a black scientist named Yacub created the devil (that would be white people in case you haven't figure it out yet) on an island near Turkey in the year 8400 B.C.E. Yacub wanted his creatures to outnumber actual humans, so he ruled that only whites were allowed to be married, and he ordered the murder of black babies. Fard also told of a giant spacecraft called the Mother Plane that was a half a mile across. The Mother Plane orbits the Earth and is loaded with 1,500 fighter craft that are armed with bombs that can bore one mile deep into the ground and explode in such a way that they will only kill white people. There is no afterlife to look forward to in

Fard's version of Islam. Salvation will be the extermination of white people from the planet. Fard humbly referred to himself as "the supreme ruler of the universe."

This may all seem too wild for anyone to believe, but some people were willing to buy into the faith. Among them were Robert Karriem and John J. Smith. Acting under Fard's influence, Karriem murdered Smith with the victim's consent, as both men believed that Smith would become the savior after his death. Fard was arrested after the homicide and admitted his religion was "strictly a racket" and that he was "getting all the money out of it that he could." Interestingly, Fard was a light-skinned man who was almost certainly of mixed race. On this and every other occasion in which he was arrested (he was also busted for battery, assault with a deadly weapon, selling booze during prohibition, draft dodging, and drug dealing) he reported his race as "white." Smith, by the way, did not return from the dead.

Fard's most important student was Elijah Poole, who would eventually change his name to Elijah Muhammed. Elijah lapped up Fard's teachings and came to understand that his teacher was God himself. "I know who you are. You are God," he told Fard to which he replied "Yes, I am the one, but who knows that but yourself, and be quiet." Fard eventually took off for parts unknown (perhaps New Zealand) and dropped out of history. But Elijah ignored the admonition to keep quiet and declared that Fard was Allah. He then dedicated himself to spreading Fard's message.

It was under Elijah Muhammed that NOI really took shape as the religion/black supremacy organization we have come to know and love. Muhammed banned music, dancing, and interracial marriage amongst his followers. Naturally, whites were banned from the faith. It was Muhammed who installed the now-famous bowtie dress code for NOI members. He wanted his people to look presentable to the world, and in his mind, dressing like Orville Redenbacher was the pinnacle of class. A group called the Fruit of Islam was created to police the members of the NOI. Anyone who wasn't towing the line was libel to be savagely beaten by the Fruit guys. One of the most common offenses that could earn you a visit from these thugs was to fail to sell enough copies of the NOI newspaper called *Muhammed Speaks*. NOI members had quotas of the paper they were required to sell. The sales of the paper were a gold mine for the NOI leadership.

Just like Fard years earlier, Muhammed wasn't bashful about his personal importance in the faith. He claimed the he was the reincarnation of King David, Lot, and Noah. He had numerous children by at least six mistresses. He claimed that all these women were his wives by divine decree.

Under Muhammed, NOI was taking off. He had a brash, confrontational minister named Malcolm X preaching the black supremacist faith and promoting Muhammed's call for a separate nation for blacks. Malcolm X's message was a stark contrast to that of Martin Luther King who was advocating for civil rights and the equality of all races at the same time. King got more followers, but Malcolm X had a sizable audience himself. But Malcolm X started moving away from his message of hate after taking a closer look at Islam. He went on the Hajj (the Muslim pilgrimage to Mecca) in 1964 and saw people of all races intermingled and getting along there. After this, he called Elijah Muhammed a "faker" whose "distorted religious concoction" and "racist philosophy" served "only to fool and misuse gullible people."

But Muhammed had another, more dependable disciple in Louis X. Born Louis Eugene Walcott in 1933 to a mother who had immigrated to the U.S from the Caribbean and a father who may have been white, Walcott was a former calypso singer who had given up his performing career and had been working his way up through the ranks of NOI for some time. Though music was banned in NOI, he recorded and released a ten-and-a-half-minute long single called "A White Man's Heaven is a Black Man's Hell," which vilified whites and became something of an anthem for the movement. He even wrote two full-length musicals with severe anti-white themes. When these productions started to generate unwanted publicity for NOI, Muhammed ordered him to end his musical career.

When Malcolm X turned against Elijah Muhammed, Louis X turned against Malcolm just as severely. In *Muhammed Speaks* Louis said, "The die is set, and Malcolm shall not escape... Such a man as Malcolm is worthy of death." Malcolm X was so worried by the threat of violence from the NOI that he asked the FBI for protection. He was right to be worried. On February

12, 1965 Malcolm was shot and killed by three NOI assailants while he tried to deliver a speech.

In the wake of Malcolm X's assassination, the NOI exploded in violence. Followers of Malcolm X who had joined with him as he walked away from the faith came under fire from those still loyal to Muhammed. In 1973, seven people (most of them children) were murdered by NOI henchmen. Two of the dead were infants who were drowned by the killers. A few months later, another mass murder claimed the lives of five more people who belonged to the Malcolm X foundation. After a NOI minister was gunned down, Louis X made a radio broadcast in which he appeared to call for the murders of those who had killed the minister. "Murder him who murders you," he said. "Smite them at the back of the neck. Take off their heads, roll it down the street and make the world know the murderer of a Muslim has been murdered." Tit-for-tat murders between the two factions followed. Some of the victims were found without heads.

All the while, Elijah Muhammed continued to run the faith from his mansion in Chicago. He loathed Martin Luther King, and after he was murdered, Muhammed challenged Christians to prove that King wasn't in hell. He also ordered Louis X to change his last name once again, this time to Farrakhan. When Muhammed died in 1975, Farrakhan expected to be named his successor, but instead the honor went to Muhammed's son, Wallace. The transfer from father to son may have seemed obvious, but Wallace was actually a pretty risky choice for a successor. When he was in prison in the 1950's, he began studying Islam, and it quickly occurred to him that just about everything in his dad's religion was not in compliance with traditional Islamic beliefs. The idea that Fard was Allah, for instance, was blasphemy in Islam. So too, was the racial hatred, his dad's claim to be Noah, and much more. Not only was NOI not traditional Islam, it seemed they didn't even know much about the way Islam had been practiced for centuries. Elijah Muhammed didn't even know how to say his own name; he pronounced it "Mack-mud." Wallace confronted his father with these tidbits of information, and they had a falling out that led to his leaving the faith. He eventually returned to the fold, however, and was in good enough graces with his old man to win the leadership job upon his death.

When he took over NOI he immediately began to dismantle it. He threw out NOI policies by the barrelful and replaced them with more traditional Islamic beliefs. He even allowed whites to enter the faith. Farrakhan had expected that he would have been given the job. He was hurt by the promotion of Wallace, but he went along with it. When Wallace announced that the Nation of Islam was no more and was being replaced with a new faith called the World Community of al-Islam in the West, it was the last straw for Farrakhan. In 1977 he quit the faith in disgust.

But you can't keep a man like Farrakhan down for long. He soon restarted the NOI and placed himself in control. He restored the old faith with the racial hate, the spaceship, the idea that the Earth is seventy-six trillion years old and all the rest of the traditional beliefs. He went even further by claiming that Elijah Muhammed was the messiah and that he had died in a conspiracy involving the U.S. government, Arabs, and the Muhammed family. He even claimed that Muhammed had been resurrected and challenged doubters to exhume his corpse to see that it was gone. To date, no one has been crazy enough to try to pry him out of grave.

The plot to murder Muhammed wasn't the only conspiracy Farrakhan was pushing. He claimed that one billion units of the AIDS virus had been shipped to Africa from Fort Meade in Maryland, presumably for a campaign of genocide on the part of the U.S. He accused Jews of injecting black babies with AIDS, and he said they had run the slave trade. His complaints against the Jews were boundless. He had the gall to say they published textbooks that removed blacks from history while at the same time NOI published *The Protocols of the Elders of Zion* as well as another hate-filled work of slander called *The Secret Relationship between Blacks and Jews*. He even compared himself to Jesus, who he said was killed by Jews. Farrakhan's attacks on the Jews were so pointed that Thomas Matzer, the former head of the Ku Klux Klan in California, donated $100 to NOI in appreciation of Farrakhan's stance on the Jewish subject.

But this was the kind and gentle version of NOI that was intended for public consumption. In 1993 NOI national spokesman Khallid Abdul Muhammad let loose in a speech at Kean College in New Jersey that didn't cling to such niceties. In his diatribe he accused the Jews of being swine, controlling black ghettos, the Federal Reserve, the White House, television, movies, newspapers, and the world's jewelry. He said Jews were cannibals and savages who had recently crawled around on all fours. He defended Hitler's treatment of them and he spoke in a mocking "Jewish" accent that sounded like a bad impression of German. Not content to only pick on Jews alone, Muhammad called Pope John Paul II a "cracker" and suggested that he wasn't male. In a throwback all the way to the medieval myth of Pope Joan, he suggested that the pope's genitals be inspected to confirm his gender.

And he presented a solution for apartheid in South Africa—genocide. He said South African whites should be given twenty four hours to leave the country and if they failed to do so...

We kill the women, we kill the children. We kill the babies. We kill the blind, we kill the crippled, We kill 'em all. We kill the faggot, we kill the lesbian, We'll kill them all... Kill the elders too. If they're in a wheelchair push 'em off a cliff... And when you get through killing 'em all go to the goddam graveyard and dig up the grave and kill 'em all, goddam again.

After this tirade, Farrakhan was pressured to react to the hate speech of Muhammad, who was one of NOI's highest-ranking officials and whom Farrakhan had once referred to as "one of the most brilliant young men I have had a chance to know." After several weeks of ignoring the issue, Farrakhan finally responded to the remarks—by further attacking the Jews who he said were "plotting against us even as we speak."

But none of this prevented Farrakhan from becoming one of the leading voices in the African-American community, although only a tiny minority of America's blacks actually joined his religion. In 1995 he parlayed his fame into the Million Man March on Washington D.C. Only black men were invited to the demonstration. People arrived from all over the country to take part in the event, which was supposedly to seek atonement for something or another. Hundreds of thousands of people (although Farrakhan claimed the real number was at least two million) turned out to hear Farrakhan speak. It is rare when one can pinpoint the exact moment in time when a man reaches his pinnacle of success and begins his downfall, but with Farrakhan it is easy. When he took the podium in front of the cheering throngs before him he was at height of his majesty; his downfall began the moment he opened his mouth.

Farrakhan avoided the race baiting and controversy that he was so well known for, but he also avoided logic in his speech. He talked in aimless circles about atonement and he sprinkled his lecture with phony history and bewildering non-sequiturs. After fifteen minutes the crowd began to melt away. By the time Farrakhan finished his blather two-and-a-half hours had passed and the crowd had thinned dramatically. His speech never did end up making any sense.

After the triumph of the Million Man March, Farrakhan hit out on what he called his World Friendship Tour. This started out innocently enough in South Africa where he denounced racism and did not call for the genocide of the white race. Things went downhill when he traveled to Iran, however. There he praised the "democracy" in the Islamic Republic and told the Iranians "God will destroy America by the hands of Muslims." He did not mention to the overwhelmingly white nation of Iran that they were a bunch of devils, and the Iranians, for their part, did not arrest Farrakhan for blasphemy against Islam, which is punishable by death there. Nevertheless, I would advise anyone visiting Iran to refrain from repeating Farrakhan's teaching that Allah was actually some guy who lived in Detroit. It might not go down well with the mullahs.

Another thing that probably didn't thrill the Iranians was Farrakhan's next stop on his tour, which was to visit Iran's archenemy Saddam Hussein in Iraq. In Iraq, he lashed out against the West's economic sanctions against Iraq as a "crime against humanity" and "mass murder." He did not criticize Saddam's unprovoked war against Iran that killed many hundreds of thousands of people.

When he got back to the U.S., he went back about his confrontational ways. Amongst his innumerable outrageous statements, he claimed that the flooding of New Orleans from Hurricane Katrina was caused by the deliberate sabotage of the city's dykes while the storm itself was "God's way of punishing America for its warmongering and racism." He claimed the H1N1 flu vaccine was actually a weapon designed for genocide. And it probably goes without saying that, in the world of Farrakhan, the 9/11 terrorist attacks were the result of a conspiracy between the U.S. government, bankers, and a Jew named Larry Silverstein.

You might think that having a black president would soften Farrakhan's hatred of the American government, but you would be wrong. He claims that President Obama is an "assassin" and a "murderer" because he ordered air strikes against Libya's tyrannical dictator Muammar Gaddafi. Gaddafi was not only Farrakhan's longtime personal friend, but also a multi-million dollar contributor to NOI despite Farrakhan's repeated denunciation of Arabs. Farrakhan has claimed that Obama was not fairly elected president and was instead selected to be president by Jews. He has gone as far as to call him "the first Jewish president."

But don't make the mistake of thinking Farrakhan is an anti-Semite. As he put it himself, "Some of you think that I'm just somebody who's got something out for the Jewish people. You're stupid."

None of Farrakhan's outlandish pronunciations are doing much to help NOI, however. It is thought that the religion has lost about half its members since the 1990s.

In 1995 Malcolm X's daughter, Qubilah Shabazz, was arrested on charges of attempting to hire a hit man to kill Farrakhan, apparently in revenge for him saying her dad was "worthy of death." Farrakhan and other NOI members rushed to her defense and claimed that the government had lured her into a trap. With the intended victim solidly allied with the defendant, the feds had little choice but to drop the charges against Shabazz. They did so on the condition that she complete a two-year psychiatric and chemical dependency program and stop claiming that the government entrapped her.

What the Hell???

Space: The Final Frontier.

As the space age took flight and science fiction like Star Wars and Star Trek became cultural phenomena, some religions quickly embraced the notion of space travel in their dogma. Here are a few examples of extraterrestrial influences on modern faith. Notice that not only do these beliefs appear to be influenced by Star Trek, but in some cases they take the terminology used on the show and use it as if it were part of the real world.

The Mother Plane

In the last chapter we mentioned the NOI belief in the enormous spaceship called the Mother Plane. But did you know that Louis Farrakhan has been on it? He claims he had a vision-like experience in which he was "beamed up" into a spaceship while he was visiting Mexico in 1985. While on board the vessel he got to meet the dearly departed Elijah Muhammed, who told him a great war was coming. Farrakhan later decided that an American air raid over Libya on April 15, 1986 in retaliation for the bombing of a German disco was this "great war."

In 2011, after a U.F.O. (it was actually the planet Venus) was photographed over Cleveland, Farrakhan said, "Wheels (his name for spaceships) are now being seen over the major cities... These wheels will be seen by the American people by the millions in a few days" He also accused the U.S. government of covering up the existence of the spacecraft.

Planet Teegeeack

As was described in the chapter on L. Ron Hubbard, the Church of Scientology maintains that Teegeeack is the name aliens use for the planet Earth. Interestingly, Louis Farrakhan has taken to endorsing Scientology and has encouraged many members of NOI to take Scientology counseling session. There are some similarities between the two faiths; they both hold that the world is many trillions of years old, and they are both big into spaceships, although the Mother Plane looks nothing like a Douglas DC-8 airplane, which is what Scientologists claim spaceships look like. But that's about where the similarities end. The rumors that Hubbard was a racist who supported apartheid in South Africa have not dimmed Farrakhan's enthusiasm for Scientology. He even has said that Hubbard represents a ray of hope for white people, "L. Ron Hubbard himself was and is trying to civilize white people and make them better human beings and take away from them their reactive minds ... Mr. Hubbard recognized that his people have to be civilized." It has been speculated that Farrakhan's embrace of Scientology may be in desperation to get his people to be worthy of the arrival of the Mother Plane and the destruction of the United States that will follow.

Planet Kolob

In Mormon theology, Kolob is the name of the planet (or star) where God lives. The Earth was created next to Kolob and was then moved across space to its present position. Belief in the planet Kolob stems from Joseph Smith's dubious translations of ancient Egyptian papyri, which form the Book of Abraham. Smith taught that Abraham discovered Kolob with the use of the same seer stones Smith used to translate the golden plates he claimed to find.

Today in Utah, you can find a geological formation named Kolob Canyons. Kolob was also the loose inspiration for the planet Kobol in the *Battlestar Galactica* television series.

Comet Hale-Bopp

Marshall Applewhite and Bonnie Lu Trousdale Nettles were a match made in heaven. She was a nurse in a psychiatric hospital, and he was a patient at the same institution. The two hit it off right away, and after he left the hospital, they immersed themselves in the study of UFOs and astrology. They convinced themselves that they were reincarnations of space aliens who were millions of years old and that they were the two witnesses mentioned in the Book of Revelation. As such, they started referring to themselves as "The Two." They left their families (in her case she ditched her four children) and began a religious ministry together.

The Two told anyone who would listen that they were destined to be put to death by their enemies, but after three days they would rise up and disappear into a cloud. "The cloud" was code for a divine spaceship of some sort.

Things for the new faith, however, got off to what may be the worst start in the history of religion when, in 1975 Applewhite and Nettles held a press conference in Brownsville, Texas to announce to the world that they were a his-and-hers pair of messiahs. They alerted the media that this would be the biggest story of all time. Thinking the event was somehow drug related, one reporter notified the police who sent a few officers over to check things out. When Applewhite and Nettles saw the cops arriving they decided to leave their own press conference, which made them look even more suspicious. The police ran the license plate number on their car and discovered that it was stolen. Applewhite spent the next ten months in jail for car theft. After he got out, the pair moved to California where they continued their ministry.

Over the years, The Two were able to put together a smattering of followers. They told the believers the time had come for them to leave for outer space. They all gathered at a campground to ascend to the stars together, but when the time for the departure came they all remained earthbound. About half the members of the Church gave up on the faith after this fiasco. For those that decided to stick it out, things got less pleasant. They were ordered to live a highly regimented lifestyle that included cutting their hair off and dressing in unisex uniforms. The theology of the faith continued to wander further off the beaten path as well. The Two told their flock that they were all related, with Applewhite being their father and Nettles being their granddad—though she was a woman). When these harsh new rules were enacted, even more people left the faith. To raise money and interest in the religion, The Two sold rides on the spaceship they were awaiting for $433 a throw. The catch of course, being that the purchaser had to wait until an unknown date to collect the trip he had paid for.

In 1985 Nettles died of cancer. She did not get up, walk around and grab a spaceship to paradise three days later as had been prophesied. This presented another challenge to the dogma of the faith. Applewhite danced around this obvious failure of his central prophesy by claiming that Nettles had gone ahead to prepare the afterworld for the arrival for the rest of the faithful. He even declared the Nettles would be piloting the spaceship that would carry everyone to the next world. Since Applewhite was on such a theological roll, he also claimed to be reincarnation of Jesus, or more specifically, he was the space alien who had occupied the body of Jesus 2,000 years earlier.

While waiting for Nettles to get her UFO pilot's license, the group settled into a mansion in southern California. They also finally chose a name, Heaven's Gate, for themselves.

Applewhite, who had a long history of sexual problems, got himself castrated, and several of his followers got themselves copycat castrations.

In 1996 the comet Hale-Bopp appeared in the skies and the Heaven's Gate bunch decided their ride had arrived. They thought the spaceship they had been waiting for was hidden in the comet's tale. The flying saucer didn't swoop down and pick them up, however, so they had to be resourceful. On March 21, 1997 the faithful all dressed up in identical, black outfits complete with badges that read "Heaven's Gate Away Team." Each member carried exactly $5.75 with him or her on the assumption they would need small amounts of American currency in the next world. The members then consumed massive amounts of barbiturates and booze, and they put plastic bags over their heads. The idea was that when they died, they would cast off their mortal shells, and their spirits would ascend up to the spaceship. All thirty-nine people who lived in the house perished. Two other members who were not there at the time committed suicide over the next several months to join up with the rest of the gang on the starship to heaven.

Sirius

Two men created the Order of the Solar Temple faith in 1984. The first of these was Joseph Di Mambro, a Frenchman who—in addition to being a convicted swindler—was an enthusiastic believer in new age spirituality. He also considered himself to be the heir to the leadership of the order of the Knights Templar, though the Templars had been wiped out many centuries beforehand. The other man was Luc Jouret, a Belgian doctor who specialized in homeopathic "medicine." A third man, Julian Origas, who had supposedly served in the Gestapo or SS during World War II and was also deeply interested in the Knights Templar, introduced Di Mambro and Jouret to one another. After Origas died, the two men co-founded their new religion. Di Mambro was the brains of the operation who laid down the faith's belief system while Jouret was the charismatic mouthpiece of the Temple with a talent for attracting new members—especially well-healed and respectable ones—to the fold. He even recruited the mayor of a Canadian town to the Temple.

The dogma of the Solar Temple is a bit hard to comprehend. Di Mambro claimed he received instructions from a group of Swiss spiritual leaders called the "Masters," but no one ever saw any of these people, and it is doubtful that they ever existed. It was most likely Di Mambro who cooked up the Solar Temple's beliefs, and it seems like he was making them up as he went along, without much rhyme or reason. He believed in unifying the world's religions—especially Christianity and Islam—and preparing the world for the return of Jesus in something called "solar glory." The number seven was sacred in the Temple and led to rituals such as the washing of food seven times before eating it. The Temple thought the world was polluted and contaminated, so they disinfected everything in sight with alcohol before touching it. They also believed that their salvation awaited them on the star Sirius (also known as the Dog Star,) which is the brightest star in the night sky.

Solar Temple ceremonies involved nude women, dramatic lighting, holograms, Wagnerian music, and other dramatic flourishes. Di Membro, in a move worthy of the old He-Man cartoons, raised a sword at the ceremonies and wailed, "By the powers invested in me, I trace a protective circle around this holy assembly."

It may all have sounded kooky, but it did bring in worshippers throughout the French-speaking world. Though the Temple only had hundreds, rather than thousands of members, their decision to target their recruitment efforts toward the wealthy paid off for them. Several Solar Templars donated $1 million or more to the cause. Di Mambro got so rich off Temple donations that he was able to buy himself a dozen houses.

But then things started to fall apart for the Solar Temple. In 1993 some of the Temple's members were arrested on weapons charges and the ensuing bad publicity damaged the faith in the eyes of the social elite that they relied upon for their funding. Even worse, a former Solar Templar named Tony Dutoit began speaking out against the faith. He even exposed the trickery the Di Mambro used to create "miracles" before his flock. In response to these charges, Di Mambro accused Dutoit's daughter of being the Antichrist. In short order Dutoit, his wife, and their baby girl were all murdered in their home in Quebec, Canada. The little "Antichrist" was stabbed to death with a wooden stake.

In the wake of the homicides, Di Mambro decided it was time for the faithful to make their journey to Sirius. Solar Templar members gathered together in various locations and killed themselves to begin their trip to the Dog Star. Unlike the Heaven's Gate worshippers, however, it seems that many—perhaps even most—of the faithful were not ready to begin their trip across the galaxy. The evidence at the scenes showed that the faithful had been drugged and then killed. Most of them had been shot though some had been suffocated. Their killers then arranged the bodies into circles and killed themselves. Incendiary devices went off sometime after the carnage and consumed the tragic sites in flames. When all was said and done, forty-seven people had died at two sites in Switzerland. When the sun rose in Canada an additional six victims were discovered in Quebec. Both Di Mambro and Jouret were amongst the dead. The next year, sixteen more Solar Templars died in France at a place known as the "Pit of Hell." Once again, many of the dead appeared to have left for Sirius involuntarily. After all these deaths, you have to wonder how anyone in the faith who was still alive could possibly be dumb enough to remain in it any longer, but people did. A suicide ceremony took place in Canada in 1997 that claimed five more lives.

The Elohim

In December of 1973 automotive journalist Claude Vorhilon was overcome with an irresistible urge to pull over and visit an extinct volcano while driving though central France. While he was there, a silver, bell-shaped space ship adorned with flashing lights silently descended from above. A "trap door" opened, and a staircase lowered from the craft. A four-foot tall, green, space alien named Yahweh emerged from the craft and introduced himself to Vorhilon. He took him aboard the craft for six days and told him the secrets of the origin of humanity.

It turns out that the aliens, who call themselves the Elohim, are an advanced group who traveled to Earth to do experiments creating life a long time ago. They divided themselves into seven different groups based upon the seven different races on their planet to do their work, because even the enlightened Elohim were apparently not above racial segregation. At first the Earth was all ocean, but the Elohim fixed that by blasting holes in the sea floor that allowed enough water to drain out to leave dry land exposed. They then started their life creation project by creating mere microbes, but gradually worked their way up to bigger and better creatures. Eventually, they created humans in their own image (although I seldom encounter four-foot tall, green people in my travels). Fearing that humans may someday turn against their creators, the Elohim also created all the world's religions to coerce the humans to worship them as gods. The aliens also told Vorhilon they were ready to appear before all of humanity, but not until he first built a magnificent embassy to welcome them. They also told him his name was to be "Rael," and he would be the world's final prophet.

In 1974 Rael wrote his experiences down in a book poetically titled *The Book Which Tells the Truth*. In 1975 another alien took Rael aboard his spaceship and took him to visit the Elohim home planet. While there, Rael got to meet Jesus, Buddha, Joseph Smith, and other religious leaders from Earth who had been preserved for all eternity by the Elohim. He founded the Raelian Movement and began to amass a body of followers, which he claimed eventually numbered into the tens of thousands. Raelians can sometimes be spotted by the Raelian symbol (the Star of David intertwined with a swastika) that they wear on necklaces.

Raelians believe that evolution does not exist. They maintain that the Elohim created all the world's life forms. They do not believe in gods or souls, but they do believe that the Elohim have technology that allows people to attain something like eternal life. They practice baptism, but only between the hours of 3:00 and 4:00 pm, as they believe that is the time when the Elohim are recording events on Earth.

Oh, and there is also sex. Raelians practice what could be considered sexually hedonistic lifestyles. Not only is open sexuality of virtually every kind tolerated, it is promoted in the faith. The group has an organization within it called "Rael's Girls," which is composed of sex workers such as strippers and prostitutes who promote promiscuity amongst women. One of Rael's ex-wives claimed he would bring home groups of female Raelians for orgies. Another Raelian group, called the Order of Angels, consists of women who have pledged to give themselves to the Elohim when they arrive on Earth. Raelians also promote "Go Topless Day" in North America each year on the Sunday that falls closest to August 26. They bill this as a demonstration for gender equality, but it has been charged that this stunt is merely one of several ways in which the Raelians use sex as a means of drawing new members into the faith. Given this emphasis on sex, it should not be surprising to learn that two-thirds of Raelians are believed to be male.

But what the Raelians are best known for is human cloning. In 2002 the Raelians claimed that they had successfully cloned a human being and that this girl, whom they named "eve," had been brought to term and born. Scientists around the world scoffed at the claim, and the Raelians have never presented any reliable evidence to support their extraordinary boast, but the ploy was a huge success for them nonetheless as mainstream news organizations around the world covered the story and gave them a mother lode of free publicity.

Rael has had decades to build his space alien embassy, and he has collected millions of dollars for the project, but he has yet to break ground for it. He opted instead to build a museum called "UFOland" that features a replica of the spaceship in which Rael rode around the galaxy. It also has the words "The Messiah is Alive Amongst Us" painted on the sides of the buildings. The Messiah is Rael in case you had failed to piece that together. UFOland is located in Canada, which is where the Raelian faith has been based since Rael abandoned France after encountering numerous legal problems there. There are plans to build a slicker, grander UFOland in Las Vegas. I guess we will just have to keep waiting for the construction of the embassy, which in turn means we will have to keep waiting to see these Elohim beings, who for some reason cannot appear before any human except Rael without the construction of this building.

Sheikh Omar Abdel-Rahman

Since traditional Islam can be considered an Eastern religion, it gets a bit of a free pass as far as this book is concerned. When an Islamic cleric moves to the United States and starts spreading his message of violence around, however, he becomes part of the religious tapestry of the West. Such is the case of Sheikh Omar Abdel-Rahman, a radical Islamic leader who provided America with an early glimpse of the pure hate of Islamic fundamentalism that would later consume the nation's attention.

Rahman was born in Egypt in 1938 and went blind from diabetes shortly thereafter. He studied the Koran passionately and went on to earn a doctorate in Koranic studies from the University of al-Azhar. He also taught Sharia law at the school for a while. But Rahman did not favor a kind and gentile reading of the Koran. He opted for a fundamentalist, take-no-prisoners approach to the faith. He felt that all secular institutions were offensive to God and deserved to be destroyed. The government of Egypt was particularly unacceptable to him, and he made no secret of his desire to see it swept away. In the 1970's Rahman threw himself into a new organization called al-Gama'a al-Islamia (The Islamic Group or IG), which was dedicated to the violent overthrow of the Egyptian government. Rahman quickly became IG's spiritual leader. The Egyptian government took a predictably dim view of IG, and Rahman found himself under arrest. He spent three years in prison where he said he was tortured. He was charged with issuing a *fatwa* (a type of religious command) calling for the assassination of President Sadat. Rahman beat the charges, however, and was set free.

Once he was out of jail Rahman traveled all about the Middle East looking for new followers and funding for his cause. In the 1980's he joined the guerilla war against the Soviet occupation of Afghanistan with his typical religious fervor. He begged God to give him his eyesight back just for a short while so he could take up arms against the Soviets. God did not comply with the request.

The battle against the Soviets was being waged by a variety of different *Mujahadin* groups who did not get along with one another. Rahman tried to get them to set aside their differences,

309

but failed. He then threw his support behind the two factions who were the most viciously anti-Western of the bunch. He made no secret of his hatred of the United States, but this did not prevent the U.S. from showering him with military support. The CIA seemed to think that by helping Rahman in his fight they could soften his attitude toward America. It would be a vast understatement to say that this idea did not pan out.

In 1990 Rahman entered the United States on a tourist visa even though he was on a terrorist watch list that should have prevented him from entering the country. He got in with the assistance of a CIA agent under circumstances that are still in dispute today. Whatever the case, Rahman left and reentered the U.S. repeatedly in the following years without any interference from immigration officials. Rahman set up shop in New York; opening a mosque that preached burning hatred against his adopted country. In his sermons he said that Americans were "descendants of apes and pigs who have been feeding from the dining tables of the Zionists, communists, and colonialists." He urged his followers to kill Westerners (especially Jews) and to shoot down planes, rob banks, sink ships, burn buildings, and do whatever else it took to destroy the Western democracies. In 1990, a follower of Rahman named El Sayyid Nosair took the blind sheikh's lectures to heart and murdered Rabbi Meir Kahane, who was the founder of the Jewish Defense League.

In 1993 a group of Rahman's followers detonated a large fertilizer fuel bomb in the North Tower of the World Trade Center. Their intent was to cause the North Tower to fall over into the South Tower, causing both of them to collapse with thousands of casualties. Their plan was completely implausible, but the explosion killed six people (including a pregnant woman) and injured thousands more. The morons who pulled off the bombing were anything but master criminals. They used a rental van to carry the bomb, and the man who hired the truck used his real name and address when he picked it up. He and his associates were quickly rounded up by law enforcement officials after the attack, and their link back to Rahman did not go unnoticed.

Actually, by this time the FBI was already looking into Rahman and his antics. They had infiltrated his group with a mole named Emad Salam, and he was providing them with a treasure trove of evidence against Rahman. Salam made hundreds of tape recordings of Rahman and his followers as they made plans for future attacks against the U.S. Amongst these plans was a plot for a "day of terror," which was to have been a series of coordinated bomb attacks against the United Nations headquarters, the Lincoln and Holland tunnels, The George Washington Bridge, and the main government office building in New York City. In addition to the tape recordings of the planning for the attacks, Salam got video of the conspirators mixing the ingredients together for the bombs they intended for use in the attacks. Also uncovered in the investigation were plans to assassinate New York Senator Alfonse D'Amato and Egyptian President Hosni Mubarak. He was to have been killed in an elaborate scheme that involved the hijacking of a military plane that would be used to drop a bomb on the president's home before being flown on a suicide mission into the U.S. Embassy in Cairo.

Rahman was arrested at a mosque in New Jersey in July of 1993. A subsequent search of his home uncovered a business card from Al-Qaeda leader Osama bin Laden's brother-in-law and a suitcase containing $62,000 in cash. It has been reported that bin Laden personally covered Rahman's living expenses while he was in the U.S.

Rahman and nine of his followers were charged with seditious conspiracy. The ten men were convicted on forty-eight of the fifty charges they faced, and Rahman was sentenced to life in prison. Lynne Stewart, who served as Rahman's defense attorney, chose to ignore the orgy of evidence that had been presented against her client and declared "He's not the first person to be convicted for his beliefs, and he won't be the last!"

Stewart was not just mouthing these words for the cameras either. She had become a true believer in Rahman's cause during her time defending him. After his conviction, she visited him in prison and conspired with two accomplices to sneak messages from him out to his followers. Among the messages that got out, were Rahman's call to reconsider a cease-fire that then existed between IG and the Egyptian government. Stewart was disbarred and sentenced to ten years in prison for her part in the message smuggling.

IG did reconsider the cease-fire and they concluded that peace wasn't in their best interests, so they went on the attack in Egypt with a ruthless bloodlust. In 1997 they attacked a tourist group that was visiting the ruins in the ancient city of Luxor. Rahman had strongly encouraged attacks against tourists because he held them in contempt for being infidels who did not adhere to his reactionary version of Islam and therefore had no business being in Egypt. Furthermore, since tourism is a vital component of the Egyptian economy, Rahman felt that if he could scare the tourists away he would undermine the Egyptian state.

Tourists had come under attack many times before in Egypt, but the Luxor attack was unlike anything seen before. After a group of fifty-eight European and Japanese tourists disembarked from their tour bus, four men armed with machine guns opened fire on them. They remorselessly mowed down everyone they could kill, including a five-year-old boy. After the slaughter was over, the killers pulled out machetes and went about the business of mutilating the corpses. They concentrated on hacking apart the females, as the women particularly offended them because they did not cover themselves from head to toe, as they believed God commanded all women to do. They took a note explaining their rationale for the slaughter and shoved it into the abdomen of one of their disfigured victims. After a battle with Egyptian security forces, the attackers then killed themselves.

After the massacre, the Egyptian public did not rally around IG as Rahman had expected. Instead, the public response was one of horror and anger at the attackers. When confronted with this reaction, Rahman tried to blame Israel for the attacks, but very few people bought that story.

In 1998 a last will and testament purportedly written by Sheikh Rahman surfaced. It is a rather unusual document. In it, Rahman says his death (no matter when or how it occurred) was murder at the hands of American infidels, and he called upon his followers to exact "most violent revenge" on the United States. His orders went on, "cut off all relations with (Americans, Christians, and Jews), tear them to pieces, destroy their economies, burn their corporations, destroy their peace, sink their ships, shoot down their planes, and kill them on air, sea, and land. And kill them wherever you may find them, take them hostage, and destroy their observatories. Kill these infidels." The will was allegedly written by Rahman and smuggled out of prison, but it could have just as easily been written by one of Rahman's sons who then attributed it to his dad.

Rahman's boys were following in their old man's footsteps and one of them, Mohammed Omar Abdel-Rahman, had by this time risen to a high position in the al Qaeda terrorist outfit. He was in close contact with Khalid Sheikh Mohammed who was the mastermind of the September 11th attacks, which mirrored the commands in Rahman's will in many ways. The junior Rahman himself may have also been involved in the planning of the attacks. He was captured in Pakistan in 2003. Khalid was captured shortly after Rahman. Rahman is thought to have been turned over to American authorities, and is being held in an unknown location today.

> The attack at Luxor was not the last time a radical Islamist used a freshly killed corpse as a vehicle to deliver a message. In 2004 the Dutch filmmaker Theo Van Gogh was shot and stabbed to death by a Muslim extremist named Mohammed Bouyeri in Amsterdam. Bouyeri was furious with Van Gogh for a short film he had made called *Submission*, which protested the mistreatment of women in Islamic culture. When he was finished murdering Van Gogh, Bouyeri attached a five-page letter to him by plunging a knife through it and into his chest. The letter was a rant against various Dutch politicians, their "Jewish masters," the United States, and so on.

Warren Jeffs

In 1890 the Mormons were anxious to see Utah admitted into the union as a state, so the LDS Church agreed to end the practice of polygamy, which had been an insurmountable obstacle to statehood. The move was successful, and in 1896 Utah became the forty-fifth state. Many Mormons rejected the change, however. They saw the concession as a betrayal of the divine revelations of the prophet Joseph Smith. Some Mormons secretly remained in polygamist relationships long after the practice was formally abolished.

But not all polygamists were willing to pretend to abide by the decision while secretly carrying on with multiple wives. One breakaway group saw the Church's change of heart on the polygamy issue as one that proved the Church leadership had forfeited their right to govern the faithful. They openly rejected the LDS as the work of the devil and founded their own Church, which they claimed was the true heir to the tradition of Joseph Smith and Brigham Young. Since Smith had claimed that God commanded polygamy, and Young had himself taken scores of wives, their claim was not a fantastical one. The splinter faction called itself the Fundamentalist Church of Jesus Christ of Latter Day Saints (FLDS). The FLDS set up a community in the remote twin cities of Hildale, Utah and Colorado City, Arizona. The towns became collectively known as the Short Creek area and were populated almost entirely by FLDS Church members. The FLDS claims tens of thousands of members in Short Creek and in other areas across the U.S. and Canada.

In 1986 a man named Rulon Jeffs took over control of the FLDS, and his one-man rule broke the FLDS tradition of having a council of leaders sharing power in the Church. He became the Prophet of the Church and was believed to converse directly with God. Needless to say, he was not a man to be trifled with. In the FLDS faith, a man's worth is largely judged by the number of wives he has, and as such, it can be no surprise that Jeffs married dozens upon dozens of women and fathered scores of children. One of them was a painfully skinny boy named Warren, who was destined to replace him.

As Rulon aged into a doddering, old man he was content to pass his golden years by marrying more young women, and he left most of the affairs of the Church in the hands of his favorite son. The Prophet Rulon predicted he would live to be 350 years old, but he fell just shy of that mark when he died in 2002 at the age of ninety-two. Warren Jeffs immediately took control of the Church upon his father's death, but it was really nothing but a formality by that point, as he had been ruling the FLDS with an iron fist long before his father had assumed room temperature.

Warren had long had a dictatorial temperament. He honed his despotic craft in his years as the principal of an FLDS school, where he often savagely berated students for the tiniest of infractions. His wives were not safe from his wrath either. He assaulted one of them (who was a teacher at the school) in front of her students. He casually walked up to her and pulled and twisted her hair until she fell to the floor. He then walked away without saying anything. The unmistakable lesson to the students was that women must be absolutely obedient to their husbands at all times.

Jeffs set up all the marriages in the Short Creek area. In 2001 Jeffs arraigned a wedding between fourteen-year-old Elissa Wall and her nineteen-year-old first cousin Allen Steed, who Elissa had hated since he had mocked her for being fat when she was a child (well, a younger child). Elissa went to Jeffs and begged him to let her out of the wedding, but Warren was resolute and forced Wall to go through with it. Wall was scolded with reminders that if she failed to go through with the wedding she would be banned from heaven and cut loose from the Church. She was eventually spirited off to Nevada and married to Steed in a secretive, extra-legal ceremony. Steed later forced himself on her. Even after the marriage, Wall sought help from Jeffs by telling him she was desperately unhappy with the man he had condemned her to spend her life with. He rebuked her for wishing to leave her "husband" and cut her off from her family. She eventually did the unthinkable; she left Steed and was banished from the FLDS. She lost all contact with everyone she knew and had to learn how to live in the foreign culture of mainstream America.

Jeffs ran the FLDS and the Short Creek area like an American version of the Taliban. He imposed a bizarre and draconian set of restrictions on his flock. He banned the sport of basketball, so all the backboards in Short Creek had to be taken down immediately. He banned movies, the color red, and ordered the library to close. Perhaps most appallingly, he forbade his people from owning dogs and forced all dog owners to shoot their pets. In 2004 he even ordered the FLDS temple to close, saying the people were unworthy of it.

He also ordered his father's innumerable widows to become his brides. Jeffs married at least eighty-seven girls and women, but it has been estimated that he may have taken closer to 180 wives. Of these brides, twenty-four are known to have been under the age of seventeen when he married them. Additionally, he has presided over 500 or so polygamous marriage ceremonies for other FLDS couples.

Of course, when you have some men taking on piles of brides, that leaves a whole lot of other guys who are going to get none. Jeffs devised a solution to that problem, however. He took to the practice of banishing boys from the FLDS for the slightest of offenses. Once severed from the Church, the boys were cut off from their families and left with nowhere to stay and no one to look after them. They were thrust out into the non-FLDS world, which they knew nothing about. The boys had received poor educations in Short Creek and were all but unemployable. They didn't know how to do many of the basic day-to-day tasks of life since the Church took control of almost every aspect of peoples' lives in Short Creek. Such kids came to be known as the "Lost Boys." The Lost Boys numbered up to a thousand in all and often wound up as drug addicts, beggars and/or prostitutes living on the streets of Salt Lake City and Las Vegas. Their families did not dare question their treatment for that would mean challenging Warren Jeffs, who spoke with the voice of God and held their salvation in his hands.

Jeffs' interference in the lives of FLDS families wasn't confined to casting their sons to cruel fates. He also used his power to rip apart families as he saw fit. Any man who displeased the Prophet was at risk of having his marriage annulled by him. When this happened, the man would have all his wives and children taken from him, and he would be forbidden from having any contact with them forever afterward. The women were assigned to new husbands who would act as fathers to the kids. Jeffs destroyed about 300 families in this manner.

In 2004 six of the Lost Boys filed a lawsuit against Jeffs for forcing them out of society to eliminate competition for wives. Additionally, Warren's half-brother Brent sued him for child molestation. The suit alleged that Warren had sodomized Brent when he was only five years old. Two other half-brothers of Jeffs who witnessed the event backed up Brent's claims, although one of them committed suicide before he could testify in court. Brent's suit also accused Warren of covering up numerous other cases of child molestation.

Jeffs didn't respond to any of the cases against him. He went into hiding instead; he would never live in the open again. The next year he was charged with two counts of sexual conduct with a minor and one count of conspiracy to commit sexual conduct with a minor. Eight other FLDS men were also charged.

But Jeffs was nowhere to be found. The FLDS community did its utmost to shield him from justice and few communities were better set up than the FLDS to accomplish such a feat. The Short Creek area was notoriously impenetrable to outsiders. The local police worked for the Church, not the public. Any visitors to the area would be shunned by the populace and confronted by the police until they moved on. Jeffs ordered Church members to fight to the death to prevent his arrest. The FLDS also had a compound in El Dorado, Texas called the Yearning for Zion Ranch. The primary feature of the ranch was a castle-shaped temple that was said to be filled with weaponry. It was widely assumed that Jeffs was safely ensconced in the ranch, but the conventional wisdom turned out to be wrong. Jeffs was actually traveling all around the country going from safe house to safe house where he would have money, supplies and wives waiting for him at every stop.

In the spring of 2006 the FBI placed Jeffs on its Ten Most Wanted list and offered a reward for his capture that eventually reached $100,000, but still Jeffs eluded justice. Finally, his luck ran out on August 28 of that same year when the SUV he was riding in was pulled over for a minor license plate infraction, and he was recognized. Jeffs was busted just outside of Las Vegas (Sin City) in a red (the forbidden color) SUV while wearing

317

shorts and a t-shirt (both forbidden in the FLDS) and carrying lottery tickets (two guesses). Other than that, he might have been a picture of the pious life that he preached.

Life in the joint did not agree with Jeffs who was accustomed to being treated as an unchallenged authority. Once the other prisoners got a load of the whole "prophet" thing, they predictably mocked him mercilessly. Jeffs refused to eat, and he lost about twenty pounds, which was a considerable amount considering he stood 6'5" and weighed a vanishingly scant 150 pounds when he arrived at jail in the first place. Furthermore, he was charged with sex crimes against children, which always dampens one's social prospects when in jail. After a few months as a guest at the gray bar hotel, Jeffs confessed on videotape that he was not a prophet and that he was a "wicked man." Three days later he attempted suicide by trying to hang himself with his own clothing.

Jeffs went to trial where he was forced to confront Elissa Wall again. She was now the centerpiece of the case against Jeffs on charges of rape as an accomplice. Whereas before, the all-powerful Jeffs had spurned Wall when she pleaded with him to be spared of the fate he had assigned to her, it was now Jeffs who was at the mercy of Wall. She did not shrink from the challenge as she laid out her devastating story to the world. The jury returned two guilty counts against Jeffs, and he was sentenced to ten years to life in prison. Furthermore, Jeffs lost the civil suits filed by the Lost Boys and his half-brother, which resulted in huge financial damages being leveled against him.

In 2008 authorities raided the FLDS compound in Texas after they received phone calls from people claiming to be kids who were abused at the ranch. The calls turned out to be fraudulent, but the cops found loads of evidence of wrongdoing when they were there. A number of girls under the age of eighteen were found to be pregnant or to have already had children. The community was tight-lipped about the identity of the fathers of these kids, but genetic testing was employed to root out the much older dads. Additionally, incriminating photographs of Jeffs were found at the ranch. The pictures appeared to be shots of Jeffs and two of his wives. The blushing brides were as young as twelve, and they were getting big smooches from the unfathomably creepy Jeffs in the pictures. One of the photos was labeled "1st Anniversary." The raid led to a host of new charges being filed against Jeffs and other FLDS members.

In 2010 Jeffs' rape conviction was overturned on appeal because the judge's instructions to the jury were deemed to be improper. Utah authorities promised to try him again, but events in Texas soon rendered a retrial in Utah rather moot.

In 2011 Jeffs went on trial in San Angelo, Texas for sexually assaulting two children, aged twelve and fourteen. The trial turned out to be one of the most shocking and bizarre courtroom dramas in the history of the United States. For starters, Jeffs fired his defense team and acted as his own attorney. It is often said that he who represents himself has a fool for a client, but Warren Jeffs lent a whole new meaning to that saying. Jeffs turned the proceedings into an all-out, three-ring circus with an endless barrage of nonsensical objections, many—if not most—of which revolved around the special connection he thought he had with God. He went on an hour-long tirade against the legal system, he read holy literature for hours on end, he demanded that the legal proceedings cease in the name of the Lord, and he threatened the judge and the "counties of prosecutorial zeal" with disease and death from above.

Jeffs had done everything possible to dig his own grave in the courtroom, but his antics paled in comparison to the jaw-dropping evidence against him that the prosecution wheeled out. They introduced a series of amateur porn tape recordings Jeffs had made in which he instructed his new, underage brides as to how he wished to be sexually pleasured. On the recordings he can be heard ordering several of his older wives to strip and then help the new kids to have sex with him. For the *pièce de résistance*, the recording captured Jeffs having sex with a twelve-year-old. Jeffs can be heard calling out the girl's name in addition to all his grunting and heavy breathing. The prosecution also showed the jury pictures of a temple Jeffs constructed featuring beds surrounded by chairs so his future brides could get lessons by watching the prophet in action. DNA evidence was submitted that showed that Jeffs was the father of the child of one of his accusers. Brent Jeffs took the stand to testify against his half-brother, and Jeffs' niece also testified that he had molested her when she was eight. Jeffs' writings were submitted to the jury as well. Amongst the volumes of self-incriminating statements Jeffs made was his 2005 comment, "If they knew what I was doing they would hang me from the highest tree." At the trial's conclusion, Jeffs was given a half an hour to make his closing argument. He used the whole 30 minutes to stand silently before the jury while staring at them before finally saying, "I am at peace." Jeffs was convicted and sentenced to life in prison plus twenty years.

Jeffs remains the prophet and unchallenged leader of the FLDS. He has issued numerous edicts to his followers from jail. He has banned corn and dairy products from the community. He ordered parents to destroy all their children's toys. He even forbade intimacy between husbands and wives. He appointed fifteen men to father all children in the FLDS. Any woman wishing to get pregnant must now go to one of them for sex. Furthermore, there must be at least two witnesses on hand to watch the carnal proceedings.

> In addition to all of Jeffs' other fine qualities you can add "virulent racist." Following in the tradition of the teachings of Joseph Smith, Jeffs preached a racial viewpoint that would make the Ku Klux Klan proud. He deplores anyone who is not white. He has railed against contemporary music as being the work of blacks, whom he thinks are trying to lead the world to immorality. He kept the FLDS a whites-only outfit; although it's not like minorities are knocking down the doors trying to get in anyway. Jeffs gave numerous speeches outlining his racial philosophies. Some examples of his worldview...
>
> *So the Negro race has continued and today is the day of the Negro as far as the world is concerned... They have mixed their blood with many peoples, until there are many peoples not able to hold the priesthood.*
>
> And
>
> *You see some classes of the human family that are black, uncouth, or rude and filthy, uncomely, disagreeable and low in their habits; wild and seemingly deprived of nearly all the blessings of the intelligence that is usually bestowed upon mankind.*
>
> And
>
> *So I give you this lesson on the black race that you can understand its full effects as far as we are able to comprehend. And that we must beware—if we are for the prophet, the priesthood—we will come out of the world and leave off their dress, their music, their styles, their fashions; the way they think, what they do, because you can trace back and see a connection with immoral, filthy people.*

In 2007 Wendell Loy Nielson was named to temporarily replace Jeffs as President of the FLDS while Jeffs awaited trail. Nielson, however, was himself facing three counts of bigamy in Texas and was also accused of abusing one of his wives who was a teenager at the time. In 2011 Jeffs got tired of Nielson's presidency and fired him. The next year Nielson was convicted on all three bigamy charges.

What the Hell???

Sexual Child Abuse in the Catholic Church

The sexual abuse of children in the Catholic Church is probably about as old as the Catholic Church itself. As we have seen earlier, Pope Boniface VIII boasted openly about the boys he had taken advantage of, and it was widely rumored during Pope Leo X's papacy that he could not be trusted in the company of boys. By the latter half of the twentieth century there had been enough arrests of clergy members to make it broadly known that there was a serious problem within the Church. In 1994 the Irish government actually collapsed after they refused to extradite a priest who had abused boys for more than forty years to Northern Ireland, where he faced criminal charges. But it was in Boston in 2002 that the dam burst on the Church, and a deluge of scandal was unleashed.

It was that in year that the *Boston Globe* broke the story of several priests who had abused hundreds of boys for years. Church officials had been notified that the priests were molesting kids, but rather than reporting them to the police or defrocking them, they transferred the suspected abusers from one parish to another, thereby throwing fresh, unsuspecting boys (and less often, girls) into their clutches. Such transfers were the standard practice in dioceses throughout the Church, but this time the scandal seemed to reach a critical mass. The outrage that erupted over the Boston cases was so severe that Cardinal Bernard Law was forced to resign as Archbishop of Boston (although he retained his position as cardinal and was given a prestigious assignment in Rome after his resignation). The enormous publicity generated by the Boston cases inspired numerous other victims of clerical abuse across the world to come forward and tell their horror stories of what had happened to them as children. Between 2001 and 2010, about 3,000 cases of abusive priests were sent to the Vatican's doctrinal courts.

It would be impossible to cover all—or even a small percentage—of the abusive priests involved in these affairs, so I'll concentrate on just one rather ordinary example, Fr. Lawrence C. Murphy of Wisconsin. In 1950 Murphy was assigned to the St. John's School for the Deaf in the town of St. Francis. It didn't take him long to get about the business of molesting the unfortunate boys at the school. His favorite activity was to pull their pants down and fondle them. He did this in his office, in the school's dormitories, in his car, at his mother's house, and at the confessional at the church. Some of his victims came forward and reported him in the early 1960s, but the reports made no impact as Murphy was promoted to be the director of the school in 1963. He served in this position for the next eleven years. Boys continued to come forward with claims of abuse, but they could not get anyone to listen to their claims. They told the police and three different archbishops, but no action was taken. After all, Murphy was a holy man, and they were nothing but some deaf kids. In 1974 several of the victims printed up mock wanted posters with Murphy's picture on them accusing him of sex crimes. They handed the posters out in front of a cathedral in Milwaukee, and this finally brought some attention to their claims. Fr. Murphy was transferred to a new job in the city of Superior where he was still allowed to have free contact with kids; he was even allowed to lead youth retreats. In 1993 Murphy was finally evaluated by an expert in sexual disorders. In his sessions with her, Murphy admitted to molesting nineteen boys, but in actuality he probably had assaulted around 200 kids. The evaluator concluded that Murphy was unrepentant; he did not understand the harm he had caused, and he would be resistant to treatment for his disorder. Murphy claimed that his acts were "sex education" for his victims and said, "There was rampant homosexuality among the older boys. I fixed the problem." So in his own mind, he thought he was something of a hero.

Three years later, Archbishop Rembert Weakland of Milwaukee, trying to defuse growing anger in the deaf community over the scandal, sent a letter to the Vatican asking them to convene a canonical trial for Murphy. The next year he wrote the Vatican again saying he received no response to his first request. The second letter was forwarded to Cardinal Joseph Ratzinger who did not respond to it. Murphy caught wind of the possibility that he could be defrocked, so he wrote his own letter to the Vatican begging for the matter to be dropped. "I simply want to live out that time I have left in the dignity of my priesthood," he wrote. This lame appeal was enough to convince Cardinal Tarciscio Bertone to dismiss the matter. Murphy died shortly thereafter and was buried in his priestly vestments. His funeral was presided over by a bishop who praised Murphy, although he did concede that there were "some shadows" in his career. The Vatican tried to keep the letters concerning his case secret, but they were uncovered and published by the *New York Times*.

Yet Murphy's death was not quite the end of the story. His victims and the victims of other predatory priests decided to slap the Archdiocese of Milwaukee with lawsuits for the abuse they had suffered. Some of the lawsuits were settled to the tune of about $30 million, but with many others still pending the Archdiocese declared bankruptcy in 2011. In so doing, they joined seven other American dioceses ranging from San Diego, California to Fairbanks, Alaska to Wilmington, Delaware in insolvency. In Boston the Church is facing $100 million dollars in judgments against it, but has so far not resorted to bankruptcy. Though bankruptcy is a humiliating step to take, it does limit the damages the dioceses have to pay to their victims, often to mere pennies on the dollar.

In Newfoundland, Canada, the diocese of St. George was able to avoid bankruptcy by selling off nearly all of the property owned by the Church. Well over a hundred buildings, including about sixty churches, were sold (or as the Church terms it, "relegated to profane use") to cover the cost of lawsuits related to sexual abuse cases. After the buildings were sold, the diocese appealed to Catholics across Canada to donate money to allow them to buy back their churches. Of course, they could have just appealed for donations to pay off the victims in the first place and thus avoided selling their churches, but parishioners have been shown to be hesitant to donate money to help pay legal claims. The sale of churches is also being considered in Cloyne, Ireland to raise money to pay off legal claims from victims of sexual abuse there.

The Cloyne abuse cases have had bigger ramifications than the relegation of churches to profane use, however. A report written by the Irish government in 2011 found that the Church took no action against nineteen priests who abused children from 1996 through 2009. Furthermore, the report found that the Vatican itself encouraged bishops to ignore the sexual abuse policies created by the Irish Church in 1996. These guidelines included the reporting of abuse to law enforcement. The smoking gun in the report was a letter from a former Vatican ambassador that stated that the Irish Church's child-protection measures violated cannon law and could only be considered a "study document." The report said this letter "effectively gave individual Irish bishops the freedom to ignore the procedures." Needless to say, the feces hit the fan in the wake of this report. Irish Prime Minister Enda Kenny lashed out at "the dysfunction, disconnection, elitism, and the narcissism, that dominate the culture of the Vatican to this day." The Irish parliament expressed their disdain by passing a resolution condemning the Vatican's role in the affair.

The weight of all these scandals has caused some degree of soul searching within the Church, but how much good it's doing is questionable. The Church commissioned a study of the abuse scandals from the John Jay College of Criminal Justice of the City of New York. In 2011 they published their results. The study concluded that it was the secular culture of the 1960's that disoriented priests and led them to sexually abuse youngsters. Ah yes, the '60s. A time when people wore their hair long, listened to psychedelic rock music, and sexually molested little kids. Or something like that. How were priests supposed to resist that temptation? Predictably, this conclusion was widely mocked and ridiculed. What's more, the study concluded that most of the predatory priests were not actually pedophiles because only twenty-two percent of the victims were pre-pubescent. The authors of the study determined that the cutoff age for "pre-pubescent" was ten. That's right, if a priest raped an eleven-year-old child he could not be considered a pedophile according to this report. By the way, most of the victims identified by the study were between the ages of eleven and fourteen. The Church commissioned this study at a cost of $1.8 million dollars, and for their money, they bought themselves a laughable document that has only increased suspicion that the Church is unwilling to address this issue seriously.

The controversy over Cardinal Ratzinger's role in the child abuse scandals didn't hold back his career in the clergy, as he became Pope Benedict XVI in 2005. The new pope was named in a lawsuit concerning the alleged abuse of three boys in Texas in the 1990s. The suits claimed that Benedict had acted to cover up the incidents. But the pope had diplomatic immunity in the cases as the head of the microstate of Vatican City, so the cases against him will never be brought to court.

Monsignor William Lynn of Philadelphia enjoys no such protection, however. In 2012 he was convicted of child endangerment after he had spent decades hiding the actions of abusive priests from worshipers. When allegations began to swirl around the priests, they were transferred to new parishes for "health reasons." Lynn even went so far as to maintain a list of all the abusive priests in the parish. The list was shredded on the order of Cardinal Anthony Bevilacqua. A second copy of the list survived, however, and fell into the hands of law enforcement officials. Lynn became the first person ever to be convicted in the United States of covering up the sexual abuse committed by priests.

Fred Phelps

In the polarized political climate that has gripped the United States in the early twenty-first century there have been few issues on which those on the left and right sides of the political spectrum can agree. There is one unifying figure left in this country, however. Just about everyone hates Fred Phelps.

Phelps was born in Mississippi in 1929, and aside from a 1951 conviction for assaulting a police officer in California; he didn't give any early hints of the viciousness that would later mark his life. Phelps took up study of the law and dedicated himself to promoting civil rights causes. He was even honored by various civil rights groups for his efforts on behalf of their causes. Alas, the semblance of normalcy that Phelps displayed was merely a veneer. It wasn't long before that peeled off, and he was exposed for what he is—cruel, bitter, and vindictive.

In 1977 a court reporter named Carolene Brady did not have a transcript ready for Phelps when he had asked for it. Phelps blew a screw and sued Brady for $22,000 although the late document had not figured into the outcome of the case. During the civil proceedings against Brady, Phelps called her to the stand and berated her for days on end. He called her a "slut" and accused her of being a pervert amongst other things. Unsurprisingly, Phelps lost the suit against her. The Kansas Supreme court then lashed out against his courtroom performance saying he had badgered Brady with the intent to hurt and destroy her. Undeterred, Phelps appealed the ruling and gave eight affidavits to the court that contained damaging information about Brady. The affidavits had been sworn to by people whom, it was eventually discovered, had not even been contacted by Phelps about the case. This stunt got him disbarred for life in Kansas.

But Phelps had another career to fall back on, because in 1955 Phelps had founded the Westboro Baptist Church. True, things have not always gone swimmingly for this Church. After he lost most of his initial flock due to internal squabbling in the Church, things got so bad that Phelps had to support himself with door-to-door sales of vacuum cleaners and baby carriages. Eventually Phelps made his kids sell candy to make ends meet. But Phelps was able to keep the Church afloat.

The Church today has a tiny congregation that consists largely of Fred Phelps and people who are related to Fred Phelps. The Church adheres to a strict Calvinist theology with an extra dash of anti-homosexuality sprinkled atop it. And by a "dash" I mean these people are utterly and obsessively fixated on homosexuals with a white-hot, burning hatred that knows no bounds.

In 1991 the Phelps gang started picketing against homosexuals and anyone they imagined to be supporting homosexuals. The protests were hateful and offensive, but in the very conservative state of Kansas they won some hearts and minds. For example, in 1990 Fred Phelps ran for governor. In the Democratic primary he got 6.7% of the vote. In 1992, after he had started his picketing against homosexuals, he ran for the U.S. Senate and got 30.8% of the primary vote in a contest in which he referred to his opponent as a "bull dike" *(sic)*. This was still not enough to win the nomination, but he increased his vote total to nearly five times what he got in his first attempt at public office.

The Church kept up the picketing all the while. They screamed obscenities at people passing by their protests. They spat on people, they bombarded their opponents with abusive faxes, and they picketed their workplaces. They filed lawsuits against those who dared to stand up to them. In all of this they benefited from a police chief in Topeka who seemed more willing to protect the Church members than the public who they attacked on a nearly daily basis. Despite all this, the Westboro congregation was still little known outside of Kansas, but that was about to change.

The Church first made national headlines following the death of Matthew Shepard. Shepard was a twenty one-year-old gay man, who on the night of October 6, 1998, was kidnapped, beaten, tortured, and tied to a fence where he was left for dead. He remained there for eighteen hours before he was discovered by a man who at first had thought he was a scarecrow. Shepard was taken to a hospital where he remained in a coma for a few days before he died. Shepard's murder became a milestone in the gay rights movement as it laid bare the murderous "queer bashing" that homosexuals still had to fear.

But not everyone was horrified by the crime. Phelps and his flock saw the work of the Lord in the murder, and they made the trek from Kansas to Wyoming to make their feelings known. The group picketed Shepard's funeral brandishing signs with thoughtful sayings such as GOD HATES FAGS, MATT SHEPARD ROTS IN HELL and AIDS KILLS FAGS DEAD. Phelps also tried to get a monument erected in Wyoming with Shepard's picture on it and the wording *"MATTHEW SHEPARD, Entered Hell October 12, 1998, in Defiance of God's Warning: 'Thou shalt not lie with mankind as with womankind; it is abomination.' Leviticus 18:22."* He was never able to get the permits for this sublime artwork to be displayed, however.

When the wars in Afghanistan and Iraq got going after the turn of the century, Phelps' people went out to picket the funerals of the soldiers who had been killed in the conflicts. In Phelps' mind, the deaths were all God's righteous retribution against the United States—a country that Phelps feels is hopelessly immoral due to its tolerance of homosexuals. But wait, I'm getting ahead of myself. I almost left out the *weird* part! Before the war with Iraq broke out, Phelps penned a letter to Saddam Hussein praising the tyrannical Iraqi dictator for his pro-Christian policies. A group of Church members even traveled to Iraq at Saddam's invitation where they staged a protest against Bill and Hillary Clinton, and anal sex.

Needless to say, the group's protests at military funerals carrying signs with slogans such as "GOD HATES THE U.S.A.," "THANK GOD FOR I.E.D.S," "PRAY FOR MORE DEAD SOLDIERS," "GOD HATES CRIPPLE SOLDIERS" and "THANK GOD FOR SEPT. 11" have not swayed the general public to view Phelps' band in a favorable light.

And it's not just military funerals that the group protests. According to the Church's website they have staged well over 40,000 protests. Whenever a major event hits the news there is a good chance the Phelps crew will pounce on it. For instance, when a bridge collapsed in Minneapolis the Church promised to protest the funerals of the victims and referred to Minneapolis as the "land of the sodomite damned." When a bus passenger in Canada was brutally murdered the group sneaked into the country to protest at his funeral. They also picketed the funerals of Frank Sinatra, Sonny Bono, Bill Clinton's mom, and Al Gore's dad.

Church members traveled to Connecticut to picket at the funeral of one of the victims of the Sandy Hook Elementary School massacre, but they left after hundreds of counter-protesters descended upon the town with the intention of blocking them. Nevertheless, Church members have publicly stated that the children killed in the school are now in hell.

Perhaps most incredibly, The Westboro clan even picketed the funeral of the vehemently anti-homosexual Reverend Jerry Falwell and accused him of praising "practicing fags." Phelps said, "On Tuesday, May 14 the old, fat, false prophet Jerry Falwell died and entered hell." His stirring eulogy went on, "Hell from beneath was moved to meet Falwell at his coming, rousing the dead, even those that used to be big shots on Earth now in hell greeting him with such words as these, 'Why hello Reverend Frogwell, you old money-grubbing pervert!' "

A group of students from Falwell's Liberty University heard about the Westboro gang's plans to protest at Falwell's funeral and decided they would not let them portray their dearly departed leader as a fag-lover. Their plans were thwarted, however, when the police stopped and searched their car, which was full of homemade bombs the students were planning to use against the Phelps protesters.

The list of events picketed by the Phelps clan goes on and on. Often the Church states its intent to protest an event and then never bothers to show up. The threat of protest alone whips up a media frenzy, which in turn gives them ample amounts of free publicity.

Encouragingly, The tables have begun to be turned on Phelps and his church. Three of Phelps' children have left the Church, as have some of his grandchildren and other Church members. Those leaving the congregation often don't hold back on criticizing both Fred Phelps' hateful dogma and his abusive style of parenting.

In 2010 a group of a dozen people traveled from Illinois to Topeka with the intention of sitting silently through a Westboro service as a protest of the group's picketing of military funerals. The Westboro Church turned them away saying such a statement would be inappropriate at a religious service. Of course, funerals tend to be religious services too, but the Westboro clan does just about everything possible to disrespect those. After the Illinois group was turned away, they took to picketing the church and were joined by several Topeka residents in the process. The protesters carried signs saying "Fire, brimstone and lunacy," and "Let our fallen rest in peace."

The Phelps clan also faced picketers when they protested at the 2010 Comic-Con convention in San Diego. The Church said that the comic book fans were worshiping false gods by reading Spider-Man comics and whatnot. They did their routine God-hates-fags song and dance, but were met by a large counter protest of people dressed as various sci-fi and fantasy characters carrying signs saying silly things such as "GOD HATES JEDI" and "KILL ALL HUMANS." The counter-protesters also chanted "What do we want? GAY SEX! When do we want it? NOW!"

Other people have started to take advantage of the Phelps hatemongering to raise money for charity. They have set up fundraising collections next to the Westboro picketers so anyone offended by them can make a contribution to groups that advocate human and gay rights. The organization Phelps-A-Thon has made an art of staging counter-protests at Westboro pickets around the country. They hold fundraisers for gay, Jewish or whatever group Phelps hates next to the Westboro picketers. They use big tote boards to tally their donations, which can reach several thousand dollars at individual events. A Westboro protest at Vassar College in New York prompted an on-line fundraiser that raised more than $100,000 in pledges to a homosexual support group.

Many of the Westboro Church's members are attorneys, and they have filed all manner of frivolous lawsuits against those opposed to their hate-mongering ways. Fred Phelps alone has personally filed hundreds upon hundreds of lawsuits. When Sears was late with a television delivery to his family he sued the company for $50 million, and he sued Ronald Reagan for posting an ambassador to the Vatican. Mostly though, the Phelps family sues their opponents to shut them up. The legal costs of defending one's self from these lawsuits can be steep while the Phelpses don't need to pay attorneys, so it means almost nothing to them to file suit after suit.

The Westboro Baptist Church has made it crystal clear that God hates America, but what about the world's other nations? Well fear not my foreign friends, for the Church is on the case! They have launched a website called godhatestheworld.com which lists hundreds of nations and why God hates them all.

A typical example is the U.K. entry in which the WBC rails against Her Majesty's realm, "Heir to the throne, Prince Charles of Wales, will certainly carry on his wicked mothers *(sic)* tradition of pandering to the fags and any other filthy, vile cause. The famous adulterer (who carried on an affair before the entire country while married to the great whore, Princess Diana) has no authority to do otherwise."

The page includes a picture of the cover of the Beatles' Abbey Road album with a WBC member inserted into the scene in place of Paul McCartney (God hates copyrights?) carrying signs that say "SIN BREEDS VIOLENCE" and "THRONE OF INIQUITY."

If you suspect that only American allies get hammered here, you can guess again. Take the virulently anti-American country of North Korea for example, about which the WBC says, "North Korea worships a little shrimp of a man. They have given over their lives and their minds to this titmouse. AWKWARD X 12! Kim Jong II is his name and perversion is his game – ugh! Just look at the freakazoid, and then quick look away. You may read his "Biography" on the North Korean "official" website, and might I suggest just a tiny bit of technical assistance on that 1985esque webpage? I mean couldn't you just send someone across the 138th Parallel to kidnap a South Korean to update your web system? COME ON!!!!"

By the way, there is no such thing as the "138th Parallel."

Most of the vitriol the WBC throws at the nations of the world seems to center around the fact that homosexuals seem to live in all of them. But what about Iran? Their president famously said there were no gays there, and they have the death sentence for homosexuality. So they must get a thumbs up from the WBC, right? Wrong.

"When Ahmadinejad told the audience at Columbia University that Iran does not have sodomites, he really meant that the Persians where jumping through so many hoops and contorting biology to such a degree that technically, no they do not have what Americans recognize as garden variety fags. Nice try, but that won't fool God! The punishment for fag-infested Iran will be the same as for the United States of Sodom."

> Fred Phelps' civil rights work may be the only bright spot on his resume, but that may not be as noble as one might think either. Some of his estranged children say Phelps routinely referred to African-Americans as "dumb niggers."

What the Hell???

The Ten Commandments in Uganda

Nothing strikes more terror into parents than the thought of their child being abducted and never seen again. So what can one say about Joseph Kony who kidnaps children on an industrial scale?

Kony was born in northern Uganda in the early 1960s. He was raised as a Catholic and even served as an altar boy for a time. In the 1980s Kony's aunt, Alice Auma claimed that she spoke for a spirit named "Lakwena" who supposedly made her bulletproof. She started something called the Holy Spirit Movement, which was a religiously based uprising against the Ugandan government. The Movement faltered, however, and Alice Lakwena (as she called herself) was forced into exile in Kenya where she reportedly became an alcoholic. In 1989 Kony stepped into aunt Alice's role by claiming that he was a prophet and that Lakwena now spoke through him. He upped the holy ante by claiming that an additional dozen or so spirits with names like "Juma Oris" and "Who Are You" also spoke through him. He put on rather elaborate performances in which he would speak in different voices to demonstrate to the faithful that he was the vessel for all these different spirits.

People bought Kony's claims, and he soon formed his own rebel group, which he called the Lord's Resistance Army (LRA). This army claims to be on a mission to create a theocratic government in Uganda in which the Ten Commandments will be the highest law of the land. The religious beliefs of the LRA include a lot of Christian traditions such as the use of the sign of the cross and rosaries, as well as Islamic ones such as the use of the crescent moon symbol and fasting during the month of Ramadan. They will not eat pork, but they do eat warthogs. The faith also includes a good amount of stuff that Kony made up himself. An example of this would be the way the group deals with HIV/AIDS. To test a person for HIV, LRA members draw crosses with a white powder all over his or her body. The person is not allowed to wash for three days. If the person is HIV positive the crosses will fall off their body in a day or so.

Foolproof right? If someone was "diagnosed" with AIDS in this manner they need not fret as Kony has a cure. The "infected" person would need to bathe in a river three times while Kony says prayers over him.

But the LRA's magic wasn't enough to overthrow the Ugandan government, so they took a more traditional military approach to that challenge. The problem was (and still is) that the LRA didn't have very many followers, so they made too feeble a force to take control of the nation. This is where Kony hit upon his big idea; if people are not coming out to join the movement in big enough numbers, why not just go out and abduct yourself an army? His forces began the practice of attacking defenseless towns and kidnapping all the children they could grab. The LRA seldom uses their guns in such attacks. They prefer to use machetes so they can somewhat silently hack people to death without creating too much commotion that would alert the villagers to their presence and thus give them the chance to run away. After the killing and kidnapping is done, the LRA invariably burns the village down. Once they have taken the kids, they put them to use in their holy quest. The girls are forced to perform the domestic chores for the group. The prettiest girls are singled out to become "wives"—or more accurately, sex slaves—for Kony and his lieutenants. Kony gets to pick the loveliest of the girls for himself before he allocates the rest to his favored men. He has taken on at least sixty wives in this fashion.

The boys are forced to become soldiers/murderers for the LRA. Discipline is harsh in this outfit. Boys are usually forced to kill prisoners, sometimes even their own parents, to prove that they are worthy of Kony's army. "Liars" (anyone who speaks ill of Kony) have their lips cut off and are forced to eat them. Sometimes Kony ramps up the horror by then ordering padlocks to be inserted through the jaws of such victims, and then he destroys the keys. Boys fighting for the LRA typically have short life expectancies, so more kidnappings are constantly required to replace the dead. High-end estimates of the number of kids the LRA have abducted have risen to more than 70,000. An additional two million or so people have lost their homes to LRA raids. The International Criminal Court has indicted Kony and his top officers for crimes against humanity. Oh, and LRA soldiers are required to pray several times a day.

This ragtag army is more formidable than its numbers (normally only in the hundreds at any given time) would suggest. The LRA is thought to have used moles within the Ugandan government who tip off Kony before any raid on his group takes place. Furthermore, the LRA has found a friend in Sudanese dictator Omar al-Bashir, who has himself been accused by the International Criminal Court of genocide, crimes against humanity and war crimes. Al-Bashir has been generous enough to supply the LRA with armaments and other types of support.

But not all is rosy in Kony's world. In 2008 President Obama signed a law committing the United States to his capture. Kony has since moved his operations out of Uganda into the lawless region of the Democratic Republic of Congo. In the DRC, Kony has kept up his same tactics of attacks on unsuspecting villages where he murders the adults and kidnaps the kids and then sends the whole place up in flames. With American money now funding the effort against him, Kony has opted to break his force into smaller pieces and has branched out into the Central African Republic, the Darfur region of Sudan, and the brand new nation of South Sudan. He has prophesied that he will never return to Uganda. I'm sure the people there were crushed to hear that revelation. In 2011 Obama sent 100 American troops to Uganda to help ensure that Kony's prophecy comes true.

But don't think that Kony has been alone in his efforts to promote the Ten Commandments in Uganda. Another religion called The Movement for the Restoration of the Ten Commandments of God also took root in Uganda and rewarded the populace with yet more blessings.

A woman named Credonia Mwerinde, an ex-prostitute with six ex-husbands, created the Movement. She set up a bar where she sold banana beer, and after that enterprise failed in 1988, she moved on to do the work of God. She claimed that the Virgin Mary started talking to her one day while she was in a cave. After that revelation, Mary regularly kept in touch with her. She told everyone about her special connection with Mary and started to gain attention. She acted in a totally devout manner, fasting constantly and spending hours at a time in prayer. Her pious ways convinced more and more people that she was the real deal, a sinner who was not only saved by God, but also given a divine hotline to Mary.

As she set up shop with her new faith, she ran into Joseph Kibwerte, a failed politician and devout Catholic who would become essential to the operation. Kibwerte was fascinated to the point of obsession with stories of apparitions of Mary, so he was naturally attracted to Mwerinde. She saw in him a man with many connections with people in high places that could help her get ahead in the world. As it would be very difficult for a woman to be the leader of a religion in Uganda, she made Kibwerte the nominal head of her new faith, but she continued to hold the real power. Kibwerte, for his part, got in on the holy visions himself as he claimed he not only overheard a conversation between Jesus and Mary, but he tape-recorded it as well. In the conversation, Mary says that people are suffering in the world because they do not follow the Ten Commandments. Eventually, Kibwerte decided he was a bishop and came to be known to the faithful as "The Prophet" while Mwerinde became "The Programmer." Nearly all the members of the faith were former Catholics. The Catholic Church dismissed the Movement as heresy, while the Movement condemned the Catholic Church as being hopelessly corrupt.

For those who decided to join the Movement, life was no picnic. They were obligated to sell off all their belongings and give the money to the Movement. They moved onto the Movement's compound and were enlisted as slave laborers for Mr. Prophet and Ms. Programmer. They got very little to eat, were forbidden from having sex, and were not allowed to even talk most of the time. They also had to listen to lengthy sermons that invariably got around to the subject of the world coming to an end. December 31, 1999 was settled upon as the date for the apocalypse when everyone on Earth except the followers of the Movement would be destroyed. When this day came and went uneventfully, things started to unravel in the Movement.

There have been innumerable religious movements that have picked doomsday dates only to see nothing happen when those days arrive. When this happens the normal strategy is to quickly pick a new date for the end of the world to stop the faithful from stampeding out of the faith. The Movement was no different in this respect as they chose March 17, 2000 as the new last day of the world.

It has been suggested that Movement members were demanding their money back, and this sparked a crisis amongst the leadership, but this is conjecture. We really don't know what was going on inside the community at the time, but things definitely took a turn for the dramatic. A church called the "Ark" was constructed for the impending Armageddon. On March 16 hundreds of the faithful poured into the Ark for an eve of destruction celebration. Seventy cases of cola were brought in, and a bull was slaughtered for the feast, which would have been sumptuous indeed compared to the paltry amounts of food the faithful normally got. Boards were nailed to the windows and doors of the Ark in order to keep out the people from the surrounding area who would be clamoring to get into the church once the apocalypse started. The next day the end of the world did arrive, at least for those in the Ark. Accelerants were poured around the Ark, and the church was set ablaze with everyone shuttered inside. By the time Ugandan authorities arrived at the scene, the Ark was a smoldering ruin with around 530 bodies inside it. Many of the corpses were incinerated into nothing but ash, so no accurate count of the dead was possible.

At first this looked like a mass suicide, but then an odd discovery was made. A horrible stench directed the police to the latrines around the Ark where they discovered six corpses in the pits below. The bodies had been poisoned, beaten, strangled, and stabbed. The theory then took hold that the inhabitants of the Ark had been victims of murder rather than suicide. They may well have been poisoned during the banquet the night before to dull their resistance to their murders the next day. As the investigation continued, new discoveries amplified the magnitude of the disaster. At a farm owned by an excommunicated priest named Dominic Kataribabo, more than 150 more corpses were found in the fields and buried under the former priest's house. The victims again showed signs of poisoning, strangulation, and beating. Hundreds of more corpses were found at other Movement sights. These people had all been killed well before March 17, so there seems to be no doubt the leadership had systematically carried out a plot to murder everyone in the faith. All told, the Movement killed about a thousand people.

But what became of Mwerinde and Kibwerte? Neither one of them has been seen since the fire. It is believed they took the money their followers gave them and like Joseph Kony, made off to the DRC. International arrest warrants have been issued for them, but there is no way to search for them in the Congo.

......

There is much disagreement about the Ten Commandments. Different religions adhere to differing versions of the Commandments. There is no universal agreement as to what the Commandments are or how they should be obeyed. That said, there is no question that homosexuality is not mentioned in the Decalogue. But that hasn't prevented a fervent anti-homosexual campaign from breaking out in Uganda.

Homosexuality is not embraced in Africa in general. It is usually seen as an American and European import into Africa where—people believe—it did not exist before contact with white cultures. In 2009 three American evangelical Protestant leaders visited Uganda and injected their own anti-gay message to this receptive audience. Chief amongst the evangelicals was Scott Lively of Abiding Truth Ministries, which is considered a hate group by the Southern Poverty Law Center. Mr. Lively is a ferocious opponent of gay rights. He was once forced to pay $31,000 to a woman he assaulted while she was trying to film one of his anti-gay tirades. In 1996 he co-authored (along with Kevin E. Abrams) a laughable piece of Holocaust revisionism entitled *The Pink Swastika: Homosexuality in the Nazi Party*. This book claims that Adolf Hitler and much of his inner circle were gay. It goes on to make absurd assertions such as Hitler using gay soldiers to commit the worst Nazi atrocities because he knew that homosexuals were without the morals that other people posses.

At the conference in March of 2009, Lively told his Ugandan audience that he "knows more than almost anyone else in the world" about homosexuality, and he regaled them with tales of the evils of homosexuality such as how gays prey on children, hoping to convert them to the gay lifestyle. He said AIDS was the appropriate penalty for homosexuality, and he said gays were probably responsible for the 1994 genocide in Rwanda. Lively referred to the presentation as a "nuclear bomb against the gay agenda." It turned out he was right.

After the "nuclear bomb" went off, a wave of anti-homosexual hatred swept Uganda. A newspaper called *Rolling Stone* (which has no connection whatsoever to the American music magazine) published the names and pictures of homosexuals under the headline screaming "100 PICTURES OF UGANDA'S TOP HOMOS LEAK." The pictures were posted next to a banner reading "Hang Them." Shortly after the publication of the list, a Ugandan gay man named David Kato sued the paper for outing him. Not long after that, he was beaten to death in his home. Scott Lively opined that Kato was probably killed by his gay lover. At Kato's funeral, an Anglican priest used the occasion to curse the mourners telling them they would face the same fate as the biblical cities of Sodom and Gomorrah.

But it wasn't just a few cranks who were out to get homosexuals in Uganda. The government took into consideration a new law that would greatly strengthen the nation's anti-homosexual laws. It would even allow for death by hanging for repeat homosexual offenders. The legislation caused an international uproar and drew the condemnation of human rights groups from around the globe. Faced with this opposition and the potential loss of aid from America and Europe, Uganda backed down and dropped the death penalty portion of the law, but it remains a stark piece of anti-homosexual legislation. The revised law still calls for the imprisonment of homosexuals, anyone who supports homosexual rights, anyone who fails to report a homosexual to the police, and anyone who even unknowingly abets homosexuality such as landlords who rent to gay tenants. Uganda's minister of ethics and integrity summed it up well when he said, "Homosexuals can forget about human rights."

When Barak Obama sent one hundred non-combat troops to Uganda to advise the units battling Joseph Kony, he managed to hit a nerve with some conservatives. The outspoken right-wing radio pundit Rush Limbaugh lashed out against Obama on his show, while praising the LRA.

"Lord's Resistance Army are Christians. They are fighting the Muslims in Sudan. And Obama has sent troops, United States troops to remove them from the battlefield, which means kill them. That's what the lingo means, "to help regional forces remove from the battlefield," meaning capture or kill. So that's a new war, a hundred troops to wipe out Christians in Sudan, Uganda, and—no, I'm not kidding. Jacob Tapper just reported it. Now, are we gonna help the Egyptians wipe out the Christians? Wouldn't you say that we are?"

Congresswoman Michele Bachmann, who was then seeking the Republican presidential nomination, also condemned the move despite admitting that she knew little about the situation.

My Cup Runneth Over

So many wretched people, so little time. I didn't want to end this book without mentioning several other men (and a woman) of the cloth who richly deserve public disdain.

Robert Tilton

After sex and money scandals swallowed up one televangelist after the other in the 1980s, Robert Tilton swooped in to fill the void they left behind. He secured a substantial loan and used the money to put himself on television across America.

His show was different than his predecessors, however. His programs were essentially infomercials in which the flamboyant Texan spoke in tongues, cried, railed against the devil and quoted scripture, but offered little in the way of moral instruction. What he did do was ask for money. He actually spent most of the time on his programs soliciting contributions from his viewers. He preached the "prosperity gospel," a religious philosophy promoted by many Protestant preachers including Jimmy Swaggart and James Bakker that basically says that God wants people to be wealthy, and through faith and atonement, one can gain financial rewards. On Tilton's shows, people were encouraged to show their faith by sending him $1,000 contributions, which they were promised would be returned to them by God many times over. People were also told their gifts could lead to miracles such as recovery from illnesses and drug addiction. The faithful sent letters and cards to Tilton along with their cash donations so he could pray over them to ensure their wishes would come true. Tilton even went so far as to roll around in piles of his viewers' letters on his show.

Tilton apparently atoned for his own sins very well because God rewarded him with vast amounts of worldly privilege. His show raked in eight million dollars a month, and Tilton bought mansions, fancy cars, and outrageously expensive suits for himself. He even referred to himself as "the apple of God's eye."

But maybe God doesn't like apples. In 1991 a story on the ABC News program *Primetime Live* called "The Apple of God's Eye" took Tilton down several pegs. The story showed thousands upon thousands of letters and prayer requests that had been sent to Tilton that had been tossed into a dumpster in Tulsa, Oklahoma after they had apparently been rifled through to remove the cash, checks, food stamps, and whatever other valuables his viewers could scrape together for the televangelist. The story implied that Tilton never bothered to look at the requests, despite his claims that he personally prayed over every request sent to him. In fact, Tilton had said that he spent so much time praying over the messages that the ink from them had poisoned his bloodstream, caused him to have strokes, and left him with a disfigured face that required plastic surgery to correct. Furthermore, the news story included an interview with a college friend of Tilton's who said that the two of them would do drugs or get drunk and then go to see Christian revival shows for laughs. The two of them joked about starting their own traveling revival shows, and they practiced ranting like preachers and speaking in tongues. After the *Primetime Live* report aired, a healthy chunk of Tilton's viewers abandoned him. He lost 85% of his television audience, and he had to call a halt to his show. He was sued for fraud, and his marriage ended as well.

But Tilton would not go down without a fight. He claimed that ABC News had faked the immense stacks of letters shown on the program, and he sued them for libel. His suit was thrown out of court, however, and other investigators found many more letters discarded by Tilton after the story was broadcast. He later conceded that he had not actually seen the letters from his viewers, but he had been given lists of the letter writers' names, and he prayed over the lists. He also bounced back on the romantic front by taking a second wife, but that marriage did not last long. The second Mrs. Tilton charged that he was an abusive drunkard who claimed that he was the pope and said that rats were eating his brain.

Through it all though, Tilton never really went away. He still had his mailing list, and he used it to solicit funds from those who still thought he was a man of God. Eventually, he was able to purchase airtime on the Black Entertainment Television network in wee hours of the morning and started his climb back. Once again the money started rolling in. It wasn't nearly as much as before, but since his shows now consisted mostly of reruns from his performances in the '80s and '90s his overhead was much lower, so his profits were still quite good. He relocated to south

Florida and built a magnificent mansion for himself and his third wife.

In 2001 a woman named Patricia Morrow, who was employed for two days opening Tilton's mail, reported that the letters he received were still being opened and tossed after the money had been removed. She described her workday thusly, "You're sat down in a cubicle and given a letter opener. You have bundles of mail and a trash bin beside you. You slice open the envelope, take the money out, and throw the letter away in the bin."

So it looks like Tilton got the last laugh in this matter. Well, maybe not literally the last laugh. In the '90s, some wisenheimers took video recordings of some of his sermons and altered them by inserting farting noises into the soundtrack whenever Tilton would grimace, squint, and make unnatural pauses in his speech. These sidesplitting videos were posted on the Internet where they went viral and remain popular to this day. A whole generation of young people who had never heard of Tilton came to know him as "The Farting Preacher" or "Pastor Gas." Of course, the suckers who continue to send him money tend to be older folks who are unfamiliar with Internet trends, so the videos haven't likely hurt his bottom line.

Oral Roberts

Oral Roberts was born into grinding poverty in 1918 in Asa, Oklahoma. As a boy he contracted case of tuberculosis that nearly killed him. His parents took him to see a faith healer and while in the car along the way to see him, Roberts claimed that Jesus spoke to him and told him to expect a miracle. Roberts would continue to claim to speak to Jesus for the rest of his life.

After that incident, Roberts dedicated his life to serving the Lord. Like so many other preachers, he put on a traveling revival show held under a large tent. In the 1940s he began faith healings after he claimed Jesus ordered him to do so. In the '50s he went on television and his show, *Oral Roberts and You* became the leading religious broadcast in America by the '70s. (By the way, do people in rural America watch *anything* besides televangelists?) In 1963 he founded Oral Roberts University.

(Are there any televangelists who *don't* found their own fundamentalist schools?)

And like so many other televangelists, Roberts got very rich. As another preacher of the "prosperity gospel" he made no effort to hide his wealth. He unapologetically drove fancy cars, lived in opulent houses, and wore silk suits. But all the money he made was never enough. In 1987 he made headlines around the world when he claimed that God told him he would kill him if he failed to raise eight million dollars in a special fundraising drive. He did not specify how God planned on killing him; I liked to envision a "hit" angel descending from the clouds to whack brother Roberts. But apparently God was employing the devil in his schemes to pressure Roberts. He claimed the devil attacked him in his bedroom one night, "I felt those hands on my throat, and he was choking the life out of me. I yelled to my wife "Honey, come!" She came in and commanded the devil to get out. I began to breathe and came out of my bed strong." Since Mrs. Roberts was able to command the devil out when Oral wasn't, I can't help but think that everyone was flocking to see the wrong member of the Roberts family because she clearly possessed stronger powers than her husband. Nevertheless, Roberts raised the money he demanded, so we didn't get to see God assassinate him.

Shortly after his holy ransom demand, Roberts dropped another bombshell. He claimed that he had raised people from the dead during his faith healing performances. He told the story of how a man had "died right while I was preaching. I had to stop and go back in the crowd and raise the dead person so I could go on with the service." He does not mention how the person died (boredom would be my guess) or how he knew he was dead. But he does imply that this resurrection was casually carried out, and the only reason he did it was because the dead guy was somehow disrupting the service. Robert's son Richard also told the story of an infant whom his dad resurrected. He claimed there were probably "dozens and dozens and dozens of documented instances of people who have been raised from the dead" by Oral. Interestingly, Oral Roberts never mentioned raising anyone from the dead in his autobiography, but he did mention that three people had died while attending his crusades without being resurrected.

Oral put Richard in charge of the University when he became too old to run the school any longer, but Richard was squeezed out of his position in 2007 after he was accused of using school money for his personal luxuries.

Two years later, Oral Roberts died of pneumonia; a disappointingly ordinary death for a man who was once on God's hit list. Even worse, no one resurrected him.

Jack T. Chick

Maybe you've seen them at the shopping mall, around a college campus or perhaps at the airport. They're religious tracts in the form of little comic books, which invariably include people finding Jesus—whom in many cases they have inexplicably never heard of—and being "saved" on the spot. The artwork is dicey, the dialogue is laughable (people routinely laugh with a "HAW HAW!" in the text,) and the dimwitted story lines range from mildly to completely offensive. The tracts are the product of Jack T. Chick. According to the Chick Publications website, more than 750 million of these tracts have been distributed in more than one hundred languages.

Chick tracts do not espouse what one might call "mainstream" Christianity. In the world where Chick lives, rock bands really do sell their souls to Satan, Dungeons and Dragons and Harry Potter teach black magic that really works, Halloween is a satanic recruiting ploy, evolution is a secularist lie, and a few seconds of blather about Jesus causes people to drop to their knees in tears and beg for his forgiveness. In Chick's tracts, God is a faceless, giant, vengeful jerk whose angels bodily toss into hell everyone that doesn't conform to a very narrowly defined type of Christianity. All non-Christian faiths—and many Christian ones—are lambasted and denounced in the strongest means possible. People who thought they were pious and good are regularly pitched into the flames of hell in drawings that seem to suggest that angels take glee in the act.

While Chick's little wads of toilet paper are filled with unintentional hilarity there is a darker side to his message. The man is one of the most prolific hate-mongers out there. A few of the groups Chick has attacked include…

—Jews

The villains in Chick tracks are often depicted as dark-skinned, hooked-nosed, scowling fiends that closely resemble the anti-Semitic caricatures of Third Reich propaganda. Chick also insists that Jesus was not a Jew. One Chick tract entitled *Where's Rabbi Waxman?* tells the story of a rabbi who is cast into hell for not accepting Jesus as the Messiah. Chick Publications also published the book *The Illegal Trial of Jesus*, which affixes the responsibility for Jesus' execution on Jewish leaders. Chick claims great love for the Jewish people and Israel, but this is based squarely on his end-times theology that says Israel will figure prominently in Armageddon and the return of Jesus. He still thinks Jews who do not convert to his theology are condemned to hell.

—Muslims

In Chick-land Muslims burn with hatred against infidels, only to realize that Jesus is their savior after hearing a few seconds of tripe from one of Chick's holier-than-thou, Bible-thumping characters. Chick attacks Islam by creating a false history of the religion in which he asserts that Allah is nothing more than a pagan deity called "the moon god" who is actually the devil. Mohammed, Chick claims, was deceived by the devil (with the aid of a Catholic) into worshipping the moon god and calling him "Allah." The tract *Men of Peace?* depicts Mohammed as a murderer, kidnapper, thief, and torturer who encouraged the rape of non-believers. Incidentally, this tract also includes several drawings of Mohammed that are far more inflammatory than any of the Danish cartoons that riled up the riotously inclined in various Islamic countries resulting in the deaths of over one hundred people. I'm amazed it's taking so long for this tract to get noticed by the embassy-burning crowd.

—Homosexuals

Chick says that God loves homosexuals. He also says that homosexuals are cursed, vile, perverted, child molesters who are terrorists under demonic control and who are filled with hate. He claims gays are murderers because they taint the blood supply with AIDS, and he says they want to throw good people into prison. He despairs that they are allowed to hold jobs in business, education, and government. He claims the average lifespan for homosexuals was a scant forty-two years before AIDS came along and lowered it to thirty-nine. So if you meet a forty-year-old gay person today, you are apparently meeting someone who has beaten the odds.

His tract *Birds and the Bees* targets his anti-homosexual message at children. In it, a righteous child stands up to his evil schoolteacher who is brainwashing him to accept a gay couple that is depicted with demons sitting on their heads. Happily, the boy summons the moral courage to call them *"Queers."* Yes, it is in bold italics in the tract.

—Catholics

No institution is as despised in the world of Chick as much as the Roman Catholic Church. As he does with Islam, Chick creates a false history of the religion, which he then attacks. The tract *The Death Cookie* claims that the Catholic sacrament of communion (the titular "Death Cookie") and the Catholic priesthood are pagan Egyptian practices devised by Satan in order to lead people away from Christianity. In a tract called *Sabotage*, the Catholic veneration of Mary is compared to Satan worshiping. Other Chick publications accuse the Catholic Church of starting both world wars, creating Islam, founding the Ku Klux Klan (a group which, incidentally, forbids Catholics from joining), writing *Mein Kampf*, conducting the Holocaust, assassinating Abraham Lincoln, conspiring with the Illuminati and the Free Masons, and using Karl Marx, Friedrich Engels, and Joseph Stalin as secret agents. Of course, the Pope is accused of being the Antichrist, the Church is called the "Whore of Babylon," and Catholics always go to hell when they die in Chickology. The list of insanity goes on and on.

So who is Jack Chick? It's hard to say. The man is a total recluse who almost never talks to the media. Even finding a photograph of him is difficult. Virtually nothing is known about him other than the scant details offered on his website. It's even possible that Jack T. Chick doesn't exist and is merely a pen name used by the writer(s) of those pathetic tracts. But Ben Kinchlow (who co-hosts *The 700 Club* with Pat Robertson) claimed he has met Chick and has "the highest regard for him."

In a way, Chick is a lot like the deity he portrays in his comics—angry, alone, and faceless.

Bishop Richard Williamson

Richard Williamson is an English Catholic bishop who is a member of the ultra right-wing Society of St. Pius X that we have met previously in this book. Williamson was consecrated a bishop in 1988 by the renegade Archbishop Marcel Lefebvre. Since Williamson and a few other priests were ordained in defiance of the wishes of Pope John Paul II, the whole lot of them were excommunicated from the Church. In 2009 Pope Benedict XVI revoked the excommunications, and Williamson was welcomed back into the Church.

While Williamson supports the fervently anti-modern views that his fellow Pius Xers share, he manages to set himself apart with radical rightist positions that make him a fringe member even by the standards of that fringe group.

For instance, Williamson is not a major fan of the United States. He has never met a conspiracy theory involving the U.S. that he didn't like. Williamson thinks the U.S. blew up the *Maine* to create an excuse to go the war with Spain, and set up the *Lusitania* in the same way to justify entry into World War I. On the same theme, he thinks the U.S. somehow arranged the Japanese bombing of Pearl Harbor to create a pretext to jump into World War II. He thinks Lee Harvey Oswald did not kill President Kennedy, and Timothy McVeigh did not blow up the Murrah Federal Building in Oklahoma City. Needless to say, he thinks the September 11th terrorist attacks were an inside job carried out by the U.S. to create another fake case for more war. This was carried out in conjunction with the Israeli government, of course.

Which brings us to another group Williamson has a problem with: Jews. Williamson believes that Catholic and Jewish power are diametrically opposed, and any Jewish ascent invariably leads to a Catholic decline. He has claimed that no Jews died in the gas chambers of any Nazi concentration camps. He thinks Jews wish to dominate the world and has declared *The Protocols of the Elders of Zion* to be a valid document that men must read if they wish to know the truth. In 2009 Williamson's anti-Semitic ranting got him kicked out of Argentina right before he was readmitted to the Catholic Church. The next year he was convicted of Holocaust denial in Germany.

He's not too crazy about women either. He has said that women should not attend or teach at universities—which he refers to as "unibrothels"—lest they "inflame" the passions of men and distract them from their serious business there. Furthermore, he claims women are only capable of "small-scale" thinking and are thus inappropriate students at universities that must teach large concepts. He even blames women's enrollment at universities for the collapsing popularity of Christianity in Europe. He thinks women are qualified only to work as nuns, nurses, and grade school teachers, but of course he apparently thinks those teachers should not have college educations.

The Jewish Anti-Defamation League and others have alleged that Williamson's bizarre views on Jews are commonly held in the Society of St. Pius X. But even if that's true, no one has been so publicly outspoken about them as Williamson.

Reggie White

Reggie White was a pro football player who did more to bring evangelical Christianity into professional sports than any other person.

He became an ordained minister at the age of seventeen and proselytized for his faith so often that he became known as the "Minister of Defense" while he was playing for the University of Tennessee. He went on to become a superstar defensive lineman for the Philadelphia Eagles and then became the first big-name star in football to change teams via free agency when he moved to the Green Bay Packers in 1993. He also was a trailblazer in the area of using his sports celebrity to promote conservative Christianity. His actions opened the floodgates for groups like Athletes in Action, an evangelical Protestant organization that today has links to nearly every professional sports team in North America.

Reggie White set himself up as a Christian role model and spoke at numerous churches spreading the good word to many people who wouldn't have bothered listening to him were it not for his talent at knocking down quarterbacks. As he put it himself, "God allowed me to use this game as a platform to proclaim the name of Jesus. ... I know some people don't like what I say sometimes, but God has called me to preach a message, and I have to preach the message." White wasn't bashful about letting everyone know where his heart was. Unfortunately, that heart was in a pretty dank place. In 1997 White spoke before a student assembly at an almost entirely black high school in Knoxville, Tennessee and used the occasion to lay out his vision of a racist conspiracy in the United States. He told the students the police wanted guns and drugs to be sold in their communities because the dealers were working for the government. He told them the police harass them and want them in gangs so they can throw them into jail because "somebody's" making loads of money on prisons. He ridiculed the use of condoms and said that some unnamed group was preventing AIDS from being cured because "they" were profiting from it. He also accused anonymous villains of wanting kids to get pregnant so they could take their babies out alive and stick needles into their brains to extract tissue they could sell for vast amounts of cash.

White's comments earned him some criticism, but not too much. After all, the man was a good football player, and he had played a crucial role in returning the Packers to prominence after decades of malaise. So in 1998 White was invited to speak before the Wisconsin State Assembly and he made sure his speech would be a memorable one. After a warm reception, he reiterated his argument that people were being sent to prison just to generate profits for someone or another. Then he said Europeans enslaved blacks because the Indians were too sneaky to be captured. He launched into a lecture dripping with racial stereotypes in which he explained the "gifts" God gave to the different races. He said Hispanics have the ability to stuff twenty or thirty people into their households, white people are talented at tapping into money, and Asians can turn televisions into watches. He didn't spare his own race either. He said most black fathers are either in prison or are dead, and he said God made blacks good at dancing. But the worst was yet to come. White accused America of shaking its fist in God's face by accepting its homosexual citizens. He said that sexually transmitted diseases were a divine consequence of this tolerance of gays. He said, "we allow rampant sin including homosexuality and lying, and to me lying is just as bad as homosexuality, we've allowed this sin to run rampant in our nation, and because it has run rampant in our nation, our nation is in the condition it is today." He went on, "I'm offended that homosexuals will say that homosexuals deserve rights... Homosexuality is a decision. It's not a race. And when you look at it, people from all different ethnic backgrounds are also liars and cheaters and malicious and backstabbers." He also suggested that the separation of church and state was a mistake, and Wisconsin should be given to the rule of God. Predictably, there were those who took offense at White's comments, but again his football prowess overcame the objections to what came out of his mouth.

White died in 2004 at the age of forty-three. Shortly before he died he lamented, "When I look back on my life, there are a lot of things I said God said. I realize he didn't say nothing. It was what Reggie wanted to do." After his death, he became the first football player ever to have his number retired by two different NFL teams and streets were named in his honor in Green Bay, Wisconsin, and Chattanooga, Tennessee.

Roch "Moses" Thériault

Roch Thériault was a Canadian man who started a group in 1977 designed to help people beat drug and alcohol addictions. Gradually he came to insert more and more of his religious convictions into his program until it finally became nothing but a religion. In 1978 he moved with his followers to an isolated area in Quebec where there would be as little contact with outsiders as possible.

Like David Koresh, Thériault was initially a follower of the Seventh Day Adventist faith, but as his religious convictions matured he was thrown out of that Church, and he started something entirely new. Thériault claimed that he was a descendant of Moses and was called "Moses" by his followers. He claimed to be the last prophet and said he could talk directly to God. His word was absolute law amongst his followers and could not be questioned in any way.

His followers included eight of his wives who bore him a couple dozen or so children. The people who chose to follow this new Moses all had to dress in identical tunics and were not allowed to wear underwear. They could not eat meat and were expected to do little talking. The penalty for crossing Thériault would include severe physical punishment including sadistic beatings in which Thériault would force other members of his flock to gang up on the victim. He once ordered a man to cut off his wife's toe with a pair of snips. He then made her cut off the finger of another woman. This was all to establish that Thériault held total control over the well being of every member of the community. In fact, he claimed that no one amongst his followers would get sick or well unless he wished it.

And to make people well he devised bizarre rituals to heal them. One particularly grim instance of this occurred after a boy was beaten by one of the group members. In an effort to nurse him back to health, Thériault partially circumcised the boy and then injected rubbing alcohol into his stomach. This "cure" proved to be fatal to the child. Furthermore, Thériault castrated the man who had abused the boy, ostensibly to cool off the passion in him. The castrated man left the group and alerted the authorities as to what was going on. Thériault was arrested and convicted of improperly practicing medicine. He served about a year in jail for this, a lamentably lenient sentence that would come back to haunt the court that handed it down.

After he got out of the jug, Thériault moved his outfit to Ontario where the legal authorities were far less familiar with him. Once there, he went about his old ways again. When one of his wives came down with a stomachache he fatally disemboweled her in another "healing" rite. Her body was then buried and exhumed three times. On one of these occasions, Thériault took one of her bones and made a necklace out of it that he kept hidden behind his unruly beard. Since the group was so secretive, no one on the outside knew the woman was dead.

Then there was the incident involving Thériault's wife Gabrielle LaVallée. He proclaimed that one of her fingers was paralyzed and made her raise her hand to show it to him. When she did so, he impaled her hand on a large knife. He then said he would need to amputate her hand to prevent gangrene. He took out a chain saw and cut off her arm instead. He then cauterized her wound, so at least she didn't bleed to death. After her disfiguring assault, LaVallée escaped the group and blew the whistle on Thériault who was arrested and finally put away for good.

In prison, Thériault dropped the "Moses" routine and claimed that he deeply regretted his actions as a prophet. The other prisoners were not all that forgiving, however, and tormented this supposed man of God. In 2011 Thériault was beaten to death by one of his fellow inmates.

Ted Haggard

Like so many others in this book, Ted Haggard is an evangelical fundamentalist preacher who started out with nothing and built himself into a highly influential brand name in the Jesus industry.

Raised in Indiana, Haggard went to Oral Roberts University and then moved on to found a church in the city of Colorado Springs after another man told him he'd had a vision of him starting a congregation there. Haggard named his church the New Life Church, and it started out very small. The initial services were held in Haggard's basement before moving up to a strip mall. Eventually the church grew into a mega-church with 14,000 members, and in 2003 he was named the leader of the National Association of Evangelicals (NAE,) a group with thirty million members that Haggard called "the counterbalance to liberalism."

Haggard was never bashful about expressing his conservative political beliefs and he pursued them aggressively with his church and the NAE at his back. He campaigned aggressively for George W. Bush in 2004, and in return, he was given the privilege of weekly conference calls with the White House where he could express his opinions on how American policy should be shaped. He also was deeply involved in promoting his version of Christianity at the United States Air Force Academy, which is located a stone's throw from his New Life Church in Colorado Springs.

The situation at the Air Force Academy reached the boiling point when the father of a Jewish cadet filed a lawsuit complaining of religious bullying at the Academy in addition to

355

the institutionalized promotion of evangelical Protestant fundamentalism. Scores of students at the Academy have complained about religious harassment. The Yale Divinity School investigated the Academy and found an environment of consistent evangelical promotion, including students who were scolded that those who were not "born again will burn in the fires of hell." The report was co-authored by Capt. MeLinda Morton, a Chaplin at the Academy. Morton was reassigned by the Air force shortly after the report was released.

Haggard threw himself into the debate headlong; strongly defending and encouraging more of the heavy-handed proselytizing that was going on at the school. He even filed a countersuit supporting the Academy's fundamentalist push. He also lashed out at homosexuals and campaigned for a ballot measure to outlaw same sex marriages in Colorado. This in turn got the attention of a man named Mike Jones who was a bit taken aback by Haggard's severe anti-homosexual rhetoric. For Jones was a prostitute who had intimate knowledge of what Haggard was doing behind closed doors.

Jones spilled the beans to the media about Haggard. He told them Haggard had been paying him for sex for the last three years, and he had purchased and used methamphetamines. When the sexual charges came out Haggard initially denied everything, then he admitted to some of it. Finally he confessed, "The fact is that I am guilty of sexual immorality. And I take full responsibility for the entire problem. I am a deceiver and a liar. There's a part of my life that is so repulsive and dark that I have been warring against it for all of my adult life." His position on the drugs also evolved over time. Early on he said he had bought the meth, but threw it away without taking any of it despite being tempted to. Then he conceded, "I bought the drugs to enhance masturbation. Because what crystal meth does—Mike taught me this—crystal meth makes it so you don't ejaculate soon. So you can watch porn and masturbate for a long time."

After Haggard admitted that the charges were true, he was stripped of his leadership at the NAE and was forced to step down from his role at the New Life Church. He agreed to undergo pray-away-the-gay type counseling for his sexual problems that had the amount of success one would expect it to have—none. In 2009 another man came forward and claimed that Haggard had sexually imposed himself on him, this time in an uninvited manner. He said Haggard had masturbated in front of him a few years earlier despite his protestations. He claimed that Haggard justified the incident by saying, "you can become a man of God, and you can have a little bit of fun on the side." In 2011 Haggard admitted that if he were twenty-one years old he would probably identify himself as a bisexual. He didn't explain why he would only use that label for himself if he were younger.

In 2010 Haggard started another church in Colorado Springs called St. James. He did a tour of television talk shows and even appeared on the program *Celebrity Wife Swap* to build publicity for it. This new church is supposed to reach out to sinners, and Haggard says everyone is welcome there including. "Democrats, Republican, independents, gays, straights, tall, short, addicts, and recovering addicts." Despite this new outlook, Haggard remains staunchly opposed to gay rights. As for the Air Force Academy, the controversy there continues, and a group called Focus on the Family has taken the lead from Haggard in promoting religious fundamentalism on campus.

Tony Alamo

Tony Alamo's story starts out a little differently than those of so many other evangelical sleaze balls. Tony was born a Jew with the name of Bernie LaZar Hoffman in the 1930s. He claimed to work as a rock promoter until one day in 1964 when God himself swung by a business meeting Alamo was involved in and told him that Jesus was returning to Earth. He also told Alamo he would kill him if he failed to spread the word. So Alamo got busy preaching for the Lord with the help of his second wife, Susan. The two of them scored a weekly television show in which Susan did most of the preaching while Tony contributed horrible renditions of gospel songs. These shows went on until Susan died of cancer in 1982.

Then things got weird. Alamo was convinced that his wife would rise from the dead, so he refused to bury her. Instead, he put her corpse on display and ordered his followers to stand around her, praying until her resurrection. After several months, he ended the forced public veneration of his dead wife, but he continued to keep her corpse on hand in a heart-shaped mausoleum.

Without Susan around anymore, Alamo's religious passions went entirely off the rails. He lashed out at the Catholic Church, which he claimed was responsible for communism, Nazism, both world wars, the Jonestown massacre, drugs, prostitution, and so on. His followers distributed millions of anti-Catholic tracts by placing them on cars in parking lots in the southwestern U.S. His screeds against Catholics eventually got Tony Alamo Christian Ministries branded as a hate group by the Southern Poverty Law Center.

During this time he also converted his Church into a lucrative business venture. This isn't to say he hadn't been successful before; he and Susan had enjoyed lives filled with every tacky luxury they desired while she was alive courtesy of donations from their thousands of followers. But now Alamo's lust for cash went into overdrive. He started numerous businesses and staffed them with church members (including children) who were required to work long hours without pay. He told them that anyone who left his Church would die, so they endured their enslavement willingly. He also dove into fraudulent business practices to turn a buck. Alamo-connected charities advertised heavily asking for material donations for the poor, which they turned around and sold for profit. This ploy came crashing down when the Tempur-Pedic mattress company found out that thousands of mattresses and slippers they had donated for distribution to victims of Hurricane Katrina were instead sold for cash by Alamo's charity. Alamo also had more mainstream businesses. He sold denim jackets decorated by his worshippers that were seen on celebrities such as Mr. T and Sonny Bono.

Alamo was making lots of money, but he wasn't too keen on paying taxes—so he didn't. The IRS eventually caught up with him, and he was convicted of tax evasion in 1994. The feds raided his house, but Alamo had emptied it of most of his valuables before they got there. Among the missing items was the corpse of Susan Alamo. It is thought he stashed her in a storage unit for the next seven years. After Susan's body was finally returned to her family, Alamo had to pay $100,000 in damages to her daughter for his bizarre treatment of her mom's remains.

Alamo spent four years in prison, and when he got out he went back to preaching. He somehow managed to get a radio show, which he used to excoriate the government and the Catholic Church. He also heavily promoted polygamy and marriage to young girls. He proclaimed that girls were ready for marriage as soon as they reached puberty, and he claimed that Mary had been as young as six when she became pregnant with Jesus. He reviled women over the age of eighteen as dried-up, old bags.

Alamo practiced what he preached. He took innumerable underage "wives," the youngest of whom was only eight years old. In 2008 he was arrested for transporting five girls across the Texas-Arkansas state line for sexual purposes. He was tried, convicted, and sentenced to 175 years in prison for his deeds.

Sylvia Browne

Sylvia Browne was widely known as a psychic. I would call her a fake psychic, but I feel that would be redundant. Despite her high name recognition, few people seem to know that she was also the founder of a religion.

Born Sylvia Shoemaker, she claimed she started demonstrating her psychic abilities in the 1930s when she was only three years old. In 1974 she founded the Nirvana Foundation for Psychic Research and got going in earnest working as a professional psychic. She claimed to have helped thousands of people with her mystical visions that she garnered with the help of her spirit guide, Francine. She also claimed that she had helped police departments across the United States find missing persons and solve crimes.

Browne became a sensational success in garnering attention and raking in money, but her rise to the top was not without its bumps in the road. In 1992 she and her third husband, Kensil Brown, were charged with several criminal counts including grand theft and investment fraud stemming from their involvement in a mining venture called "The Sylvia." Investors claimed that Sylvia told them her psychic powers told her the mine was going to pay off, but it did not. Furthermore, she took the money they had invested in the mine and used it to support the Nirvana Foundation for Psychic Research. The money was used to pay the Browns' salaries as well as those of others. Sylvia pled no contest to six counts of wrongdoing, and in the wake of that fiasco she dropped her husband, but kept the name "Brown" —although she added the "e" to it at this time. She continued to call herself "Browne" even as she went through her fourth and fifth husbands.

Browne claimed she had a success rate of between eighty-seven and ninety percent on her predictions. But in 2000, a magazine called *Brill's Content* examined thirty-five cases in which Browne assisted as a psychic detective and found that, "In twenty-one, the details were too vague to be verified. Of the remaining fourteen, Law enforcement officials or family members involved in the investigations say that Browne had played no useful role." In 2010 *Skeptical Inquirer* magazine did a larger study involving 115 cases for which Browne made predictions. Their findings showed that, "of the 115 cases reviewed with LexisNexus and newspaper sources, Browne was wrong in twenty-five, and the remaining ninety either have no available details... or the crime is unsolved." In other words, Browne's actual success rate was somewhere between zero and zero percent.

But that didn't stop her from becoming a frequent guest on television programs such as *Larry King Live* and *The Montel Williams Show*. She made innumerable predictions on these programs and many of them proved to be wildly wrong. One legendary case involved Shawn Hornbeck, a boy who was abducted by a stranger while he was riding his bike in 2002. Browne had the nerve to tell his parents on national TV that Shawn was dead. She also told them a tall, dark-skinned man with dreadlocks who was possibly Hispanic and who drove a blue car had abducted him and dumped his body in the woods near large, jagged rocks. Hornbeck was found in 2007. The kidnapper was white, his skin was not dark, he drove a white truck, he did not have dreadlocks, he was not tall, and he did not dump Hornbeck's body in the woods. In fact, Shawn Hornbeck was found alive.

She pulled the same stunt in 2004 when she told Louwanna Miller that her daughter, Amanda Berry, was deceased. She callously told the desperate mother "She's dead, honey." Miller said she "98% believed" Browne and "It seems like the God-honest truth." She was devastated by the prediction. When she returned home she seemed to give up hope. She took down Amanda's pictures and gave away her computer. She died in 2006. Her daughter was found alive in 2013.

Or take this exchange that also occurred on *The Montel Williams* show when another distraught woman asked Browne for help in finding her missing boyfriend.

Sylvia Browne (in a grating, frog-like voice that bears witness to every cigarette she has ever inhaled): The reason you can't find him is because he's in water. And to find him in water, it's like the girl in Aruba. You can't find somebody…

Distraught Woman: Well, it was September 11th. He was a fireman, but…

Sylvia Brown: Well no, you see. I keep seeing him in water. (Long pause) Is there any way he could have drowned in water? Some way?

Woman: They never found a piece of him—nothing.

Montel Williams (helpfully interjecting): From 9/11.

Browne (after another long pause): Cause, cause he says he couldn't breathe (she is now waving her impossibly long fingernails in front of her face) and he was filled with water.

Sure Sylvia, the man died in the famous water balloon attack on the World Trade Center. And speaking of the September 11th attacks, Browne appeared on Larry King's show on September 3, 2001 and made no mention whatsoever of any terrorist blitz that was about to occur. The list of Browne's spectacular failures like this goes on and on. She even predicted that cures for breast cancer would arrive by 1999 and for the common cold by 2010.

So ok, Sylvia Browne may seem like a shameless clown (or "clowne") who had as much psychic power as the average bag of potato chips. But this never stopped her from being invited onto television and radio shows, and it never diminished the number of people willing to believe in her alleged powers. It didn't prevent her from publishing scores of books including *Afterlives of the Rich and Famous*, which includes "intimate afterlife accounts of Princess Diana, John Lennon, Heath Ledger, Marilyn Monroe, and other charismatic celebrities" and *All Pets Go to Heaven*, which explains what happens to our pets after they die. SPOILER ALERT: They go to Heaven. And it didn't prevent her from founding her own religion.

In 1986 she launched the Society of Novus Spiritus. In it, Sylvia taught that there is a male God, named Om, and a female God who answers to the name of Azna. Om loves you constantly, but if you require any assistance in your life you need to ask Azna for it because she's the one who actually gets things done. Om sounds a bit like a deadbeat dad to me; he says he loves you a lot, but he can't be bothered to actually help you out. Novus Spiritus recognizes the Bible as an important moral guide, but they do not recognize the divinity of Jesus. The Church also does not acknowledge the existence of sin, the devil or Hell. They do believe in Heaven (or the "other side") obviously, because that's where your pets go after they get run over by cars. They have a list of holy days they observe that includes all the equinoxes and solstices each year, but strangely their website got the dates wrong for every one of them when I checked it.

They also recognize the almighty dollar. They respect the power of cash donations to the Church and the IRS's gift of tax-exempt status to religious organizations. Novus Spiritus sold diamond jewelry to the faithful for years that turned out to have a "quality issue." The issue was that the "diamonds" were actually cubic zirconium. Browne somehow failed to sense this fleecing of her flock with her psychic powers. Novus Spiritus also encouraged people to get psychic readings from Sylvia that cost $850 for a twenty to thirty minute telephone session. If you wanted to go the cheap route, you could get your reading done by Sylvia's son Chris for a mere $500.

Browne predicted she would live to be 88 years old. This prediction failed in 2013 when she died at the age of 77.

She never saw it coming.

Select Bibliography

Ahlberg, Sture, *Messianic Movements*, Almquist & Wiksel International, 1985

Bennett, Richard E., Black, Susan Easton, and Cannon, Donald Q., *The Nauvoo Legion in Illionois*, Arthur H. Clark Company, 2010

Boston, Robert, *The Most Dangerous Man in America: Pat Robertson and the Rise of the Christian Coalition*, Prometheus Books, 1996

Boureau, Alain, *The Myth of Pope Joan*, The University of Chicago Press, 1988

Brooks, Juanita, *The Mountain Meadows Massacre*, Stanford University Press, 1950

Carrasco, David, *City of Sacrifice*, Beacon Press, 1999

Chamberlin, E.R., *The Bad Popes*, The Dial Press, Inc., 1969

Corydon, Brent, *L. Ron Hubbard, Messiah or Madman?*, Barricade Books, 1987

Essen, D.M.R., *The Curse of Cromwell*, Leo Cooper Ltd., 1971

Gaunt, Peter, *Oliver Cromwell*, New York University Press, 2004

Gorenfeld, John, *Bad Moon Rising: How Reverend Moon Created the Washington Times, Seduced the Religious Right, and Built an American Kingdom*, PoliPointPress, 2008

Hardman, John, *Robespierre*, Addison Westly Longham Ltd., 1999

Helfferich, Tryntje (editor,) *The Thirty Years War*, Hackert Publishing Co. Inc., 2009

Hunter, James, *Smile Pretty and Say Jesus*, The University of Georgia Press, 1993

Johnson, Marion, *The Borgias*, Rinehart and Winston, 1981

Kertzer, David I., *The Kidnapping of Edgardo Mortara*, Alfred A. Knopf, 1997

Klineman, George, Cohn, David and Butler, Sherman, *The Cult That Died: The Tragedy of Jim Jones and the Peoples Temple*, G.P. Putnam Publishing, 1980

Knecht, Robert J., *The French Civil Wars*, Pearson Education Ltd., 2000

Levak, Brian P., *The Witch-Hunt in Early Modern Europe*, Longman Group, 1987

Magida, Arthur, *Prophet of Rage*, Basic Books, 1996

Marcus, Sheldon, *Father Coughlin*, Little, Brown and Company, 1973

Martin, Sean, *The Knights Templar*, Thunder's Mouth Press, 2004

Misciattalli, Piero, *Savonarola*, W. Heffner & Sons Ltd., 1929

Norwich, John Julius, *Absolute Monarchs: A History of the Papacy*, Random House, 2011

Oberman, Heiko A., *Luther, A Man Between God and the Devil*, Severin und Sieder Verlag GMBH, 1982 – Yale University, 1989

O'Shea, Stephen, *The Perfect Heresy – The Life and Death of the Medieval Cathars*, William & Company, 2001

Paine, Michael, *The Crusades*, Pocket Essentials, 2005

Phayer, Michael, *The Catholic Church and the Holocaust 1930-1965*, Indiana University Press, 2000

Remini, Robert V., *Joseph Smith*, Viking Penguin, 2002

Sabatini, Rafael, *Torquemada and the Spanish Inquisition*, Stanley Paul & Co. Ltd., 1913

Segal, Binjamin W., *A Lie and a Libel*, University of Nebraska Press, 1926

Singular, Stephen, *When Men Became Gods*, St. Martin's Press, 2008

Smith, John Holland, *Constantine the Great*, Hamish Hamilton Ltd., 1971

Sobel, Dava, *Galileo's Daughter*, Walker Books, 1999 and Penguin Books, 2000

Starkey, David, *Six Wives*, Harper Collins, 2003

Wright, Larence, *Saints and Sinners*, Alfred A. Knopf, 1993

The following newspapers, periodicals, and websites also provided valuable information for this book.

The New York Times, The Los Angeles Times, The Washington Post, The Times of London, The Atlantic, The Anti-Defamation League, The Oregonian, BBC News, ABC News, CBS News, NBC News, CNN, PBS, Religious Movements, Skeptic Tank, The Telegraph, The Christian Science Monitor, The Independent, Working For Change, Common Dreams, Slate, Time Magazine, Newsweek, National Geographic, Infosect, The Skeptic's Dictionary, The Catholic Encyclopedia, Live Science, The Miami New Times, The Tulsa World, The Dallas Observer, The Skeptical Inquirer, The New York Daily News, Politics Daily, The Southern Poverty Law Center, The Village Voice, The Texarkana Gazette, God Hates Fred Phelps, Comics Alliance, Foreign Policy, USA Today, Scientific American, The New Yorker, Positive Atheism, The Spartanburg Herald Journal, The Smoking Gun, National Public Radio, The Salt Lake Tribune, Failed Messiah, Media Matters for America, Paliban Daily, Daylight Atheism, Positive Atheism, Mother Jones, The National Catholic Reporter, Ideofact, History Review, History Today, The Catholic Education Resource Center, The Guardian, Netreach, History Times, The Age, The James Randi Educational Foundation, TruTV, The University of Southern California, The Cleveland Plain Dealer, The Chicago Tribune, The Raw Story, Euronews

Finally, I would like to thank Nicky Torkzadeh and Sara Donohue for their assistance with my writing efforts!

Manufactured by Amazon.ca
Bolton, ON

38785804R00201